ANSWERS UNLEASHED

The Science of Unleashing Your Brain's Power

Olympia LePoint

Praises for *Answers Unleashed*

"With personal, real-life examples, Olympia LePoint cleverly uses storytelling to explain the thinking patterns she used to transform her chaotic experiences into a successful rocket science career. With ***Answers Unleashed®: The Science of Unleashing Your Brain's Power***, I am convinced readers will unleash their success too. ***Answers Unleashed*** is inspiring, and one of the best self-help neuroscience books on the market. Professionals, parents, college students, and everyone who desires to overcome challenges will benefit from reading this book. I support Olympia in her passion for helping shed light on how the human brain works through her own powerful, triumphant experiences. This book is not only excellent for S.T.E.M. education, but is also excellent for anyone who desires to take ownership over their brainpower and launch to great feats."

— Robert Curbeam,
Retired U.S. Astronaut

"Olympia LePoint in ***Answers Unleashed*** masterfully uses a storytelling style to direct the attention of readers to what she calls the *Triabrain,* in reshaping one's brain thought process. She uses faith, science, psychology, and intuition to reshape the brain in mindfulness and decision-making. It directs the attention away from bad thinking habits and pushes forward the skill of awareness and strategic innovation. Such skills positively impact one's life as it allows one to develop a solution-oriented thought process. ***Answers Unleashed*** is an inspiring book that easily connects to its readers. I recommend this book to anyone who wants to overcome hesitations and achieve a brighter mindset."

— G. Ali Zakeri, Ph.D,
Professor of Mathematics
California State University Northridge

"It has been an honor to work with Olympia LePoint in her journey of creating ***Answers Unleashed.*** It has been a privilege to watch Olympia LePoint take what she has learned from many sessions, as well as her own personal insights, to define the *Triabrain* and develop the ***Triabrain Theory of Relativity*** in this book. I truly believe that her discovery of the three-sided brain, along with its theory, will help many people develop a basic understanding of intuition and how to access it."

—Sean Wolf, Body Restoration Expert,
Founder of The Body Restoration Clinic
San Jose, California

"Very few people understand the complexities of brain science. Even fewer understand the complex nature of launching rockets. No one has combined rocket science, brain science and faith to help people unleash their life's power, until now. ***Answers Unleashed: The Science of Unleashing Your Brain's Power*** by Olympia LePoint does a phenomenal job in explaining how faith and free will embeds in science. Olympia LePoint is the first person to create a ground-breaking, chaos-science discovery that helps anyone take ownership over their free will. Through her brilliant chaos-induced stories that temporality threaten stability, Olympia LePoint cleverly exposes that every situation is a brain-changing gift. Although packaged in a way that one would not expect, life's chaos is explained as a tool to unleash the power of one's life.

I have known Olympia LePoint as a spiritual leader at Bel Air Church, and I am thankful for her service to God and fellow people. She is a person who sees the big picture both spiritually and logically. Olympia LePoint helps others move toward personal greatness. I am proud to endorse the ground-breaking ***Triabrain Theory of Relativity*** in this book. And, I look forward to Olympia LePoint's lectures as a regular guest speaker on TV, at universities and in faith organizations. "

—Reverend Dr. Drew Sams,
Lead Pastor, Bel Air Church,
Los Angeles, California

"Olympia LePoint has created an amazing book everyone will sincerely appreciate. ***Answers Unleashed*** highlights how hidden memories can affect current behaviors in invisible ways. More importantly, Olympia LePoint has brilliantly explained complex psychological brain structures in simple ways. With the various mindfulness-driven exercises included, ***Answers Unleashed*** can help anyone lessen, or even remove, pain brought on by hurtful memories and replace it with awareness. Olympia LePoint has done a phenomenal job in showing that spiritual growth, emotional health, and logical thinking are vital for successful brain function."

—Athena Dhawan, M.A. M.F.T.,
Marriage and Family Therapist & Nationally Certified
Trauma-Focused Cognitive Behavioral Therapist

"***Answers Unleashed: The Science of Unleashing Your Brain's Power*** by Olympia LePoint describes a new and innovative approach to the process of healing the brain and recovering from traumatic experiences by reshaping your brain—neuroplasticity. Founded on her faith, her own traumatic experiences in life, her education as a mathematician, and work as a NASA scientist, Olympia discusses a new structure of the brain function, the *Triabrain* and ***Triabrain Theory of Relativity***. Anyone can use this theory to reshape their brain during the trauma-healing process. The ***Triabrain Theory of Relativity*** is unique and can ultimately transform lives."

—Dr. Ramin Vakilian, Ph.D.,
Professor of Mathematics
California State University Northridge

"I had the honor of helping Olympia LePoint construct the emotional mind-to-body foundations of this book by guiding her through my VOILA Method Therapy sessions, where people learn to bridge the gap in healing from the inside out. This healing is a two-way bridge. I support Olympia LePoint as she has been my mentee for over three years. She ventures into this work to help men and women overcome mind-to-body emotional trauma and unleash the real power from their mind. Plus, she offers ways for women to listen to their intuitive selves and their bodies. Many people are looking to outside sources for healing like Cupping, Tape, Needling, and the list goes on. And this way of thinking is not beneficial to the people who need help. It is a backward approach. These methods may seem easier, but they are certainly not long-lasting nor sustaining.

Real empowering change happens from the inside, and it extends out. As I teach in my VOILA Method courses, the body's decision to heal occurs from the inside. Olympia LePoint has taken the VOILA philosophy and added her feminine touch for explaining the healing-based thoughts and decisions women can achieve in their decision-making power. Olympia LePoint helps women overcome emotional challenges, so they can embrace the power that lies within."

—Joel Crandall,
Kinesiologist and founder of the *VOILA Method*,
Physiocare Center, Los Angeles, California

ANSWERS UNLEASHED

The Science of Unleashing Your Brain's Power

OLYMPIA LEPOINT

OL Consulting Corporation & Publishing
Los Angeles, California

ANSWERS UNLEASHED: The Science of Unleashing Your Brain's Power

Printed in The United States of America.

Published by:
O.L. Consulting Corporation & Publishing
Los Angeles, California 91325
310.272.4293

Address all inquiries to:
RomanCharles@OLConsultingCorp.com

Includes bibliographical references.

Library of Congress Control Number: 2017914106

ISBN: 978-0-9885376-2-0 (Paperback)
ISBN: 978-0-9885376-6-8 (eBook)

Editor: Penny Scott
Cover Design: Michelle Manley
Interior Design: Carla Green, Clarity Designworks
Cover and Author Photos: Todd Tyler
Illustrator: Christen Cushing
Printing: David Gagnon and Rene Gagnon, Allura Printing

I dedicate this book to God, and my mother, Pamela.

Thank you, God, for everything.

Mommy, thank you for everything.

I am honored to fulfill my life calling with you both.

ACKNOWLEDGMENTS

I would like to acknowledge the key people in my life who helped me write this book. First and foremost, I thank God who gave me the vision and mission to write this book. I also thank His Son who came to me in a dream and told me how the brain truthfully operates. All of which I have been defining scientifically ever since.

And in the Earthly realm, I would like to thank first and foremost my loving mother, Pamela, who always helps me to stay focused on my purpose no matter the challenges that I experience. She endured a catastrophic brain injury in 2004, and she is a walking miracle. It is to her that I dedicate this book. I thank Psychologist Dr. Bonnie Collins who came into my life shortly after my mother's brain surgery. She helps me embrace the power as a woman and how to make integrity-filled choices in the world, as well as take ownership over reprogramming my brain with spoken aloud affirmations. Many of her suggestions I include in this book. Dr. Collins has helped my family, and I make wise decisions and assisted us in understanding the human brain and its powerful thoughts for the last 15 years.

I want to thank my Bel Air Church Pastor, Dr. Drew Sams, who prays for me and always explains key spiritual concepts. Dr. Sams' teachings on how God exists in the time-space-continuum are life-changing. These Godly truths have been applied in my own life, as well as translated for others into science. I interweave many of these healing aspects (independent of time and space) from his church sermons in this book. I also thank Third Tuesdays Pastor Jeff Perry and his wife Patsy Perry for reminding me of my power in the entertainment world. The influence of this exceptional group is a pivotal reminder how the media is an asset in ultimate healing work. And I thank neuroscientist and fellow "Third Tuesdays" church member, Jeffrey M. Schwartz, M.D., who continuously encourages me to speak and write about my own experience in rewiring the brain.

Thanks also go to Kinesiologist Joel Crandall who stuck by me through thick and thin as I broke through the barriers of mind-to-body trauma. He showed me the meaning of healthy love, and the strength I could harness in my body and soul through his ***VOILA Method*** of physical therapy. You will find numerous concepts of the ***VOILA Method*** incorporated in this book. I thank ***Body Restoration Expert*** Sean Wolf for teaching me to direct intuition into practical ways. Sean teaches energy principles and guides how energy and science overlap concerning healing the human brain. I've included several fun exercises within this book.

I would also like to thank my older sister, Crystal, who underwent brain surgery like my mother, but 12 years later. It is through Crystal's near-death experience that I received confirmation regarding my purpose in helping people heal their brains. I'd like to thank Nick Johns, my younger sister, Auriel, and her daughter, Isis. I love them more than they know. I'm thankful for my spiritual family; Dustin Marler, Fran Irvin, Justin Phillips, and Petina Pervis: for praying me during the creation of this book. Carrie Starbird has been a true confidant during my sister's brain surgery. I also thank my friends and colleagues at Pasadena City College, California State University Northridge, Bel Air Church, Third Tuesdays, and the Rotary Club of Los Angeles.

And I would like to thank my editor Angela "Penny" Scott who has patiently helped me translate painful memories into empowering stories designed to inspire millions of people. She has been so patient with me! Lastly, I would like to thank Andrew Pearce who came into my life when I decided to remove physical trauma and replace it with self-love. Through his unorthodox actions, Andrew opened my eyes to understanding the power of relationships, freedom, my self-worth, and love.

Thank you to everyone who had supported me, especially when I needed it the most.

Contents

Acknowledgments ix

Foreword
by Neuroscience Researcher Jeffrey M. Schwartz, M.D xiii

Introduction to Answers Unleashed xvii

Chapter 1: What Can You Do? 1

Chapter 2: The Triabrain Theory of Relativity 25

Chapter 3: The Meaning of Chaos 43

Chapter 4: Brainbrink: When Chaos Separates Your Brain 69

Chapter 5: The Truth: The Power in Your Triabrain Connections ... 93

Chapter 6: Unleashing Your Faith Brain Power 121

Chapter 7: Building Your Intuition 155

Chapter 8: Unleashing Your Right-Brain Power 193

Chapter 9: Unleashing Your Left-Brain Power 225

Chapter 10: The Power in a Woman's Touch 261

Chapter 11: Successful Endings 277

Bibliography 283

About Olympia LePoint 289

FOREWORD

By Neuroscience Researcher and Author Jeffrey M. Schwartz, M.D.

Answers Unleashed takes a step forward in offering a fresh, innovative work that is a genuinely new approach to self-directed neuroplasticity – which means changing your brain. Much has been written about the process of healing the brain from traumatic situations, but Olympia LePoint describes a new perspective on the brain, which she calls the ***Triabrain*** and the ***Triabrain Theory of Relativity***. She profoundly describes how anyone can use science and faith to reshape their brain and ultimately transform his or her life.

As you will read, ***Answers Unleashed Triabrain Theory of Relativity*** introduces a new aspect of brain function, which Olympia calls the "faith sector." In addition to the brain's left and right hemispheres, the faith sector introduces the understanding of intuition and its assistance in decision-making abilities. This concept combines faith, science, and intuition, which is a new combination in how to understand the workings of the brain. Readers explore the ideal function of the ***Triabrain*** and learn how chaos induces it into a process called *brainbrink.*

In this way, ***Answers Unleashed*** helps a person become aware of painful memories and habits that turn off the brain's powerful executive mind.

For many years now, I have worked to explain the power of mindfulness, which is the ability to have a clear-minded awareness of your own thoughts and actions. When people become aware that they have choices, they can make decisions that reshape the brain – this is called self-directed neuroplasticity. There are bad habits and unhealthy thinking that can take control of people's thoughts and actions. Unbeknownst to them, the brain's habit center, called the striatum, can run their behaviors without any conscious awareness. One common example is someone who chain smokes cigarettes. He may be totally unaware that he has lit another cigarette, and has actually held a flame burning inches from his face, until after the cigarette is already being smoked. Unless a person is willing to use mental awareness to change their automatic habit drive, and replace it with healthier operations in thinking, there is no way to overcome a person's chronic deceptive brain messages.

Olympia LePoint explains how the *Triabrain* helps a person create a new method of thinking, to redirect thought in a powerful way. With practical applications using the *Triabrain Theory of Relativity*, a person can learn to utilize their executive brain thoughts for innovation. She provides the recipe to jumpstart the brain with a unique combination of faith, intuition, psychology, and science. This ground-breaking approach serves to connect the prefrontal cortex (which contains the executive brain) and striatum's habit center together for mental awareness. This mental awareness helps break destructive habits.

With personal, touching anecdotes, Olympia cleverly uses storytelling to explain the thinking patterns she used to transform her chaotic life into a successful rocket science career. Furthermore, she takes the reader on a journey as she witnesses the futuristic minds of brilliant NASA engineers. Through inspiring stories, Olympia shares the methods that she utilized to help her mother and sister overcome two separate accident-induced brain injuries. Olympia's inspiring, passionate energy and infectious enthusiasm jumps off the pages and into the reader's brain.

Answers Unleashed explains how science, God, and chaos work collaboratively to give individuals the opportunity to transform their brains. This combination is one that will empower many people to harness the power of their brains. Olympia shows that our brains have directive energy available for life-changing innovation. Olympia LePoint explains this process using her profound *Triabrain* approach to communicate easy-to-understand concepts for everyone to grasp.

Olympia LePoint's ***Answers Unleashed*** helps everyone understand that wise decisions can introduce brain change at any age. Anyone who reads this book will unleash hidden power in reshaping their brain from the inside out.

I highly recommend ***Answers Unleashed*** as a fun, easy to read self-help neuroscience book for every young adult. This book helps audiences understand the power of mindfulness. I truly believe this text will be an excellent contribution for university campuses, counseling centers and within professional development curriculums. The readers are empowered in making life-changing decisions. I support Olympia LePoint as she continues her efforts to help people to get the most out of their brains.

Jeffrey M. Schwartz, M.D.
Author of ***You Are Not Your Brain***, ***Dear Patrick,*** ***Brain Lock,*** and ***The Mind & The Brain***

INTRODUCTION TO ANSWERS UNLEASHED

Photo of Olympia LePoint in the ROSC Mission Control. Credit: Lee Choo.

I am not a brain surgeon. I am not a psychologist. I am not your classically-trained neuroscientist. I am Olympia LePoint, a rocket scientist, and mathematician who has been through hell and back in becoming one of the first female women of color to launch NASA rockets. I had to overcome horrendous early-life challenges, plus learning difficulties. I wondered, "Why on Earth did I have to endure so much energy in changing my life?" Although I experienced chaotic obstacles, I became an award-winning rocket scientist, who helped launch over 28 NASA Space Shuttle Missions. Many people across the world refer to me as the "*Modern Day Hidden Figure*," a person who has developed a genius brain. But very few people know that anyone can develop a genius brain. At any age, you can unleash your powerful brain force if you allow chaos to reshape it.

Everything in your life is connected. The spiritual side of you is connected to the emotional side. The desiring side energizes your scientific, logical side. Your brain is connected in the exact same way. You were born with a life-long connectable brain. But chaotic situations will trick you into unleashing true powerful force against yourself. If you do not know the truth, chaos tricks you into separating the most powerful force that you have at your immediate disposal – your *Triabrain*. It is your three-sided brain that uses thoughts to perform "superhuman" feats. Your *Triabrain* is able to foresee events with accuracy, guide you into safety with its intuition, increase your pleasurable feelings and help you build things that will change the world. But no one tells you the truth. The truth is that your brain is a chaotic and divine blueprint of your life's journeys. And as you reshape your brain, you reshape your physical life. As you experience chaos, your brain mathematically recalibrates itself faster than chaos, so you can overcome any situation meant to stall you. Your thoughts are cleverly designed to serve as tools. Thoughts transform chaotic energy to unleash YOUR power. If no one has told you this fact, keep reading.

"Faith brainpower" is underestimated, and often ignored. But the truth is that there is a part of your brain that can accomplish unimaginable tasks that you would never physically believe. That is, until now. As I developed methods to overcome my life challenges and to launch Space Shuttles, I witnessed how the same math principles used to launch rockets to Mars also explains your ability to remap your human brain. When your brain remaps, it unleashes a powerful force. And this unstoppable force changes your thoughts, feelings, actions, and every physical obstacle in your path. Your new associated action pulls you into success.

A chain of events in 2004 forever defined my view of how human brain function completely works. My mother was a pedestrian in a traumatic car accident. She survived. However, this traumatic accident led her to an 11-hour brain surgery. After brain surgery, my mother relearned how to walk, talk, eat and sleep again. She embodied infant-like characteristics. But oddly enough, this chaos provides answers that will transform your life as you read this book.

During that time, I nearly lost my sanity – witnessing my mother in this infantile state, while spearheading the details of her recovery. Throughout the course of Mom's brain healing process to regain critical function, I began to research how the brain truly works. After all, I was a rocket scientist, not a neuroscientist, yet. From the frontal lobes to the neuron connections, my knowledge was not for myself. Ultimately, this "research" was purposeful: it would help my mother's life. In the process, I found myself developing a branch of Neuroscience that will transform science as we know it. As I worked with Neuroscientists and psychologists to help explain the interworking of the brain, none of them could explain *HOW* the brain heals and reconnects itself. All the specialists said, "Well, no one fully knows yet. The brain is still a mystery."

When I helped launch rockets, my eyes opened to how my fellow scientists used their brains to develop awe-inspiring technology that seemed to defy gravity. I witnessed the brain's countless functions. Not just the basic ones we use to walk, eat, sleep and talk like my mother was regaining, but more sophisticated brain processes that create something from thin air. And these innovative people simply used a mental vision! Such inventors were envisioning their inventions through a new light in their eyes. It was in a way that other people do not. And this intuition guided them to break through. As I connected with these fellow scientists more, I realized anyone could powerfully use their brains to create something out of nothing, "aka" innovation. It wasn't just rocket scientists who could use these intuitive parts of their brains. Anyone has the capability as long as that person knows the steps to direct the power they harness.

After leaving the role of launching rockets, I became a math professor and professional speaker. I wrote the math book, ***Mathaphobia: How You Can Overcome Your Math Fears and Become a Rocket Scientist,*** in an effort to help people remove fear and ace math. Success requires reprograming the brain. The book was a major hit. I appeared on several TV shows and radio programs. ***Mathaphobia*** became well-used on college campuses to help students remove their fear and relearn math. One day, while I was delivering my book to a PBS producer for an upcoming TV appearance, pure chaos occurred again. I experienced a car accident which left me with a concussion. I lost my ability to talk and walk upright for a full two weeks. Upon returning to my college classes, I found it difficult to communicate most words. Oddly enough, the math flowed out my mouth and brain flawlessly. Little did I know, math was healing my brain. Math was restructuring how my brain was being reshaped after the accident. The accident, together with past physical experiences, provoked me to seek physical therapy as a means of regaining my full range of motion. Placing my mind over the situation, I regained full communication abilities. Six months later, I would be asked to give the now famous *TEDx Talk*, "Reprogramming Your Brain to Overcome Fear," which has been viewed by millions around the world.

Like you, I am a person who knows that self-improvement requires a commitment to healing. Something had to still change in my brain. Thus, I returned to physical therapy where I learned that my brain and body were intricately connected through sacred *VOILA* mind-to-body pathways. To my surprise, these *VOILA* pathways resemble the chaos mathematics I learned in graduate school. While receiving *VOILA* Method therapy, my consciousness changed. I was hit with the profound question: Why is it that our brains select certain memories while others stay hidden? Why do some people succeed in overcoming life's chaos and other's do not?

Unfortunately, for 30 years of my life, I didn't have this brain reshaping knowledge. After a traumatic situation in childhood, my brain "stalled." For the next 30 years, I turned off my feelings, but the trapped energy manifested in my body and chaotic actions. I excessively turned to sugar and baked cookies for years thereafter. Unknowingly, I was using sugar as a self-medication! I turned to math and science because I knew "math" would not lie to me. In my teens, 20's and 30's, I had absolutely no feeling in my abdominal area. My gut feelings turned mute. So, I overate so I could experience feeling stuffed in my stomach area. Pain was better than no feeling at all. For me, it served as a warped sense that I was still alive. In my 20's, I threw myself into launching rockets and graduate school to avoid working through the deep-seated emotions. I completely avoided committed, romantic relationships. Although I had high intellectual an intuitive intelligence, my brain was chemically-stuck in the emotional state of being 8-years-old in regarding relationships. Through the *VOILA Method*, I discovered how to remove painful memories and replace it with a new energy. This new energy filled my *Triabrain*, causing it to work faster. I share more about this experience in Chapter 8. I am 800% better now!

Mouth-dropping epiphanies came alive. But when you experience any life changing epiphanies, the most unpleasant experiences are most probable to occur. That is the role of Chaos. And the events will want to make you pull your hair out! When you are at your highest state of brain reshaping, capability chaos hits you. But the chaos is for you to make a choice, in what I call a fractal moment. And these decisions fuel your life-transformation.

While undergoing a transformation with my coaches, I did not always encounter the most pleasant experiences. There were severe ups and downs. At times, I am sure I made my therapists pull their hair out! Other times, therapists were there to help maintain my sanity as horrific memories fully resurfaced and were finally replaced. Initially, my intent was to regain full range of motion prior to the concussion. But, therapy delved deeper and led to toxins releasing from my brain.

Each time you are healed, your insight and perception become clearer. More importantly, your intuition overwhelmingly increases. Things like déjà vu became regular occurrences. You can sense when someone is about to call.

Your dreams become extremely vivid. And, you can foresee future solutions with clarity. After I healed from my concussion, I recalled traumatic memories I unknowingly hid deep within the crevices of my brain. Although you go through rough times, you can cling to faith – believing that your cumulative experiences are going to help you and others in profound ways.

At the time of my own therapy, I had been teaching as a math professor for 10 years. My role was 50% math, and 50% psychological. Teaching math concepts were an effortless task. I memorized over 20 math texts from cover-to-cover, and easily explained the concepts with mathematical rigor. However, helping people overcome fear was more complex. It required an added layer requiring extraordinary skill. In each case, I had to probe inside of students' minds to pinpoint the first time their world crashed. Usually 99% of the time, these moments were triggered by chaos. Discovering "hidden trauma" was an acquired skill used to guide the next generation in reprograming their brains to foresee solutions.

Typically, students run to the first person willing to help them rise from pure chaos. Counseling students after class often lead to helping students make life-changing decisions such as: overcoming breakups, planning wisely upon learning of unexpected pregnancies, encouraging a student to consider cancer treatment options, proposing ways to negotiate school loans, and suggesting on-campus mental health therapy for one student determined to burn down my classroom! Teaching served to demonstrate that I wasn't the only person experiencing major chaos! Everyone experiences chaos and a whole new generation needed answers on how to transform this often debilitating chaos into unimaginable success.

Chaos has a way of mimicking the same lesson in other areas of life. My epiphany was driven home again at my church. Countless people struggled to overcome severe hardships. Nevertheless, when you tap into faith in the midst of chaos, you are empowered to create situations that defy the odds. From bankruptcies, to divorce to exiting abusive situations, your brainpower can withstand any circumstance. You can overcome cancer, become CEOs, and give birth after being told of barrenness. When embodying faith, you can harness a powerful life-changing positive energy that's unstoppable by negative forces.

As you sleep, your brain opens the door to find answers. My life is no different. One night as I slept, I was given the science of how the brain unleashes its power. In the dream, I was on what I call the "Other Side." It was a heavenly place, tranquil and completely peaceful. Within this location, there was a training ground for people who harnessed their brainpower. I was a part of the group. Everyone was divided into various rooms based on levels to practice talents. Like Karate, various levels are demonstrated by belts. One room was for telekinesis (moving objects in mid-air with the brain). Another room was for telepathy (reading thoughts), another room was for foretelling the future, another room was for healing the body, etc.

I was in each room, mastering the assigned brain exercises. Excited, I would zip from one room to the next, practicing various skills. I could play piano with my brain, and change the color of fabrics. I searched for my mother in one of these rooms. To my surprise, she was there, too! She was a senior master in a particular room – the room of faith. I mastered my talents in every room. And when I exited the rooms, I went into this place that resembled a Greek amphitheater.

The amphitheater was empty. The seats circled downward into the center ground. Up from the center rose a man by the name of Jesus Christ. He looked at me and said, "You have graduated: You now know all the ways to use the brain." He looked at me in pure peace.

Then as I awoke, God said something loud and clear. I continued to hear, "Now that you have graduated from here, your assignment is to teach humanity on Earth about the power they harness in their brains." God said, "Show them through me." Then I woke up. The content of this book was downloaded into my brain.

Little did I know that in order to write the book and share the process with you, I would personally undergo intensive learning and healing! And what you will learn will blow your mind. Personal healing is required. Honestly, the transformation is not easy. It is designed for people personally committed to transforming their lives. In the first chapter, you will read my own personal journey. When you read the chapter, think about what you would do in your own life if you were placed in my shoes. Ask yourself, "What would I do? Would I do the same?" Then in Chapter 2 and Chapter 3, I provide extremely technical explanations. Chapter 2 explains the *Triabrain, Triabrain Theory of Relativity* and how the *Triabrain* scientifically operates. In Chapter 3, you will understand the mathematical meaning of chaos, so you can recognize the patterns that happen on Earth and in Space. In Chapter 4, you will see how chaos can separate your brain into unrecognizable parts. There is a self-test for you to know when you are unknowingly giving your ultimate power away to others.

In Chapter 5, you will know the truth of what was shared in the dream I experienced. It further expounds on the *Triabrain Theory of Relativity* in a way that applies to you daily. This pivotal chapter shares the ultimate truth how Science, God and chaotic forces work together for your success in profound ways. Be ready, that chapter will expose the internal power that you can unleash. In Chapter 6, I provide tips on how to reconnect your brain, so you can regain your power. If you've ever wondered about intuition, Chapter

7 is for you. You have intuition, but chances are you don't know how to use it. This chapter shows the types of intuition that can be unleashed daily in your decision-making process. Are you experiencing an emotional cycle, where everything, including relationships, feels overwhelming? Chapter 8 empowers you to take hold of those emotions and transform them into powerful feelings designed to help you take action. In Chapter 9, learn how to use your resources to build your desired future logically. Chapter 10 is dedicated to the ladies. If you are a woman reading this book, you have a feminine force that unleashes powerful innovation. You will benefit in knowing the power that you bring to this world and recognize that you are not alone. Lastly, in Chapter 11, you will receive the last brain exercise to help unleash your brain's power.

Healing your brain is not an overnight process: it is a lifelong, awe-inspiring experience. ***Answers Unleashed*** provides a jump start to help unleash your ***Triabrain*** force. It provides baseline tools to begin the process of reshaping your brain from the inside out. This process is a form of self-directed, neuroplasticity that my mother's doctors, at the time, could not explain.

You can achieve anything you desire. Do you believe that you have a life worth living? Do you believe that you are here on Earth to contribute something powerful that no one else but you can accomplish? Do you want to reshape your brain to unleash its power? If the answer is "yes" to any of these questions, keep reading. This book is 100% for you.

It's time for you to know the truth.

What Can You Do?

CHAPTER 1

WHAT CAN YOU DO?

"I've been in an accident!" My sister, Auriel, screams, as Mom picks up the phone and places it on speaker.

Panic runs through my system.

Mom yells, "Where?"

Auriel cries loudly, "49th and Main!"

Immediately, I grab my purse and run out the house, telling Mom, "Come on!"

We leave the entire house unlocked as we travel two blocks from my mother's home in South Los Angeles. Panic and adrenaline simultaneously run through my veins, as I drive. "*No, No, No*," I think. I did not want to repeat the accident mentally. Two years earlier, I experienced a similar horrible car accident myself.

The night poured with sheets of rain. Auriel was driving a Ford Explorer when the airbags deployed. She blacks out due to the force of impact. Her 2-year-old daughter experiences convulsions and vomits on herself in the back seat. Moments later, Auriel awakens in the damaged vehicle, realizing she needs to save her baby. Auriel had no idea she was hurt because her brain's powerful response pumps enough adrenaline to move her injured body and limbs.

Mother and I arrived. We see Auriel's silver Ford Explorer, partially mangled, on the curb. It was located just a few inches from the traffic light post. I look at the center of the street where I see the green; four-door Honda Accord was crushed into a shred of unrecognizable metal. The drunk driver blew through a red light and slammed into my sister's truck as she carried my 2-year old niece. While fleeing the scene, the drunk driver leaves his passenger in the mangled wreckage.

I open my car door and run toward the accident. I scream, "Where is the baby? Where is the baby?" In panic mode, I was asking anyone to tell me where my family was located. My brain pumps adrenaline. When I see my niece, I grab her. I feel no pain in my back despite experiencing muscle issues earlier that evening. Now, I only feel the need to survive. The need to help my sister and niece survive. I quickly grab Auriel. I throw my arms around her and held her shaking body. Pain enters my soul.

Despite being a rocket scientist, launching over 28 NASA missions to space and performing expert *TEDx Talks*, my brain was struggling. This trauma introduced fear which repeatedly attempted to shut my brain's solution-finding ability off.

Mom approaches us. Pain enters her soul as she sees her children and grandchild traumatized through the actions of another irresponsible person. Mom is worried and doesn't know what to do: she nervously stands there patting my sister's back. She then grabs her grandchild and takes her to my car to wait for the ambulance. Heavy rain soaks through my military wool pea coat.

Understandably, my sister is an emotional wreck. Her nonstop, inconsolable tears match the harsh downpour. It's an extremely traumatic time. Nevertheless, I chanted, "It will be okay. It will be okay. It will be okay." I hold them until the ambulance comes where they are rushed to the hospital's emergency room.

Image 1-1: Photo of the rain-soaked accident scene taken January 2015.

While Auriel is in transit, I look for my cell phone. I cannot find it. I must have dropped it while running to rescue my sister and niece. I frantically try to problem-solve, and my brain begins shutting down while straining to remember simple things. Cleverly, I ask to use someone else's phone. When I do, my brain begins to work again. I then recognize fraudulent tow people who try to take my sister's car. Because we hadn't made a call to our AAA Company yet, we knew these companies were illegally attempting to tow her car. Disastrous auto accidents are prime opportunities for fraudulent tow companies to seize cars illegally. For a quick second, I found the answer to this problem by "verbally beating" them off.

Then, I manage to get the brilliant idea of returning to my mother's house to grab her phone. We return for the phone, and I arrange the AAA tow service to haul my sister's truck. I stand in the rain to take pictures of the accident from every angle. My wool pea coat and shoes are getting heavily soaked: I feel the water against my skin. My hair is completely wet. As I feel water on my neck, I continue in corresponding with the officers about the police report and next steps. My brain slowly turns back on to continue problem-solving, despite the fear caused by this traumatic accident.

Next, my brain struggles to remember the correct directions to the hospital. I have no GPS. No maps. My phone is lost. I have trouble paying attention to the road. I barely follow the traffic signals. Mom and I become lost. Then my brain turns back on. I receive the idea to stop and get directions. My mother and I stop at a local taco stand for directions. We receive instruction from a person who barely speaks English.

Thankfully, Mom and I arrive at the hospital. After a few minutes, we find Auriel and my niece. This resilient 2-year-old is singing her ABC's for the doctors. Auriel is wearing a neck brace. My brain goes into "empathy mode" and starts to shut down as I feel their pain. I pray for a miracle. I get the brilliant idea to use Mom's phone to post a prayer request on Facebook and leave her number for friends to call. My brain turns back into problem-solving mode again. And, I request the right diagnostic tests for my sister (CAT scan and X-rays of limbs/body parts). After a series of tests, no life-threatening damage is observed by the doctors. Thankfully, they are released but with strict orders to rest and recover. From this accident, I learned one of the most valuable lessons of all time that I vowed to share with the entire world.

Painful memories have no place in our brains ever again! Your painful memories have no place in your life ever again! Pain memories have no place in my life ever again!

My mission became to do anything and everything possible to help myself and others change traumatic memories that create fear into answers that people need to change lives. Rebuilding natural intuitive brainpower is the key that unlocks your ability to create innovative answers that bring success.

I was experiencing the same type of brain processing issues many people face across the world. When we were born, we were born with a sound mind. Throughout life, chaotic situations, bad relationships and physical/emotional attacks make our brains go haywire. The brain struggles in finding solutions. It loses the innate power that it is designed to exude. Within time, peace of mind disappears. Consequently, our brains fight to restore its natural ability in creating answers to life's toughest situations. Answers are not only found in science, technology, engineering or math fields. You can also find answers using intuition. I have experienced similar circumstances. Have you ever found yourself at a loss for answers or words?

Chaos is a force. Fear is a distraction. Success is a decision. Painful memories (often called trauma), is an opportunity to reshape your brain. While dealing with my sister's car crash, I was struggling to remain calm and regroup. Each of us is given the ability to overcome situations by discovering creative solutions. However, we cannot see these solutions when certain thoughts overpower our brain.

Brilliant answers arrive once you consciously decide to reshape your thoughts. Only you are in charge of reshaping your brain and healing yourself from painful memories. No one else has this life-changing power except you. You and only you have the ultimate power to change your thoughts. In making the decision to do so, you successfully reshape your brain.

What will separate you from people who fail to beat the odds? Why can you heal after disturbing accidents, while other people do not? How can you invent brilliant science technology without any viable resources? How can you change a painful situation into one that brings peace of mind? Keep reading.

1 out of 31,000 African-American Women earn a Ph.D. in math or sciences and even fewer become rocket scientists. As a woman of color, I had a better chance of being hit by lightning twice than beating these odds! Nevertheless, I did it! I became an award-winning rocket scientist. I was a rocket scientist for nearly ten years, launching NASA's Space Shuttle Rockets helping NASA's *Mission Control* protect astronauts and deliver life-changing technology to Space. I used mathematics and science to calculate the probability of catastrophic explosions within the flight. I authorized multi-million-dollar engine tests and helped secure over $55 million dollars in new, engine contracts with innovative scientific approaches. I not only had to find scientific solutions earning my degrees in mathematics, but I first had to find answers in my personal life.

More importantly, how can you take your brain, reshape it, and defy your odds? Are you able to literally go inside your brain to reshape its interior, so it operates for you differently? Can you take neuroscience concepts and apply them in an easy way for your success? And, can you take actions to witness measurable differences that will produce life-changing results?

For years, these questions haunted me. And for years I did not know the answer. In neuroscience, the ability to reshape the brain to overcome any challenge is called *Neuroplasticity*. When you take ownership over your thoughts to reshape your brain, it is called self-directed neuroplasticity. Neuroscience is the branch of science that attempts to explain how your brain reorganizes itself by forming new brain nerve cell connections. The neuroscience process explains how neurons compensate and adjust in response to your new and different situations. Interestingly, I did not become an expert on reshaping the brain through the conventional methods of medical school. Instead, I was educated through years of facing obstacles in my own life. While working as a rocket scientist, I learned how genius brains connected. Thirdly, I helped both my mother and sister recover after two separate accident-induced brain surgeries.

It is through these rare combinations of life-challenges that I found the recipe to change the brain by changing thoughts. These ideas or "brainwaves" are actually energy, forever traveling through one of the most powerful energy converters that exist – your human brain. Three personal situations have allowed me to become an expert on how the brain unleashes its power. But, chances are you're clueless as to how your brain truly works. You are not alone. Scientists have yet to determine how brainwaves can change your exterior situations fully.

If you think of the brain as being a single organ within the human skull, delete that thought. If you believe that whatever happens in the brain – remains in the brain – shift your thinking. Stop believing that the brain has no influence over situations that happen within the body or events that occur in the world. There is a more powerful way to think. ***Answers Unleashed*** will expose how your brain is not just an organ independently operating within your skull. Using scientific theory, you'll learn how the human brain has three forms. You will discover how the brain is like a tree. When a tree has deep roots, it is strong. Your brain is similar. It has roots that branch out like a tree. Your brain's roots extend through your nervous system and continue outside of your physical body. Your brain's intuition will act as a flashlight within your thoughts. The energy within your emotions will be transformed into your powerful feelings. And these feelings will cause you to take action which pulls you into your desired success. These three parts of the brain renew life. When we understand how to increase the power of each brain part, we can then merge it together. In doing so, we can change lives and create the inconceivable.

Your thoughts have power. Your brain creates these thoughts, so you convert energy from chaos into energy needed for life. This process can be seen in many forms. The process can be used for inventing, overcoming, and healing. Each result gives identical, powerful outcomes. If you want to be an inventor and create a new product, you must envision the technology before any evidence of it exists. Then, you must decide to pursue it despite any fear or obstacles. You are also required to use scientific principles to bring your invention into existence. These are the identical steps that you take to overcome challenges.

If you want to overcome a horrible situation, you must envision a "way out" before anything in your situation changes. The concept "way out" is used because you may see many doors. However only one door truly leads to freedom. Other doors lead to additional traps and obstacles. Therefore, you must decide not to let your current restrictions trap you. Then, you successfully find a way to use physical, mental, and situational resources to access a path out of chaos. These steps are also used when you desire to heal your body. If you want to heal the body, you must decide that healing will occur despite any of your doctors' prognosis. You must realize that your thoughts – healthy or unhealthy – exist outside of the skull and in a field around you, which triggers healing or pain. It's imperative to reshape the way your brain and body work together and remove any doubt or fearful thoughts about the ability to heal while using science and practical steps.

But the problem is you do not know how to harness this skill. Or, more importantly, you may not know the science behind these miracles. Unfortunately, you do not possess the knowledge to overcome, invent or heal. You can become trapped in a "mentally stalled" state, where you are paralyzed and unable to make decisions. During this moment, you are unconsciously allowing fear, traumatic memories, and physical pain to interfere with being able to move forward powerfully. Fortunately, there is a method to move past this "STALLED STATE." We move forward by unleashing and applying the true power that moves through us. But, chaos can almost be full-blown crippling. The following personal stories will help serve as examples to the power of chaos.

OVERCOMING

You may falsely assume that I had a great foundation to do such amazing things in life. Some may say that I was always prepared to achieve great feats, but that response would not be the truth. In fact, I experienced every type of challenge in reaching my goals. If I had not seen the good that came out of every challenging situation, I would have crumbled under the types of pressures I endured.

You may ask, "Wasn't rocket science hard?" My honest answer is that rocket science had its own set of challenges. My difficult upbringing in the grand scheme of life helped me to stay in a rocket environment where it wasn't always easy to handle as a woman.

A dear friend suggested I should document my experiences in a book. So I am taking his advice. I will be candid and share with you the truthful challenges I endured in childhood. The wisdom gained from each experience helped me to free my spirit to overcome and unleash brainpower. Once your spirit is aligned, then your brain power unleashes – you go *POW*!

However, instead of me writing about myself, what if I asked you to be in my shoes? I wonder if you would've made the same life choices. Envision yourself in my life.

Changing Your Thoughts = Building Your Power

Suppose from day one; you were born with a challenge to overcome. At infancy, your biological father left your mother. You see him a total of 5 times while growing up. You never comprehended the meaning of a two-parent home. Suppose while watching "The Facts of Life" (a TV sitcom in the 1980's), you were first introduced to the term, "parents." While struggling to define this new term, you think about the two dominant leaders in your home. You ask Mom if she and your older sister, Crystal, are your parents. You distinctly remember their puzzled look. Nevertheless, you have vivid memories of Mom repairing roof shingles on top of the house, and Crystal welding together pipes, along with fixing other plumbing issues around the house. You think they were your parents: unbeknownst to you, this was a single-woman-run home. Despite going through life without a father present, you manage to embrace the fact that women can do ANYTHING, even without a man present!

When you turned 4, your grandfather (aka "Papa") the only positive male figure in your life, passes away. He was the one who taught you how to count. Papa provided the most support to mom when providing for you and your siblings. And when grandpa passes, you begin to feel a deep sense of loss that never seems to go away. Your mother deals with her own grief. Now, you realize she was battling her own type of depression while struggling to raise three girls (Crystal, Caprice, and you). The blessing from that situation is that you also understand that your grandfather has always watched out for you from heaven.

When you were 6, you take a life-changing field trip. Your first-grade class visits the Jet Propulsion Laboratory (in Pasadena, Calif.), to see where rockets and jets are built. Ironically, Papa was a janitor in Pasadena for more than 30 years before he retired. That trip alone inspires you to one-day launch rockets like the men you saw in the pictures on the wall.

Two years later, when you were 8, your whole world changes and the unthinkable happens. Mother befriends two men who become "friends of the family." This situation is quite disconcerting: you are a naive female. You admire and look up to one of the men until he mistook that trust. He rapes you at 8-years-old! The good news is that your brain literally erases the memory until 30 years later. You finally confront and remove the trauma that those painful memories caused for more than 3 decades. In doing so, you learn that despite your age, painful memories caused by traumatic experiences can be removed.

At the age of 9, your mother gives birth to your youngest sibling (Auriel), and then your mother suffers from post-partum depression. Mom stays in bed all day. The good news is that you and you sisters learn to raise yourself in the most difficult situations. You learn to bake and cook delicious dishes, along with learning to make household repairs.

In the 4th grade, you experience many challenges. You develop severe acne, have trouble digesting food and coping with stressful situations (unknowingly due to sexual trauma). You start struggling in school. But to deal with situations, you learn to take yourself out of reality and start envisioning the future. To your surprise, things in the future start happening. Many things that seemed like déjà vu occur. So you start spending most of your time in the future instead of the present. You become very good at predicting what will happen next.

At 10-years-old, your family falls deeper into financial hardship. You and your sisters chew on ice regularly to trick your brains into thinking it's food. Fortunately, Mom decides to return to junior college at night, as she attempts to educate herself for a better job. Mom is training for a position where she could actually pay for daycare. But upon entering night school, she must drop out abruptly. A crack house opens in your neighbor's back house. Daily, you watch unsuspecting people light up crack pipes on the outside of your bedroom window. Mailmen. Teachers. Prostitutes. With each moment, a portion of your childhood is stripped away. On the bright side, you begin having a deeper relationship with God, while praying for addicts outside your window.

A few months later, while in your fifth-grade classroom, you are stabbed in the face by a boy. Unbeknownst to you, he's filed down a ring so it would cut like a knife. You and he get into an argument over a piece of paper. This young gang member finds pride in disfiguring your face. On the other hand, you nearly lose your left eye. Hope is restored at the hospital. While stitching up your face, the surgeon shares the good news. He looks into your eyes and says," I will stitch your face up so well that when you go on TV, all there will be is a little line on your face." His words excite you. For a few hours, you forget about your face, and you become excited. No one knows that you had this dream of appearing on TV.

Mom pulls you out of school and finds a way to enroll you in a gifted magnet school across town. You soon learn that you were four grades behind your peers, due to the lack of educational resources in your former poverty-stricken school. Once a star math pupil, you now fail Algebra and Geometry. A false belief enters your mind: Thoughts of no longer succeeding in math clouds your brain. Nevertheless, the greatest outcome of that situation is you learn anyone can succeed: no matter her heritage, "race," or socio-economic background. The pivotal variable in this solution is having mentors who expect students to succeed at a certain pace.

At the tender age of 13, you enter 10th grade, by finding a way to attend Alexander Hamilton Performing Arts High School (near Beverly Hills, Calif). Your friend, Teveya, and her father show you how to complete the magnet school enrollment application. For you, Hamilton is the only option. The high school in your neighborhood is gang- and drug-infested. To ensure acceptance into Hamilton, you learn to sing and act in order to pass the audition. Since the age of 5, dancing had always been a favorite pastime. For Hamilton's audition, you give an "applause-worthy" rendition of "Somewhere Over the Rainbow" from the movie, *The Wizard of Oz*. The judges are impressed and accept you as one of the youngest performing arts students. By this time, you've learned to express yourself and escape the outside world in doing so.

Simultaneously, Mom returns to school and your older sister, Crystal, leaves home. You find yourself caring for your two younger sisters alone at night. Now, you've taken on the role of "second mom." Daily life is filled with cooking, feeding the dog, doing laundry, and other household chores. Schoolwork becomes an overwhelming abyss. Sadly, you begin failing Calculus and Chemistry.

Following a 30-day experience, your life dramatically changes at the age of 16. Mr. Provencio is a Calculus teacher who offers complimentary tutoring for anyone in Advanced Placement (AP) Calculus, planning to take the final AP standardized exam. You take him up on his offer. And you borrow $1.35 each day from the kind gas station attendant. He knows you have no money to attend school while on Winter break. The bus ride is 2-hours each way. Every sacrifice is well-worth Mr. Provencio's empowering one-hour tutoring sessions.

Mr. Provencio serves to be your first "brain power" life coach. An epiphany occurs during this transformational experience. You discover your brilliant capacity to learn and retain information. Problems now appear as "silent messengers" designed to point to life's answers. You realize the divine power of connection. When connecting with the right help, you can eventually learn to accomplish any goal. But it requires you to stop clinging onto fear as an excuse.

You take the AP Calculus test and still fail. However, the lessons you relearned from that Winter 1993 would change the course of your entire life into the direction of success.

The divine path has now been formed. Teveya and her father help you complete college applications. Among the many colleges, you are accepted into California State University Northridge and received a $1000 scholarship. But since your mother was on governmental assistance (and your father never paid child support) they threatened to cut your sisters off welfare unless you turned your scholarship money over to the county. If you stayed at home, your sisters would starve. But if you leave home, you could help save the only way they had an opportunity to eat.

Being the toughest moment in your life, you choose to sacrifice time with your family. You decide to leave your 8-year-old sister, Auriel, who you vowed to protect, in order to help them. So, you leave home at the age of 16. You instantaneously grow up, learning to budget, while living on your own. You now have the responsibility of grocery shopping, purchasing toothpaste, toilet tissue, and other personal items. Looking back, you have never lived at home since. Fortunately, throughout this time, you have learned to use your intelligence to keep a roof over your head.

At the age of 17, you survived one of the most catastrophic events in California history. On January 17 at 4:31 in the morning, the 1994 Northridge Earthquake occurs. Your college friend dies in the collapsed apartment building across the street. This is the first time you have experienced death since your grandfather. More importantly, you had never experienced an earthquake of that magnitude. You and your younger sisters barely make it out alive. Fearfully shaken, Caprice, 12, and 8-year-old Auriel follows closely behind as you navigated dark stairways riddled with shattered glass to escape the collapsing building. It would take you almost two years before you learn to no longer sleep in tennis shoes and street clothes. You would lose everything you owned. But at the same time, you felt thankful. You were alive: you had survived a horrific event. But thankfully you were only 17 and realized there was still much to live for. The gift of life was the most powerful opportunity you realized you owned.

When you turned 18, you became a math tutor and started working as a student orientation director on campus, leading student tours around the institution. You find yourself enjoying this role because you can use your performing arts skills you acquired back in high school to inspire people to be committed to learning. You are hired by a woman, Shellie Smith, who would later say to you in a conversation, "One day I want to work for you." Little did she know that her words shaped the way you see yourself as a future business mogul.

Image 1-2: Photo of Olympia LePoint using math and science. Photo courtesy of California State University Northridge.

At the age of 18, you try to live back at home with your mother during a Summer Break. You didn't anticipate an extremely difficult commute. Nor did you foresee the next challenge heading your way. Mom lived two hours and twenty-five minutes away from the college campus where you worked. You try to make an effort because you want to spend time with your mother, and you didn't have money to live anywhere else. She is dating a man who drinks way excessively. One day, Mom's boyfriend becomes agitated because you've been talking on the phone too long. You're deep in conversation and ignore his commands to hang up. Without warning, he approaches you like a child and attempts to intimidate you. Although you stand your ground, he's intoxicated and enraged. Within seconds, you're gasping for air as he clenches your throat while pushing you into the back door. Your head jolts against the door's glass window, shattering it into pieces. You look up as jagged pieces of glass fall toward your eyes. You close your eyes and pray to God (like you did with the crack addicts) that God saves you, too. Miraculously, none of the glass scratches your face, and the glass misses your eyes – the same eye that received stitches following a childhood stabbing.

You leave immediately following this incidence with your Mom's boyfriend, vowing never to be around an alcoholic again. You also tell your mother that you would never live at home again. You do everything you can you to keep a roof over your head as you work and go to school. This mission results in finding friends willing to let you sleep on sofas for a couple of days each week while over Summer Break until the semester started. Traveling from friend-to-friend, you sleep on couch-to- couch. Oftentimes, you repeatedly wore the same clothes. Your mission was to get an education: no matter what because you know that an education will change the pattern of your life. Fortunately, your mother wakes up to the value of her own choices and throws the man out after he does the same thing to one of your younger siblings several months later.

At age 19, you take classes in a Calculus II class and encounter other school mates, who were sexist, and question whether you "belong" in the right class on the first day of school. After all, you are the only female in the class. To top it off, you have a professor who suggests you should no longer be a math major since you do not understand the homework nor did know how to complete assignments. Yet, you are the only person who showed up for tutoring at the time. You find a way to politely put this professor in his place. Yet you go home to your roommate and cry your eyes out, wondering if all of this hard work in Science, Technology, Engineering, and Math was worth it.

But in this process, you encounter three people who remind you of your worth in science. Although you barely made enough to pay for dorms, tuition, books, and supplies, you had the support of the late Jane Pinkerton who saw your gift of teaching. Through the guidance of your first college math professor, Dr. Schilling, and an amazing German Linear Algebra professor, Dr. Michael Neubauer, you graduate as one of the Top 5 students in a 6,500-graduating class receiving a Mathematics degree.

Would you have chosen to go endure this chaotic path, in order to reach your first accomplishment of your journey?

INVENTING METHODS FOR SUCCESS

How can you birth greatness? This is a theory that many philosophers have discussed for centuries. How does someone invent something out of nothing? How does someone take an idea and birth it from simply a dream? Is there a way to consistently do this for success?

Well, I saw this process close up when I entered rocket science at the age of 21. I earned an advanced degree in Mathematics. While working as a rocket scientist launching NASA's Space Shuttles, I witness Einstein-like minds create out-of-this world inventions. Imagine being in my shoes once again.

On the first day of work, you enter excitedly. You are proud of yourself. For the first time in your life, you feel as if you have earned something that no one can take away from you: a university education. More importantly, you manage to overcome every obstacle in your path to graduate at the top of a 6,500 California State University Northridge senior class. You complete this goal after sleeping on people's couches, nearly starving, studying all night, and practically living in the library. You feel like you are on top of the world.

Now, you find yourself hired by the Boeing Company. The aeronautics company hires you as a mathematician to use statistical knowledge for helping engineers create correct engine parts without causing waste. Little did you know that you would be in this role for a couple of months.

On the second day, you are both excited and disturbed. Your eyes open in awe over two events that would set the tone for your nearly decade-long run at the company. First, you are brought across the street to see the Space Shuttle Main Engine up-close. It is being constructed by skilled engineers. It is a 2-story tall huge engine that had thousands of tubes running in one direction, and over 100 fuel lines running in others. You attempt to get close and are advised to stay back. Any fingerprint oils on the metal could eat through the specially heat-treated material in Earth's upper atmosphere. Picture acid eating through mold: that's the damage human fingerprints could cause when touching alloy metal. You are amazed to know that your math knowledge is now going to help launch this enormous piece of machinery. At the picture below, I am looking at one of the three Space Shuttle's main engines.

Image 1-3: Photo of Olympia LePoint next to the Space Shuttle Main Engine. Photo courtesy of California State University Northridge.

As you walk back to your desk, you experience an epiphany. You are a woman of color working in the predominately-white, male aerospace world. You would have never thought of this until you walked down a hallway. A gray bearded, tall lumber jack-sized man greets you in the hallway. He looks at you, and his mouth drops open. You wonder why he has such an expression by examining your clothes to verify there are no stains, and ensuring no tissue is on your feet. Then, you realize the gentleman is gazing at you in complete disbelief. He stands, while his eyes circle around you as if you are a museum piece. Without saying a word, the man suddenly walks away. You have no idea how to respond. As a "new hire," you're careful to feel out the environment before saying or doing anything. To top it off, you've never met this man.

Seconds later, a few women whom you also don't know pull you into the lady's restroom. They introduce themselves as "secretaries" for the major executives on your floor. The women describe how excited they are to see you because a female engineer had not been hired in their area for over 15 years. The secretaries state that they are supportive of you. They also warn you of a major issue. This issue is one that you would encounter from select people during your entire time at the company.

One lady turns to you and says, "He was one of the nice guys. You are a woman. And some men, not all, will do anything to make a woman upset and cry. This is their tactic to get you emotional. If you get emotional, they use this as a reason why you can't handle the job. Their ultimate hidden agenda is to find one of their male friends to replace you. So, if you ever get upset, never let the men see you cry. Never let them know how you feel. You can grab one of us here and take us to the restroom. Talk it out with us. Whenever you go out there, stay calm." You grab this wealth of knowledge and run with it for the next 20 years.

You encounter both exhilarating and horrific circumstances that tested the fabric of your brain power.

One day, you are working, and you are introduced to a man by the name of Zhao who is overworked. And there is only one other person at the company of 3,500 employees who could do the same calculations for him. You ask him to help you in your graduate school homework. He graciously helps you. And in turn, you become his friend. You offer to help him do the math calculations after work since you see piles of incomplete calculations on his desk. He becomes one of your major mentors who would introduce you to other technology leaders. The friendship with Zhao tremendously helps navigate your way through the engineering world. He is a man from China who was married to a kind woman. And his daughter was close to your age.

Together he and you learn about great engine designs. You are brought along to meetings, where you gain the ability to see how all the fascinating rocket engineering is formed. You discover the right oxidizer and propellant combinations like intricate cooking recipes. This scientific "recipe" would ensure the whole engine does not melt like butter in a sauce pan. You discover how the turbo pumps needed to rotate, so the energy could drain an Olympic-sized swimming pool in less than 5 seconds. You would help plan how the blades would move in bending moments[1] so high vibrations during engine launch would not rip apart the engine.

You discover how to create a rocket design from scratch. And you are pulled to more advanced projects, where you are literally working with engine designers. These engines were designed from a person's imagination. Some dreamt about the designs. One designer, Jeff, would see movement in 4 dimensions, and used his vision to explain the complex design that engineering software had trouble modeling. You see how many brilliant men's vision turn into reality. They use a faith portion of their brain to see the design, how it could operate, and how it could be built.

---

1 Bending moment is the reaction induced in a structural element when an external force or movement is applied to the element causing the element to bend.

And you are able to get inside of the minds of people who literally create massive 2-story tall rockets from simply an idea that came to them in a dream.

Then you are promoted to the position that authorizes engine tests. Your signature is the System Safety and Reliability signature for the program. This meant that no engines could be tested without your signature. At this time, you are working with another mentor named Dennis who takes you under his wing to show you every weld, nut, and bolt that had to be considered within hot fire tests. No person could test the Main Engine without your signature. Your signature would mean a lot. Your signature would ensure that you knew the health of every single duct and line, the location of every tube, knew all testing factors and the performance history of every component within the Main Engine. You were like a doctor knowing a patients' health before going into surgery. Except the human was the rocket. Your signature meant that you had memorized books of information regarding that one test. You were 100% confident that no human lives would be lost if a malfunction were to occur. This research was required to authorize engine tests. And at nights, the stress from the role would inspire you to pray that everything would test successfully.

Later, you graduate to the next leg of your career with Dennis. You rise to a new position supporting Mission Control. You sit in this dark room called the ROSC for 12-hour time frames. For 12 hours straight, you are looking at numbers roll past your eyes on 5 screens in front of you. One screen is for the turbo pumps. One screen is for valve pressurization. One screen shows the controller and electrical signals of all the engines' red lines[2]. Another screen shows the pre-launch pneumonic pressures of the freezing gasses that kept the oxidizer from immaturely combining with the fuel. You needed to prevent a launch pad explosion as well as a launch explosion.

You have every single engine function categorized. You are looking at component health information. You have a unique role different than everyone else's. Your job is to understand how all of other people's parts were going to connect and map together during launch. You predicted issues before they happen. You are paid to predict the future like a fortune teller. And you would have to devise ways for your brain to see simultaneous futures at once. Your role was devised in a way to pick the future that would ensure flight. Your work is a success. So much so, 20 years later your desk and seat become an exhibit at the California Science Center visited by millions of people per year in Los Angeles, California.

---

[2] Redline refers to the maximum engine speed, temperature or pressure at which an internal combustion engine or traction motor and its components are designed.

Image 1-4: Photo of Olympia LePoint's desk an exhibit at the California science Center ROSC exhibit in Los Angeles, California.

While experiencing innovation, simultaneously, you are battling a chaotic situation. You are often treated as if you do not know what you are talking about, even though you oversee authorizing high levels of technical procedures. Remember, you are a woman: the only woman in a room filled with 200 men, at times. During one instance, a man even tries to present your work in lieu of you because, "You are young and a woman." But, you stand your ground to present your own work instead of being pressured into letting this one man take the credit. He later apologizes.

Another time, you win a national award, *The Modern Day Technology Leader Award*, as part of the Engineering of the Year Awards. You are extremely honored and excited. Then you find your car keyed from end to end with racial slurs from a disgruntled envious employee. You cannot believe how some people could fear you, or be fooled to think success is not for everyone.

To top matters off, you are grilled when you give presentations to the same individuals the women in the restroom warned you about. You discover you always must know twice as much as the next engineer. Some of your mentors pull you aside and tell you what was said about you behind closed doors. Your brainpower is being tested. And there are times where you seek comfort with your secretary friends, and cry with them in the restroom.

The two worlds collide. On the one hand, you encounter frustrating challenges of being a woman in a male-dominated world. On the other hand, you're experiencing pure joy and feel purposeful because your scientific work was helping millions indirectly through Space exploration and science innovation. Despite the challenges, you make a choice to brave another day. You do this for nearly 10 years. And it pays off. And what encourages you is the ability to invent ground-breaking science. For what you were creating made UFOs seem like cartoons. You have faith that you are working there for a powerful reason: one in which you would not know fully until 20 years later. In both cases, choosing success was a decision made every day. The path to success was in scientific innovation. Another purpose was to change the way men perceive women, race, and age in the workplace. Unbeknownst to you, your life would eventually inspire millions of people. Countless would later pursue Science, Technology, Engineering and Math (STEM) careers around the globe simply because they would hear your story through a *TEDx Talk*.

HEALING LIVES

When I was working a rocket scientist, my mother endured a terrible accident. This event opened my eyes to see we can change our lives by changing the way we see opportunities. Life is about experiences. Now, allow me to share my experiences. Imagine being in my shoes, traveling on my path once again.

On July 8, 2004, you got this phone call while working on NASA data. It is your sister, Caprice. She tells you that your mother was in a dreadful accident. You drop everything and run to the hospital to find out what happened. You discover this horrific accident caused severe brain trauma, requiring immediate surgery. You go into panic mode: anxiously wondering how things will turn out. Your entire life is turned upside down.

The securities that you enjoyed one minute were taken away the next. It feels like pure chaos. You turn to God and ask for a miracle. Despite the intricate 11-hour surgery, you mother survives. Yet, you remain in shock. Your mother experiences major brain damage and must re-learn to walk, talk, eat, and sleep again. You wonder how anything good will come out of this situation. Nevertheless, you're committed to your mother's recovery. You're also committed to perform in your dream job as a rocket scientist successfully. In fact, you are the only person in your family who can take on the financial burden of this situation.

You find yourself returning to work a week later, and the whole world appears different. All the disagreements you previously encountered have very little meaning in the big picture. Your true friends step up to help, while some "close best friends" now choose to become acquaintances. They shy away from you and your life. You turn to God for help. And you wonder, "If your life will forever remain this way?"

Your intuition becomes unlocked. You begin dreaming of foods that will help your mother's brain heal faster. You accompany her to doctor's appointments. You read everything you can find regarding the brain. You sit down with your mother, and she begins to have coherent conversations with you. Then, you realize the act of talking things out is a way that her brain heals. You form a deeper relationship with your mother. She speaks affirmations: she says she sees herself healed. She sees herself better and doing things she loved.

You see your mother trusting God and committing herself to recover. She performs her physical therapy homework every day without fail. Meanwhile, you are working 10-hour days, and taking care of your mother at night. Your younger sister, Auriel, travels daily on the bus 2 hours each way to watch your mother during the day.

There is an added layer to this situation. You are required to finish your graduate work and write your thesis. Otherwise, all of your classes will be wiped from your records. No more emergency exceptions could be applied. You find yourself working days, caring for your mother at night, and then staying up until 3 a.m. writing your Master Thesis. You are surviving on three hours of rest per night. You wonder how on earth you will survive this ordeal.

Your mother's faith is powering her. And you start to recognize that her brain is firing faster. She is starting to speak faster. Now, your mother is able to stand up on her own, as well as notice things that escape YOUR attention. Your mother is healing. Her faith is healing her life, and it is offering you the power to heal your life. Meanwhile, you are working steadily, taking care of your mother, and deciphering how much permanent disability will exist.

She gradually makes progress. Your mother continues to envision herself returning to various tasks. Then, a huge test comes for both of you. As you are two days from submitting your thesis to earn your advanced degree in mathematics, you experience an unforeseeable situation. You go to the grocery store and unknowingly buy a tainted batch of salmon. You take it home. Cook it. And upon eating the first bite, your intuition goes into action. This is the same intuition that awoke through the chaos of your mother's accident. Intuition tells you to stop eating the salmon even though seconds before you were starving. You decide to follow your intuition.

Three hours later, you wake up with uncontrollable vomiting. Blood spews out of your mouth. You manage to call your friend, Marguerite, who takes you to the hospital. Upon arriving at the hospital, you collapse in the Emergency Room. You wake up five hours later after receiving six IV bags. The Emergency Room physicians say, "You are lucky. Had you eaten any more of the poisoned salmon, there's a high possibility you would've died from poisoning." You are purely thankful to be alive, yet distraught. One day remains until your thesis is due. Otherwise, years of hard work will go down the drain.

During this time, your mother is witnessing your faith in her recovery. She values all of your work with her, and your dedication to receive your master's degree. While you're still recovering at the hospital, you inform your mother of an important document requiring multiple signatures prior to submitting your thesis. Still fighting food poisoning, you go in and out of consciousness at the hospital. Simultaneously, your mother takes a huge leap of faith. Unbeknownst to you, she calls her medical driver and asks to be guided through your college campus. Although in her recovery state she slowly walks, inch-by-inch across a vast university campus. There, she finds the offices of your thesis advisors and has all three professors (whom she never met) sign this last document.

As you lay in the hospital bed, your mother comes in the room and says, "Look, honey, I got the paper signed for you. I brought my driver with me, and I found your teachers."

Your eyes tear with complete gratitude that you were helped when you needed it most. Your mother's brain power unleashes a strong faith. It gives you the courage to take IV needles out of your arm, and check out of the hospital to complete your thesis. After submitting your thesis, you collapse in the hallway. That moment in time, you realize faith fueled you to this point. Faith gave you the power to heal your life and your loved one. Faith was far more powerful than you ever could have imagined. It is through embodying faith, lives powerfully change their trajectories.

Later, you would learn that your future depended on that moment in time. With that advanced mathematics degree, you would later use that knowledge to help create innovative rocket launches, prevent billion-dollar currency processing issues at a national banking institution, teach tens of thousands of university student's overcome their fears in mathematics, and later write a series of books about the brain.

SUMMARY

As you can tell, those stories embody chaos at its truest applied form. These stories are meant to heighten your awareness that chaos can lead to amazing results in the end. Chaos is pivotal to what you are about to read. As an adult who has conducted years of rigorous mathematical training, I have found the answer to the brain reshaping process. The answer is ready for unleashing. Extraordinary skills required within inventing new science are identical skills necessary within overcoming situations. Exceptional abilities mastered while overcoming horrific situations are similar skills used to heal the body. And, the same decisions used to heal the body are equal attributes that transform external environments for the better. These situations all require chaos to act as a catalyst.

In the process of overcoming situations, we create a new life. And in the case of inventing scientific solutions, we find new life. But the process to triumph is not achieved overnight. Nor is the ability to make overnight scientific discoveries. But, solutions are revealed. When a solution arrives, you must usher it into existence through the intuition of your brain. However, you may not be aware of how to birth this success.

Through this book, you will learn details to reshape the brain and unleash its power. You'll also realize that every circumstance is designed for your unique purpose. You are never stuck in a terrible situation. You have been gifted with a powerful brain and the ability to change situations. You have the power to alter your life. You have been given a brain to recreate health. You have the mental capacity to succeed.

The answer revolves around the theory of reshaping your brain's thoughts, unleashing its intuition and feeling the joy during the process. During my *TEDx Talk,* "Reprogramming Your Brain to Overcome Fear," I first introduced fear, but didn't understand the complete picture. Overcoming fear was just one part of the brainpower unleashing process.

Within ***Answers Unleashed***, you will see how painful memories and fear separate your three-sided brain, which I call the *Triabrain*. Painful memories create brainbrink, which occurs when chaos hits your brain. A separation occurs and disrupts communication between your brain's hemispheres. This disruption "divorces" your brain from changing the environment. Your thoughts can direct chaos into two paths: "success" or a "stalled state," which sends you into a repeated cycle of frustration or propels you into a complete success.

Your *Triabrain* channels your solutions. When you are in a chaotic state with faulty thinking, you experience brainbrink. This is when your thoughts are used against you, thereby allowing chaotic energy to become trapped in your brain. Your ANSWERS are hidden.

But there is good news. Brainbrink can be overcome by reconnecting your brain's three most vital sectors to form the *Triabrain.* This unification is achieved by repowering the faith, right, and left-brain hemispheres using the exercises in each chapter. This system is devised with Mathematical Chaos Theory, Science applications, Psychology, Energy principles, and foundations rooted in Faith. When you merge your *Triabrain*, you reach successful states in your life. Successful CEOs, billionaires, athletes, and inventors all have use of this brainpower too! There is a science to selecting brain paths that lead to solutions. Brilliant answers equal unimaginable success.

When you reunite the three sectors of the *Triabrain*, you transform any energy to invent solutions in your life, allowing your problems to work together for you instead of against you. After reading this book, you will look at life challenges as opportunities to test out your new brainpower. Every situation is an opportunity for you to create your success. This book is simple, yet profound. If you realize that you are the only one in charge of changing your brain, you will change your life. No one else has this power except you. But first, let us understand how the brain is SUPPOSED TO work by understanding an important theory I call the ***Triabrain Theory of Relativity*** in Chapter 2, and ***The Truth in Your Triabrain Connections*** in Chapter 5.

Let's unleash some knowledge…

The Triabrain Theory of Relativity

CHAPTER 2

THE TRIABRAIN THEORY OF RELATIVITY

"Olympia! Mommy has been in an accident," Caprice yelled.

"What?" I frantically replied from my office phone. It was July 8, 2004, and I was in the middle of running calculations for launch STS-114. This was a pivotal step toward ensuring *Space Shuttle Discovery's* launch a year later. Nevertheless, when an emergency family matter occurs, you drop everything.

"I got a call from the hospital. Mommy was hit in a car accident, and a light pole fell on her," Caprice screamed in panic. "She is at County USC Hospital."

"Is Mommy okay? Can she walk? Does she have all her limbs? How did it fall on her?" I demanded in a panic.

"I don't know! I don't know!" My sister responded in hysteria.

"I am coming. I will be there in 40 minutes," I assured Caprice. "I am leaving work now. I will be there to pick you up, and we will go to the hospital together." I responded with determination to get to the hospital as fast as possible.

I looked at my computer, and I prayed, "God, please let Mommy be okay."

I grabbed my purse and keys, left my computer on, and passed my work manager, yelling out the door, "I am leaving. My mother has been in a horrible accident."

This traumatic call came during the most hectic time at my job. We were preparing for the first shuttle launch planned after *Space Shuttle Columbia's* disastrous event upon re-entry into the atmosphere Feb. 1, 2003. At the time, I was working for Boeing's Space Shuttle Main Engine Program. My calculations helped authorize *Discovery's* return flight.

But, fear ravaged my brain. I had trouble driving. As I went to fill up my car tank with gas, I was so nervous I couldn't place the nozzle in the gas gauge until the fourth time. I just couldn't hold my hands steady. As I continued driving on the freeway in route to retrieve my sister, I found myself speeding. Now looking back, speeding was the most dangerous action I mistakenly took.

While I drove, I heard a clear, distinctive man's, authoritative voice in my ear. He powerfully commanded, "Do not endanger other people as you travel to the hospital." It was a voice I could not ignore. I followed the directions immediately and without question. I lifted my foot off the gas, pursuing at a slower pace toward my mother's home. I picked up my sister, and we silently drove together. Although estranged for seven years prior to this incident, we were bonded by that moment to help save our mother. Once we discovered we had no clue where we were going, we began speaking. Sure, we had an address. But this was before GOOGLE phones, and handheld GPS was available. Needless to say, we struggled to find to the hospital. About an hour later, we arrived at County USC Hospital. We parked in a multi-layered parking lot. Then, we walked on a concrete bridge to the hospital.

Once we were in the hospital, we were faced with the mission to find our mother. It felt like time stood still, as I traveled to the Emergency Room. Around me, I saw people with stab wounds. I saw people on their "death beds," with a dark; gray aura encircled around them. Life was slowly separating from their bodies. On the other hand, healthy people experiencing illness seemed to have a beautiful, white aura around them. For some powerful reason, I instantly knew who was going to make it, and who would leave this Earth in death.

We walked through a long set of hallways and open areas. While experiencing mental chaos, we walked down a tranquil Spanish-style lobby, with blue and yellow tiles lining the walls. Hoping for a miracle, we walked through a tight, closed corridor. We started on one corner of the huge hospital complex, and we winded through pathways in search of the Emergency Room. Once there, we found the people who were overseeing our mother's care. Now, we would learn the severity of Mom's accident.

My mother was an Administrative Assistant in Downtown Los Angeles. She decided to walk across the street to get office supplies. While on her way back from the store, the unthinkable happened. A red, pickup truck made an illegal move against a traffic light. An oncoming SUV swerved to avoid a head-on collision with the pickup truck. As the driver of the SUV took measures to avoid one accident, another was caused. The SUV came to the curve, hitting the traffic signal, which in turn ripped it out the ground. My mother tried to escape from the corner. The traffic signal fell on her head, cracking her skull and slicing it open. My mother was catastrophically injured and remained alive despite the horrific blow to her head.

Seen by many people as "random," an off-call ambulance was just 2 blocks away from the accident. Drivers responded immediately when onlookers called 9-1-1. Fortunately, Mom's skull cracked in many places including the base of her neck. Although this news seemed horrible at first, these fractures allowed severe bleeding to release the over-pressurization in her skull.

Emergency Room doctors had her sedated for surgery by the time my sister and I finally arrived. My older sister, Crystal, was already there. Little did she know, years from now, she too would undergo brain surgery from a surgery-related accident. Caprice and I greeted her. Though our youngest sister, Auriel, had yet to arrive, we were happy to know she was on her way. During this time, the Emergency Room doctor told us that, in order to stop the bleeding, they had to transport Mom into neurotrauma brain surgery. All of us gasped in panic when attempting to answer a few questions posed by the Emergency Room doctor. He wanted to know if we had any clue regarding Mom's final requests if her heart should fail during surgery. I was speechless as I heard these questions. Tears filled my eyes with the thought of losing Mom. I could not live with that reality. None of us responded.

The doctor said, "We can't wait for your decisions, we are taking her in NOW to stop her brain from bleeding."

As the doctor turns away walking, I run after him asking, "Will she be okay?"

His answer burns in my memory.

And his answer to my question is given in Chapter 6. All the subsequent problems that had to be solved in the coming ten years would serve to emerge my expertise in knowing about the brain. My expertise did not come from a formal neuroscience educational background or a prestigious psychotherapy curriculum. Rather, my mother's traumatic brain injury (and later Crystal's brain surgery) forced me to understand the human brain, its internal workings, and functions that people have yet to discover. If Mom were to survive, I would have to know how I could help her overcome this horrific ordeal. I became a brain – specialist for the sake of my mother's survival. This moment in time would forever shift my focus from just rocket science to encompassing the power of the human brain in everything we do here in this universe.

THE BRAIN'S OLD OPERATION MANUAL

If you were to buy a new blender, chances are you would open the instruction manual only when you encountered a problem. If you bought a new car, you would definitely make sure you had the newest and latest version of the operational manual. It would include specifications, horsepower, type of maintenance required, and offer guidance on recommended repairs. The more expensive the machinery, the more inclined you are to ensure you can handle its operation. I guarantee you that every luxury sports car owner knows about his vehicle inside and out.

How more valuable is our brain than a luxury sports car? Do you have your brain's operation manual? Unfortunately, when I was tasked with taking care of my mother, I did not own an operational manual. In fact, I did not know how to use my brain fully. In fact, very few people understand how to use their entire brain either completely. At present, a 100% accurate general operational manual for our brain does exist. Furthermore, you are unaware of the true power your brains harnesses. Using the car as an analogy, we are the equivalent to an 8-year-old trying to drive a manual transmission Bugatti at 520 miles-per-hour. But, our tires blow out at 250 miles-per-hour because we've haven't figured out how to match the tires to the engine's performance level. If not shown how to master such fine biological engineering, we are bound to crash.

At first, I learned some basic information about the brain to help Mom. I could write books upon books based on what I've read about the brain. Many expert neuroscientists study hundreds of books on this concept. And for years, many psychologists and neurologists have attempted to define some basic functions of the brain. With a multitude of research, trials, and errors, brain specialists as a whole have come to agree there is one brain with a left and right side. Within each brain, there is a set of hormone responses and neuron synapses that allow the brain to function in its intended operation. I've decided to expound upon this concept. My goal is to explain how the basic "old way" of viewing the brain doesn't help you change your life. Instead, it is my hope that this newly-proposed brain structure provides an alternative way to view the brain in your daily life.

Just to break down a bit of scientific knowledge, I will share some basics. Your brain is divided into two halves (hemispheres). The left half of the brain controls the right side of your body. Connecting both hemispheres in the center is the **corpus callosum**. The right half of your brain controls the left side of the body. The brain function was investigated by Roger W. Sperry, a neuropsychologist, whose experiments examined the way the human brain hemispheres operate independently and together (Sperry, 1945). The right brain-left brain theory by Dr. Sperry won the Nobel Prize in 1981. While studying the effects of epilepsy, Sperry discovered that by cutting the corpus callosum, seizures could be reduced or eliminated. However, these patients also experienced other horrible symptoms after the communication pathway between the two sides of the brain was severed. In the study, patients faced many difficulties: some describe it like human torture.

It was found that your brain's right hemisphere controls the muscles on the left side of your body, while the left hemisphere controls the muscles on the right side of your human body. The left side understands the use of language (listening, reading, speaking and writing). It triggers memory for spoken and written messages. Your left hemisphere initiates detailed analysis of information, clarifies steps in mathematical calculations, and composes music. When you retrieve facts, your left brain pulls it from your memory. How individuals relate to others is also associated with the left hemisphere of the brain.

Similarly, your right hemisphere judges the position of things in space, which includes knowing your body position and self-orientation. So, if you frequently bump into things, you are not aware of your position in space and time. Your right brain recognizes faces and processes music. Your right hemisphere understands and remembers things you do and see. It also connects pieces of information together to make an entire picture for you to understand. Your right hemisphere also controls the left side of your body. It performs some math, but mainly geometrical relationships and comparisons. The brain's right side also helps you comprehend visual imagery and to make sense of what you see. Additionally, the right brain hemisphere plays a role in your language, particularly in interpreting the context and a person's tone of voice. So, if you think someone is mad at you, it is a matter of perception.

As mentioned earlier, your corpus callosum is a bridge between your left and right brain hemispheres. A bundle of nerve tissues, your connection contains over 200 million nerve fibers that carry electrical impulses from the neurons' cell bodies. These cells facilitate communication between both sides of your brain. This corpus callosum part is the largest collection of "white matter" within your brain. It has a fatty, protective coating around the nerves that facilitate quicker transmission of your brain information. White matter within the brain allows different parts of the brain to communicate. Please note: gray matter within your brain is "different." Gray matter is for computation, thinking, memory storage, and other conceptual processes. The corpus callosum is located above your thalamus but under your cortex. In short, the corpus callosum is part of your brain that helps your left and right side of your body to move together.

THE NEW BRAIN – THE TRIABRAIN OPERATION MANUAL

Have you ever thought about someone and they called seconds later? Can thoughts heal your body? Is the brain able to predict new technology? When I first wrote my HuffPost ***Lucy*** (LePoint, Movie Review: Lucy, a Thrilling Science Misinterpretation, 2014) movie review, people around the globe commented about what I shared regarding the human brain's power. But that article was simply the "tip of the iceberg." As you recall, I first became knowledgeable about the brain when my mother was in a catastrophic accident, which required emergency brain surgery to survive. After the surgery, Mom was tasked with relearning how to eat, walk, talk, and recall present events. She suffers short-term memory loss. I have been by her side ever since. Through years working with neurologists, neurosurgeons and therapists, I discovered how the human brain reshapes and heals itself.

During my mother's major recovery, I was tackling numerous responsibilities. It took every ounce of my strength and sanity to endure my mother's ordeal while working as a rocket scientist and graduate student. Through these life-altering experiences, I realized that Space and the human brain were nearly identical. Many math concepts about Space are similar to the brain's complex structure. Interestingly, the same math that we use to launch vehicles to Mars is the same math concepts that we use to reshape the brain. I was further floored when I recognized Albert Einstein's famous *Theory of Relativity* explained more than Outer Space. It not only described physics on Earth: but also describes phenomena that happen within and outside of the brain. The true power that we harness within our brains' structure can be mathematically represented as well. This epiphany allowed me in helping my mother's brain heal faster. Through it, the new structure in the brain and how energy is traveling through it can be characterized.

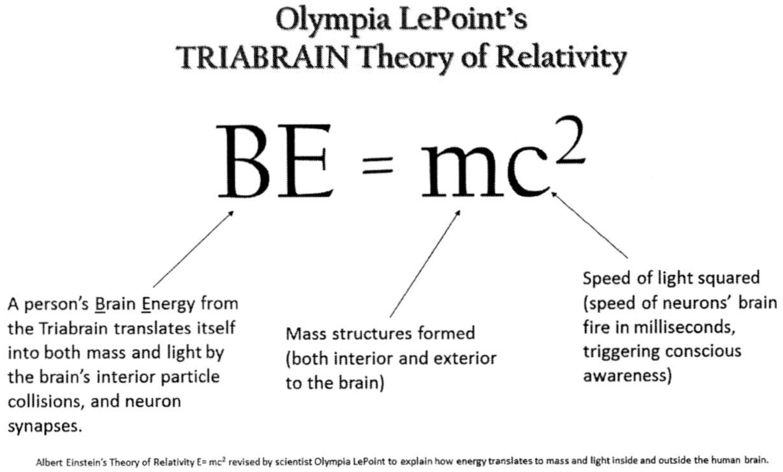

Image 2-1: Olympia LePoint's Triabrain Theory of Relativity

Through personal experiences, my understanding of mathematics, neuroplasticity, and Einstein's *Theory of Relativity*, I have discovered the ***TRIABRAIN***, and the ***Triabrain Theory of Relativity*** (LePoint, The Triabrain and Answers Unleashed, 2016). A *Triabrain* refers to the brain operating in three main modes. And, a person's brain energy from the *Triabrain* translates itself into both mass and light. Brain energy from its interior particle collisions and neuron synapsis form both interior and exterior mass structures to the brain. This is multiplied by the speed of light squared. Light, in this case, is characterized by the neurons' brain fire in milliseconds, which triggers conscious awareness. I will break down this concept with more clarity.

Nearly twelve years after my mother's accident, the unthinkable happened. In May 2016, my older sister, Crystal, experienced a medical accident that required emergency brain surgery for her survival. Painful history seemed to repeat itself. However difficult, both my mother's and sister's brain surgeries created inspiration to explore brain trauma. Life-changing knowledge was exposed through their ordeals.

The *TRIABRAIN*: Everyone Has It

The *Triabrain* is composed of three main sectors; left hemisphere, right hemisphere, and the "Faith Sector." As long as humans are alive, the brain naturally reshapes. But in some, it reshapes faster. It reshapes the fastest when a person consciously uses their full three sectors: the left (scientific logical) side, the right (emotional and creative) side, and a newly-discovered third side I call the ***faith*** (foreseeing side) that connects both sides of the brain, itself. The faith sector is responsible for branching the brain through limbs and organs, and by means of the nervous system. The energy that travels through the faith sector does not end with limbs. It extends outside of the body, creating a circular energy field that can be reprogrammed based on changing thoughts. When the brain is linked to all three sections, the brain reshapes, unleashes answers and regrows. One important fact to grasp is how the faith sector operates. As the third brain sector, it operates independently – without the constraints of time and space.

During my sister's ordeal, I was teaching as a college mathematics professor, and appearing live on my radio show, ***Answers Unleashed***. (LePoint, http://answersunleashed.com/, 2016) The talk show was originally designed to encourage college students to overcome situations by reshaping their brains. By using science and faith, students were able to recognize the answers in front of them. I share more information about "The Triabrain" in the first episode. But little did I know that my informative talk show would contribute to a new dimension of neuroscience.

Image 2-2: Olympia LePoint executive produces and hosts the talk show Answers Unleashed.

The Triabrain's Faith Sector

Now, let's take a closer examination of the newly-discovered third side of the *Triabrain* known as the ***faith sector.*** When you consider its physical structure, the faith sector is the largest white matter segment in the brain. It consists of 200–250 million contra-lateral axonal projections. Most envision the brain as a series of connections separated by a left and right side. However, the faith sector is a combination of the corpus callosum that connects the left and right sides together, plus the entire nervous system that extends into the body. Like a tree has roots, the brain roots into the body. Energy passing within these roots extends outside of the physical body and forms an energy field. This energy can be focused toward any direction. The faith sector also facilitates interhemispheric communication between the left and right sides of the brain. Such communication then extends beyond the body through the energy field. The faith sector allows thoughts to exist not only in the brain but also within the body. Thoughts can be in an arm, hip, foot or in the brain. A painful hip may silently signify a hidden belief of never being supported – physically or emotionally. The faith sector also connects the brain to the outside world. It helps people overcome major obstacles, and inspires people to create new technology. Plus, it appears to initiate significant body healing.

Consider a tree and its numerous roots. The deeper the roots, the more power the tree possesses to thrive. A tree's roots run deep into the ground, connecting to a power *source*. The faith brain also houses roots to the brain. These roots are comprised of the physical corpus callosum structure and the nervous system that extends through all organs, muscles, and limbs. Essentially, the brain is in the entire body and thoughts can happen anywhere that connections occur. Energy from this connecting nervous system also extends outside of the human body into an energy field that will be later explained.

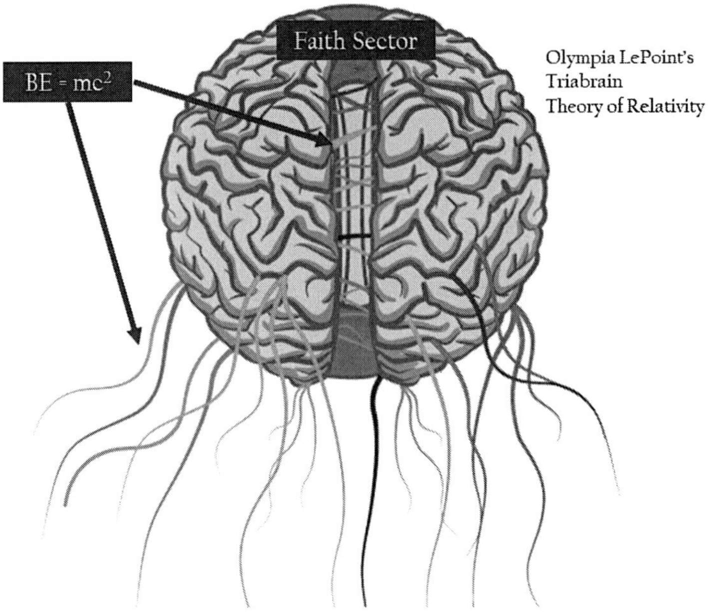

Image 2-3: Illustration of the Triabrain.

Highly-innovative and triumphant people use the faith sector of the brain to accomplish insurmountable tasks, independent of time and space. Let's consider some examples. Olympic athletes often envision themselves winning the gold medal before the Olympic Games begin. Inventors have visions of new technologies before they are created. People who miraculously heal are often the ones who knew "beyond a shadow of a doubt" that they would recover. During my *TED x Talk*, I speak of how I overcame life challenges despite every odd against my favor.

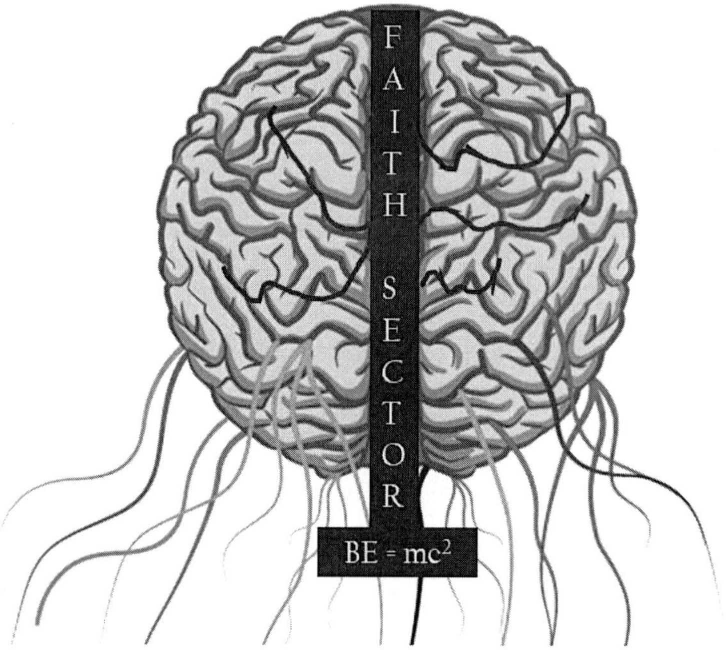

Image 2-4: Illustration of center connections which compose the Faith Brain sector of the Triabrain.

Let's consider the brain composition of one of the world's most notable scientist, Albert Einstein, with respect to the article, "The Corpus Callosum of Albert Einstein's Brain: Another Clue to His High Intelligence," published in the journal ***Brain*** (Men W, 2014). The study released on October 4, 2013, found Albert Einstein's brilliance may be linked to the fact that his brain hemispheres were extremely well-connected. The ability to use right brain's creativity and left brain's logic simultaneously is what made Einstein a genius. The corpus callosum contains a bundle of neuronal fibers found in humans and other higher-order mammals that allow the two hemispheres to talk to one another.

The research was led by Dean Falk, an evolutionary anthropologist at Florida State University. Falk and her team discovered that Albert Einstein had significantly more extensive connections between certain parts of his cerebral hemispheres compared to both younger and older control groups.

For another scientific example, consider the October 27, 2013, ***Medical Press*** article, "Neuroscientists discover new 'mini-neural computer' in the brain," (Falk, 2013) dendrites which are the branch-like projections of neurons, were once thought to be passive wiring in the brain. However, scientists at the University of North Carolina at Chapel Hill are showing that these dendrites are more powerful than once believed. Dendrites relay information from one neuron to the next. These neurons actively process information, multiplying the brain's computing power.

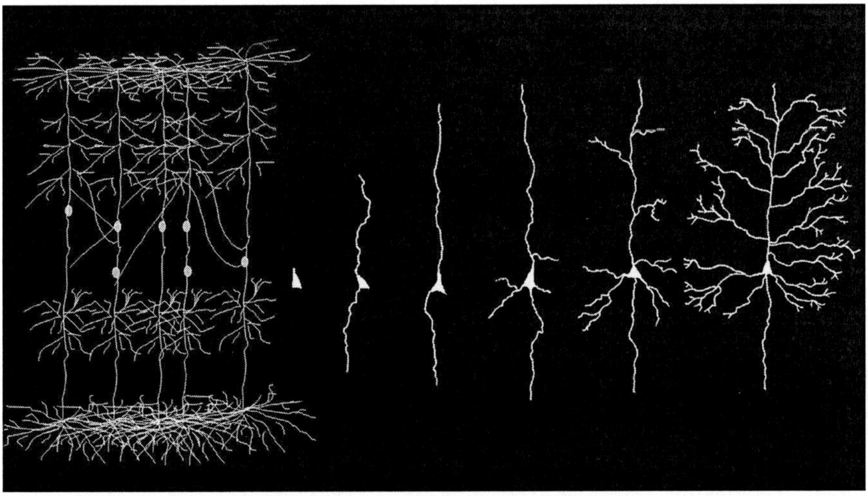

Image 2-5: A stick figure drawing of multiple dendrites (to the left) with a single cell body (to the right) that branches off into numerous dendrite structures connecting in the brain.

According to the February 22, 2016 *Science New Journal* article, "A 'Neuroscience Bombshell'— Human Brain is Capable of Storing the Entire World Wide Web," (A Neuroscience Bombshell - Human Brain is Capable of Storing the Entire World Wide Web, 2016) the brain with its connections is far more powerful than the web and is far more powerful than scientists have projected. The article states:

> *"An average human brain contains around 100 billion neurons, and each neuron is capable of making around 1,000 connections (synapses) with the other neurons. These 1,000 potential synapses created by each neuron*

are responsible for data storage inside the brain and body. Now if we multiply the count of neurons (100 billion) by the number of connections (1000) that each of them can make, then we get a whopping 100 trillion data points — which can at the very least account for storing about 1000 terabytes or 1 petabyte of information."

From my personal experience assisting my mother in her brain therapy support groups, I witnessed that the people who typically recovered fastest were the people who saw themselves healed before test results returned. Naturally, while working with brain specialists, I needed to know the science behind such phenomena. I was surprised when I discovered the brain's reshaping science had yet to be fully understood. So as a scientist, I started applying my own tools of math and science to find answers.

Image 2-6: Image of Olympia LePoint and her mother, Pamela, after Pamela's brain surgery.

THE SCIENCE BEHIND THE TRIABRAIN AND BRAIN RESHAPING

Space and the human brain are almost identical in its structure through the application of Chaos Theory Mathematics. It takes a specific method in order to fly to distant locations in our solar system with a fixed amount of fuel. This technique includes taking a "freeway" through the solar system, which resembles a vast array of virtual winding tunnels and conduits around the Sun and planets. Sticking to this method has allowed engineers to fly to distant planets like Mars and Jupiter. With all the crooks and turns used to transport rockets as I describe in my *Huffington Post* ***"Martian Movie Review by a Rocket Scientist,"*** (LePoint, Martian Movie Review by a Rocket Scientist, 2015) there are identical unknown crooks and turns in the human brain. These crooks and turns transfer knowledge from one area to another faster, igniting the frontal lobes as a result. Once ignited, these frontal lobes are responsible for creating solutions.

Image 2-7: Artist's concept of the interplanetary superhighway. Image credit courtesy of NASA/JPL.

According to Dr. Caroline Leaf, a neuroscientist and author specializing in brain neuroplasticity and cognitive therapy, when a person experiences fear or trauma, dark tar-like mass forms in the brain that bind brain tissue together. The mass functions like glue, provoking cognitive issues whose infectious properties grow with the presence of fear and trauma. It is through my scientific understanding that these infectious masses block the original pathways and force the interior of the brain to alter its superhighway pathways. New crooks and crannies to certain pathways are thereby created. As a result, massive structures block the physical space and "brain fire." However, through my chaos math analysis, the brain fire is similar to a rocket traveling in space. Brain information travels on two types of pathways: where information can stall, or accelerate to an intended destination. And unlike brain synapses that consist of a presynaptic ending containing neurotransmitters, mitochondria, and other cell organelles, these brain neurons are specifically impacting each other through collisions caused by blockages.

Through the blockage caused by the dark-trauma-mass, neurons form several collisions on a miniature scale to us, but it constitutes a large collision in the brain space. And Einstein's *Theory of Relativity* characterizes their action. Ideally, all neurons are electrically excitable, maintaining voltage gradients across their membranes. Neurotransmitters tell a neuron either to fire, or not.

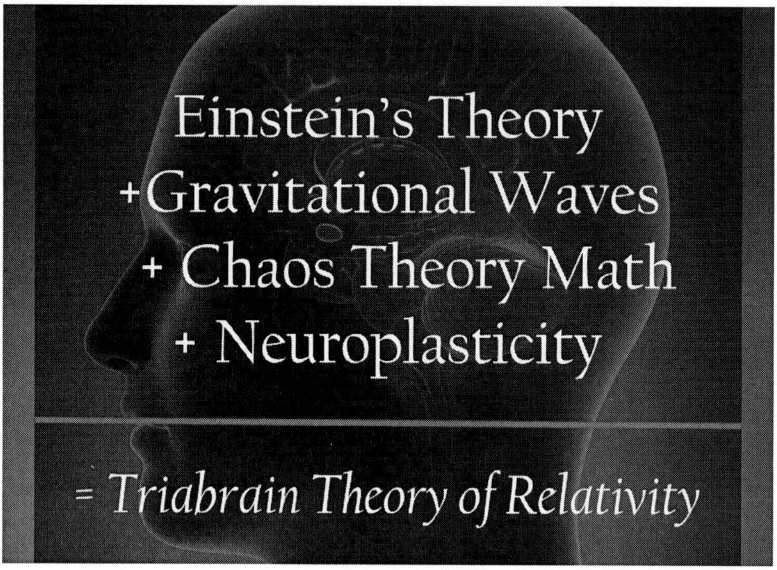

Image 2-8: Triabrain Theory of Relativity Calculations solved by Olympia LePoint

Neuroplasticity science has yet to incorporate Einstein's *Theory of Relativity*, gravitational waves, chaos theory mathematics together within understanding how the brain reshapes itself. As a result, through my understanding of the brain, this led to the *Triabrain Theory of Relativity*, which says that the brain is composed of three sectors and the third sector consists of all the brain connections transferring energy inside and outside of itself using principles of Einstein's *Theory of Relativity*. In this faith sector, it converts energy to mass in conjunction with light. Light can be defined as the way in which a person is consciously aware of the world based on their location in space. Religious officials may call this "c" in the equation the effects of "holy enlightenment." And some energy workers may refer to this "c" as "awareness."

Einstein's theory hinged his proof on the fact that gravitational waves existed, which was recently proven when audio recordings captured two black holes colliding in January 2016. The ***Scientific American Special Report*** on February 14, 2016, titled "The Discovery of Gravitational Waves" gives a detailed account of all The Laser Interferometer Gravitational Observatory (LIGO) gravitational wave discoveries. As a background, LIGO has an L-shaped antenna with perpendicular arms 2.5 miles long. LIGO is composed of layers of steel and concrete which create the world's largest vacuum chamber measuring a couple of feet wide and containing 2.5 million gallons of empty space. At the end of each arm are mirrors hanging by glass threads, isolated from the bumps and shrieks of the environment. It catches movement in Space light years away.

Let's briefly review the background of gravitational waves. These particular waves are "ripples" in space-time produced by violent events in the cosmos, such as the collisions and mergers of massive black holes. Their existence was predicted by Einstein in 1916 when he showed that accelerating massive objects would shake space-time so much that waves distorted space.

On Thursday, February 11, 2016, a team of scientists announced they had proven the last prediction of Einstein's general theory of relativity by using LIGO technology. This discovery changed all science, and it solidifies Einstein's century old theory. When Einstein announced his theory in 1915, he said that matter and energy distort the geometry of the universe, producing the effect we call gravity. Further, Einstein's published work in 1916 explains what we perceive as the force of gravity is the curvature of space and time. Einstein proposed that objects such as the sun and the Earth change this geometry.

Like the way two black holes collided in space, the brain has similar space in it. Comparable to the phenomenon that happens in space, brain neurons and dark brain masses collide and merge. These collisions are considered massive in the brain's space. Thus, they exert a force in the brain's space, resulting in brain gravitational waves that I call ***Triabrain Waves*** (LePoint, The Triabrain and Answers Unleashed, 2016).

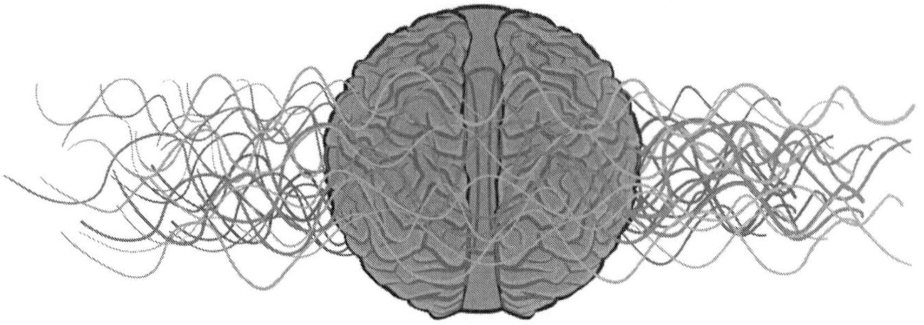

Image 2-9: The brain creates its own gravitational waves, known as 'Triabrain Waves' as depicted in this illustration.

These waves are part of the brain energy structure that directly builds (or destroys) mass in conjunction with brain light. Brain waves travel from the brain and nervous system. When you have a thought, this thought takes energy from the situation and converts it into a *Triabrain Wave*. This energy wave moves time and space just like gravitational waves. When this energy is beneficial, it works together to connect the left and right brain, thereby reshaping the brain's interior. The *Triabrain Waves* are part of the brain's energy system that also sends waves from the brain throughout the body. These powerful waves can also be directed outside of the body. This is the reason why a person may call when you are thinking about him or her. Or, friends may know each other's thoughts for a split second. This energy is sensed by all living organisms. *Triabrain Waves* reshape the brain and its physical properties similar to how gravitational waves in space pierce through all matter. But most importantly, I believe these *Triabrain Waves* are the foundation of all future neuroplasticity science, human intuition studies and are the method in which prayer and faith work to change the exterior world. This concept is explained more in Chapter 5, Chapter 6, and Chapter 7.

For more information about the *Triabrain*, listen to my ***Answers Unleashed*** talk show episode "Triabrain" by visiting the link AnswersUnleashed.com/podcasts.

Image 2-10: Olympia LePoint shares how to reshape the brain with science and human experiences.

So instead of looking at my two-family members' situations as tragedies, I chose to interpret these brain surgeries as blessings. My family members' continuous recovery efforts shed light on our brains' powerful reshaping capabilities, as well as the energy we have yet to harness fully. There is still much for us to understand about the brain. And I welcome other scientists to help in developing this knowledge. Hopefully, this research is a significant introduction to unlocking a new way of thinking about the brain's true capabilities, outside of a science fiction movie seen in theaters.

Next, in Chapter 3, we will understand ***The Meaning of Chaos*** and what happens in the *Triabrain* as chaos unfolds.

The Meaning of Chaos

CHAPTER 3

THE MEANING OF CHAOS

"Olympia, it's an earthquake!" My 8-year old sister, Auriel, yells, while shaking my body, attempting to wake me from a deep sleep.

"Okay," I drowsily respond, thinking the earthquake would end soon.

KA-BOOM! The bed is thrown three feet across the floor, while my sisters and I are waking up in my campus apartment.

The jolt rips pictures from the wall, throwing them like frizz bees 10 feet across the room.

"Olympia," Auriel screams at the top of her lungs, while hysterically shaking and attempting to wake me.

I look around and realize, "*Oh my GOD! Where do we go for cover???*"

The cabinet doors become possessed, continually swinging open and closed until the hinges break from the wall. The glass window behind the bed shatters. We are being hit with every flying object. I shield Auriel with my body.

We hear transformers pop. Meanwhile, the refrigerator is tossed from the kitchen into the living room, throwing milk, raw meat, and ketchup 10 feet across the floor. The sliding living room door shatters, leaving tempered glass scattered across the floor. The TV is thrown directly on the floor, in the exact place where my youngest sister would have slept in her sleeping bag.

It is January 17, 1994, and 4:31 a.m. I am 17 years-old and caring for my younger sisters, 8-year-old Auriel, and 12-year-old Caprice. We are experiencing the catastrophic Northridge Earthquake. My sisters decided to spend a night with their older sister (me) at the university. Although they hoped for an exciting adventure with me, experiencing an earthquake was not on their bucket list.

"Olympia, Olympia!" I hear Caprice screaming from the living room where she slept. She runs into the bedroom near my sister and me. But the vicious swinging door clocks her in the temple, knocking her down.

"Olympia, Olympia!" My youngest sister fearfully yells, while clinging to me.

After 31 seconds, the shaking stops. Car alarms are ringing. Power transformers are popping. The putrid smell of an earthquake permeates the air and almost makes us vomit. Shrieks can be heard from our building and nearby apartments across the way. Although the ground is not shaking, it feels unstable.

Immediately, I hear crackling. I cannot determine if it is fire or a broken water main. In any case, I immediately say, "We have got to get out of here!" Caprice grabs blankets. I take Auriel's coat. Our shoes are nowhere to be found. In the rubble, I somehow manage to find my keys.

We quickly exit my apartment, and enter a dark hallway toward a well-lit EXIT sign, swinging back-and-forth viciously. I knock on my neighbor's door. She answers and says she is okay.

My sisters are in the hallway, gazing at blown-out windows. Hallways are nearly pitch-black, except for neon green, EXIT signs. The signs are powerful indicators, reminding us the importance of leaving the building. A few hours earlier, Northridge had experienced 30-mile gusts of winds. For some reason, wind gusts dissipated, leaving an eerie stillness within this disastrous situation.

My sisters and I proceed to the stairwell. We travel down the first flight of stairs. As we reach the second story, a large aftershock occurs, jolting us forward. The aftershock is almost as strong as the initial quake. Panicked, we look at the wall, checking its sturdiness. Our blood curdles as we see stairs curve. I look back to see the stairwell bolts rip away from the wall. The stairwell starts twisting. Stairs were separating from the wall – we were on these twisting stairs. We had one more story to descend before exiting the building. However, the building was beginning to collapse on itself. I prayed to God for help.

I look at Auriel and throw her on my back. I take Caprice's hand and yell, "We are going to jump!" Crying, they follow. We jump from the second floor to the first floor, landing on the cement in the stairwell. I jarred the door open as the stairs separated from the wall. The bolts, metal, and wood made a horrible groaning sound of destruction. By the grace of God, we didn't break any bones. The bottom stairway door did not become jammed, while we exited the stairwell.

We make it into the lobby. Immediately, I run for the emergency exit door located between two buildings. I quickly realize that if we were to run out this exit door, we would be killed by sheets of falling glass from the floors above.

"No!" I yelled, "We have to go this way!!!!"

I then led my sisters, through a long way over broken glass. It is a miracle we are not cut as we escape into the cold night. We watch part of our building's floors collapse. We escaped at the right time. We look around, and all we see are flames. Over ten of our surrounding buildings are blazing. The flames light the night sky as we hear fire truck alarms in the distance.

We are thankful to be alive.

We were the ones who could escape the building, and we huddled together outside. Only one person had a cell phone, and he let others call home. My friend, Wendy Yost, looks around and sees how many escaped our building. Snapping is heard from the flames. The water main is broken. Car alarms are still going off. My sisters are cold. I am cold. All I have on is a T-shirt and panties. I have no shoes. Caprice is clothed with a blanket, and Auriel is hysterically crying. All I can think about is, "*What's next? God help us!*"

Around 20 minutes later, I foolishly returned to the building with my neighbor, entering a side of the building still standing. I needed to grab clothes for my sisters and shoes for myself. I also decided to use the bathroom. My neighbor and I took turns holding the door open: just in case another earthquake occurs. Looking back, I see I made a crazy choice. We could have been caught in the tragedy. I was fortunate. In the *Northridge Apartments* across the street, people were not as lucky. The complete 3rd and 2nd floors collapsed into the first. On that building's first floor, people were crushed and killed. My friend, Jaime, ultimately suffocated and died a gruesome death. He and I were freshmen students at California State University Northridge and met in the 1993 Summer Bridge Program.

Many survivors camped out on the grass directly outside of the apartment. Mom came to pick us up. Upon her arrival, she was not sure if she would meet surviving daughters or dead corpses. Tears streamed down her face, as she discovered we had survived and safely escaped the collapsed building. We traveled home to our mother's house. I was okay. But the next day, something horrific happened. Trauma finally hit me.

I woke up at my mother's house and realized that all my belongings were destroyed. I had nothing but the clothes on my back. Everything I physically owned was thrown across a room that began to collapse. Reality sunk in, and I cried for hours. Although I was quick on my feet during the earthquake, my brain stopped solving problems the next day as I sat in my mother's room uncontrollably crying. *Where will I finish my degree*? I wondered. *Am I ever going to get my things back? How will I know my friends survived?*

The months following were difficult. I was emotionally traumatized. I had insomnia. When I fell asleep, I didn't feel comfortable unless I was wearing jogging clothes and street shoes. In fact, I insisted on wearing shoes 24 hours a day. I never sat next to windows. I always wanted to be ready for the next emergency. When I decided to return to California State University Northridge, the campus had been completely leveled. As a result, we learned complex math in trailers spread over the entire campus.

Although I took my college studies seriously, I had a challenging time taking care of myself. I found myself taking more risks outside of my character. While I never became reckless, I felt reckless. I began dating more often without prioritizing time appropriately. I went to social gatherings more: I wanted to occupy my mind to prevent replaying that tragic earthquake in my head. Deep down inside, I did not know if I would be guaranteed a "tomorrow." For months, I sat on the edge, not knowing if another earthquake would kill everyone.

After Jaime died in the earthquake, my *LIFE* seemed so fragile. Inside, I secretly felt my time on Earth was limited. I was focused on my math classes. However, in my other classes, I struggled to concentrate 100%. My stomach was constantly in knots. The only regular food I could digest was hamburgers, French fries with tons of ketchup, and water all day. My stomach had a low toleration for other foods. Ironically, I lost over 15 pounds. But then, my hair started falling out at the temples. I needed help. So I did something that very few people are strong enough to do, I sought mental assistance.

The trauma from the event was tough to overcome. For the first time in my life, I had evidence that showed I needed psychological counseling. I experienced something traumatic, and the world was verifying this trauma in the News. However, I did not realize that all the events I endured before the earthquake was also considered "TRAUMA." With the counseling that followed after this earthquake, I became enlightened on how chaos, trauma, and painful memories affect our human brains. It took an earthquake to begin to understand life is not about living through painful memories. The earthquake was a blessing. It helped me to take ownership over reshaping my thoughts about how to handle chaotic events. Surviving an earthquake exposed three major concepts: 1. Chaos Mathematics represents life events; 2. Chaos works together to determine your success or failure; and 3. Chaos Mathematics can represent your decision-making.

PAINFUL MEMORIES

Basically, painful memories are formed from different types of traumas. There are different types of traumatic situations to consider. As these situations occur, it causes your *Triabrain* to separate. *Triabrain* separation is what can occur when your brain interprets chaos. These difficult situations cause severe mental processing issues when your brain unconsciously or consciously relives painful memories.

- **Single Blow Acute Trauma** – A one-time traumatic event like sexual assault, a car accident or death. It can cause severe, emotional damage to children and adults. Other such events can be robberies, planes crashes or criminal violence. Oftentimes, these distressing events are unexpected but leave agonizing memories for everyone experiencing the event first hand.
- **Repeated Chronic Trauma** – Such circumstances are recurring events. Some examples include caring for an ill spouse or a loved one. While many experience extremely stressful work environments daily. As they're summed together, these events cause an accumulated negative memory effect in the brain. Prolonged and repeated exposure to these circumstances can also result in more severe mental health problems than single blow trauma! Incidentally, most traumatized women in abusive relationships experience repeated chronic trauma on a daily basis. Within this traumatic environment, they lose self-confidence and give the decision-making power to another person – often the abuser.
- **Complex Trauma** - Repeated events that frequently occur during childhood. Some examples include, a parent neglecting a child for days. Or, repeated exposure to an alcoholic or drug-addicted parent or sibling. This experience becomes ingrained in the brain. When a child experiences trauma, oftentimes, they interpret trauma as love. As a result, these adults seek out love relationships based upon the trauma they experienced as children. Many living in foster care experience this type of trauma due to the absence of a parental figure.
- **Naturally-Caused Trauma** – Natural disasters can produce painful memories. Hurricanes, earthquakes, floods, ice storms, avalanches, volcanic eruptions, and Tsunamis are all capable of inducing trauma. If this is the only "trauma" to overcome, studies have shown the recovery is the shortest when compared to other types of trauma. Recovery is faster because natural disasters are often considered as outside of a person's control, and could happen to anyone. There's no, "Why me?" because this trauma happens to everyone else. Oftentimes

people who survive experience guilt, and question why God allowed their survival.

The vast majority of people who experience trauma and survive are able to heal and lead productive lives afterward provided they understand how chaos from these situations has affected their thinking and feeling process. But first, you need to understand Chaos in its scientific definition before it can be aligned to your thought processes within the brain.

CHAOS THEORY
THE SCIENCE OF UNIVERSAL MADNESS

Why do tornadoes destroy an entire block of homes, and yet the next block is spared? Why do some people experience accidents or illnesses, while others remain healthy? How do some people win big money in the stock market and others lose their fortune? The answer is Chaos. Chaos is the science of surprises. It is the study of nonlinear and unpredictable events. Chaos explains how to expect the unexpected. While most traditional science deals with predictable phenomena like gravity, electricity, or chemical reactions, Chaos Theory deals with nonlinear occurrences that seem to have no order to the human mind. It predicts events that seem impossible to control, like turbulence, weather, the stock market, our brain states, and many other situations. Such phenomenon is often described by fractal mathematics, which captures the infinite complexity of nature.

Chaos Theory demonstrates how circumstances work together to produce breakthrough growth or untimely death. Growth is when there is a successful outcome yielding some new form of resource, product, or life. A caterpillar transforming into a butterfly, or raging brush fires are such examples of chaotic transformation. On the other hand, death and destruction lead to a "stalled state" which only stops any growth made. These examples include widespread Ebola outbreaks killing millions, or when a space ship unexpectedly stalls in Space and is unable to return to Earth. Both success and stalled events can occur, but a sequence of events between the two leads you to success or stall. The events determine what state will be eventually reached. In this section, you will discover how the brain works to make order out of chaos. You will also see how chaos serves to remap your brain's thoughts and create a successful future path to your success.

CHAOS THEORY 101 – FRACTALS AND CHAOS

Chaos Theory basically does this: it takes seemingly rare events and maps them together in a beautiful pathway through a series of interactions. The combination of these interactions creates a new energy force within itself. The power (energy force) of the interaction selects certain paths that eventually lead to one of two final outcomes: growth (innovation) or "a stalled stated" (death). Chaos studies movement and represents it in mathematics. Meteorology, sociology, physics, engineering, economics, biology, and philosophy all use this concept. This chapter explores Chaos Theory and its role in how your thoughts create dynamic energy to change physical situations in your life and restructure your physical brain. Nothing in life travels within a 100% straight line – except for light. Reaching from Point A to Point B is not a straight forward shot. Hence, you will understand the power of Chaos.

Image 3-1: Chaos in turbulence. Picture Source: NASA - Langley Research Center.

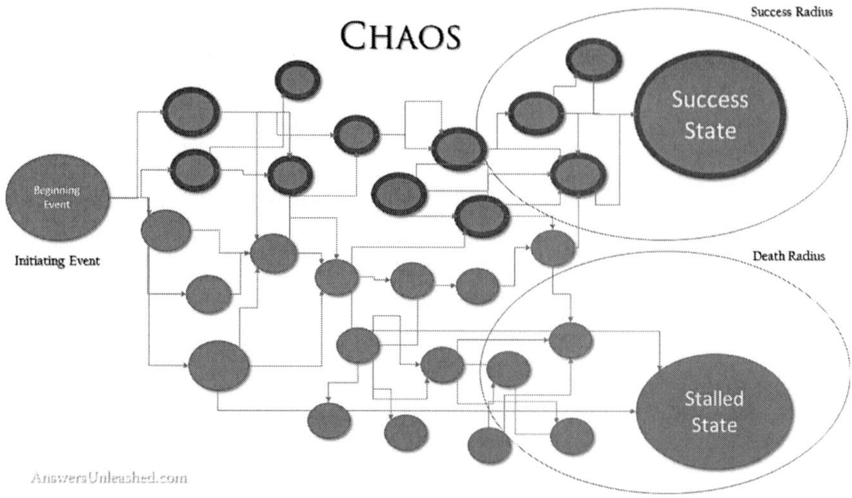

Image 3-2: Chaos Leads to Different Outcomes through nonlinear events.

The figure above shows how there is an initial event. There are different ways the event can play out. Each point in the chaos map links to another event. Subsequently, that event links to another. There are events that solely link to a successful state. On the other hand, there are events that specifically link to an undesired outcome ("stalled state"). More importantly, certain events can map to both a success and a "stalled state." When an event is close to the desired outcome, a force "pulls" the event into the outcome seen above as the ***success radius***[3], and the ***death radius***[4].

Most textbooks describe chaos with the same principles. There are some basic principals in Chaos Theory that must be understood. Everything in the universe falls into these basic principles. Whether it concerns interpersonal relationships, how the brain fires, or how the wind flows in the sky, these principles are applicable to all matter in the universe ("FractlMan"). Let's consider the following principles of Chaos Theory:

1. **(Butterfly Effect)** – Small changes in one area can lead to dramatic or ripple effects in another area. An example is a match being thrown into bushes which start a brush fire that ultimately ends a fireman's life.

---

[3] Success Radius is known as the radius convergence in mathematics when an event within a series of interactions absolutely converges close enough to the positive result. Overtime, any event occurring after its predecessor on this path will result in success.

[4] Death Radius is known as the radius convergence in mathematics when an event within a series of interactions absolutely converges close enough to the negative result. Any event occurring after its predecessor on this path will result in a stalled state.

2. **(Order vs. Disorder)** – Chaos represents both order and disorder simultaneously within the same space. Think of a city protest as an example. If a riot happens in the city, there is order represented by law enforcement, and disorder represented by the rioters in the same space.
3. **(Unpredictability)** – Chaos models pure unpredictability. For instance, if a person is abused as a child, that person can later become an adult abuser, victim, civil rights advocate or mentally-resilient. No one knows how the initial abuse will impact the future.
4. **(Feedback)** – Chaos has a consequence loop. Some things make the situations worse. For example, when stock prices fall, perceptions intertwine into outcomes. Investors are experiencing panic, sell stock which in turn causes stock prices to plunge deeper.
5. **(Fractals)** – Chaos repeats patterns but in new areas. For example, waves in the ocean travel identically to "air waves" in jet streams; crooks and turns in an oyster are identical to the crooks and turns leading to Mars in space travel.
6. **(Mixing)** - Chaos demonstrates how adjacent events end in two different outcomes. Two adjacent points in the system can eventually end in completely different locations after time passes. One example would be identical twins who share the same DNA, yet one ends up fighting cancer, and the other one lives.
7. **(Growth or Stall)** – Chaos classifies two outcomes life (success) or death (stall). Exemplified in the Russian Study for Innovation known as - TRIZ Principle, one event can have two varied outcomes: either leading to the creation of innovation or destruction. When destruction occurs, you are "stalled," and forced to start back at square one. For instance, a technical product can be created. It will either evolve or become irrelevant.

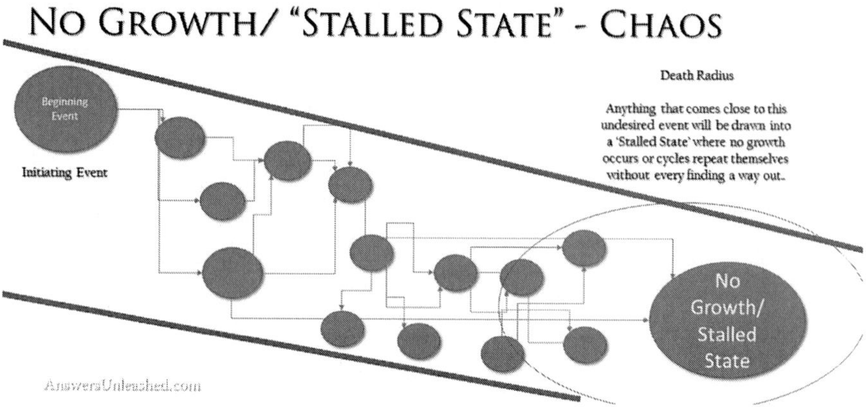

Image 3-3: Chaos Leads to a No Growth/Stalled State.

With reference to the preceding images, please consider the "stalled state." Oftentimes, many experience a "stalled period" when funds crash in the stock market, a tsunami destroys a city, or you fail an important exam. In each case, these are undesirable events. Each outcome leads to a form of destruction or disappointment. Or, the outcome may require you pick up the pieces and start over.

The more desirable pathway leads to success. I call this Divine Chaos. When Divine Chaos occurs, events connected in a path always lead to a beneficial outcome. Both negative and positive events work together for an outcome that is 100% desired. Consider a driver that gets lost, asks for directions and meets the love of her life. Think of the man who gets turned down for his number one job position, but is later hired for another job that makes him famous. Such outcomes may leave you in complete shock, due to the "fairytale" endings. When "negatives turn into positives" most are thankful for the divine outcome that was completely beneficial.

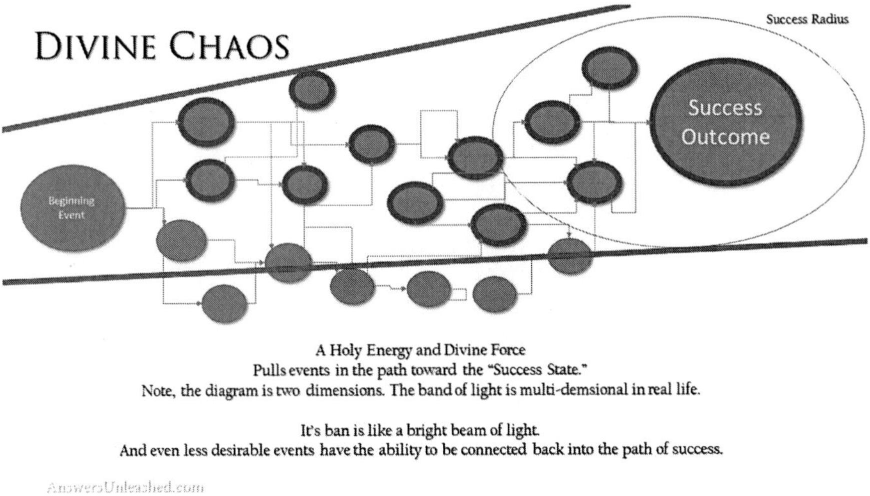

Image 3-4: Chaos Leads to a Successful Outcome.

Periods - When Situations Repeat Themselves

Periodicity is a common part of everyday language. For example, the Olympics happen every four years. Some women experience fertility every 25 days. A person has a birthday every year. These events repeat until there is a change in the system that forces a new outcome. If a person were to die, there would be no more birthdays. If a woman begins menopause, there are no more menstrual cycles. And, if mankind ends, there would be no more Olympics. Periods are events that repeat over and over until there is a change in the overall interactions that produce a new cycle.

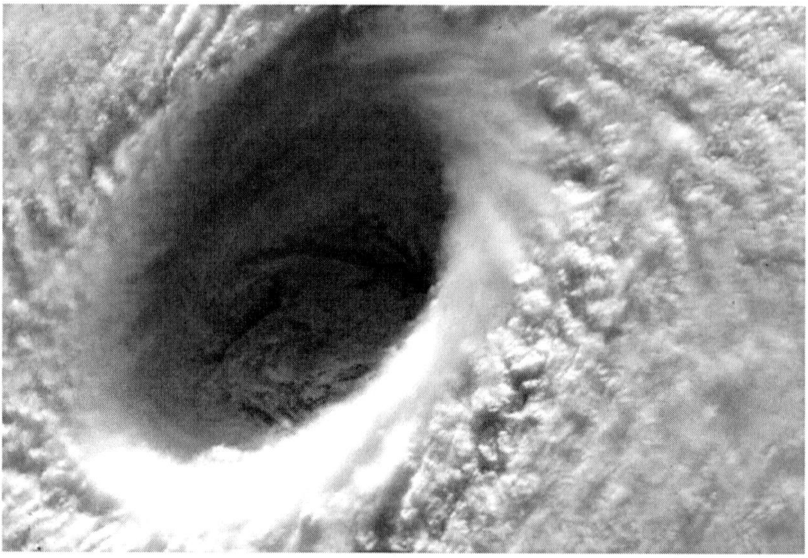

Image 3-5: NASA Photo of Typhoon Maysak in April of 2015. Such weather systems have a repetitive cycle until a change in interaction breaks the storm free.
Credit: Courtesy of NASA

For instance, if you fail Calculus three semesters in a row, each time you retake the class, you gain a deeper understanding of the subject. During your fourth attempt, you eventually ace the class. In essence, the energy of a period event induces more intensive energy. Also, consider the wind in a hurricane. The wind repeatedly rotates in a circular formation. As it continually rotates, more power is generated leading to an excessively powerful outcome once the cycle breaks free of its current repetitive constraints.

FRACTALS - The Boundary between "Hell" and "Heaven"

What if the *Titanic* took a slightly different course avoiding the iceberg? What if the World Trade Center Terrorist attackers never gained flight training? What if a Stage 4 cancer patient discovered the illness earlier and received treatment? Why do certain situations occur and others don't? Have you ever seen a pattern that seemed to apply to a completely different situation? Or, have you ever experienced déja vu, where time seemed to mimic itself through an event you previously envisioned? If you have, congratulate yourself.

You are experiencing fractals, which is a point in time and space that determines either success or disaster. In the chaos, fractals are specifically the boundary between order and disorder. It describes how order and random events can exist in the same space, and a breakthrough is on the horizon.

There is always one point in time where a situation can go either way. It is the defining moment where one move can change the course of history. Or, this one direction can change the course of the future. What would have happened if your parents never met and gave birth to you? What if you never accepted the job offer? Would you be in the same place? What if you never married your spouse? Never took that class? Would your life be different?

In Chaos Theory, such cases are considered "fractal moments." This is where the future depends on this moment (present). It is a place in Chaos Mathematics, where there is a boundary between order and disorder. It will either result in the desired effect or an undesired outcome that brings pure stalled, chaos. (Miller and Swinney)

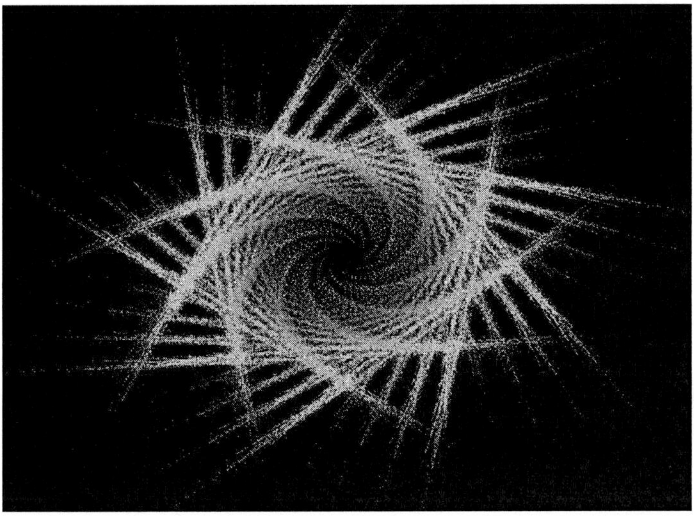

Image 3-6: Chaos Mathematical Diagram of Reoccurring Patterns. Credit: Courtesy of NASA

Chaos Theory stems from the concept of fractals, which are repeating patterns that continue infinitely. Consider the following classic fractal example of the triangle illustrated in Image 3-7. There is one big triangle with a smaller, inverted triangle located in its core. This new interior triangle breaks the larger triangle into separate, equally spaced areas that also form identical triangles. So, with each of the three areas, we repeat the process of drawing an upside-down triangle. This process now creates nine new areas of the original triangle. When we repeat this process forever, it is called a fractal.

Image 3-7: Chaos Fractal of an Equilateral Triangle known in Mathematics as the Sierpinski Triangle

A fractal is an infinitely complex pattern that creates identical patterns in a smaller dimension. They are created by repeating a simple process in an ongoing feedback loop. Fractals are also images of dynamic systems. In Chaos Theory, these images (interactions) are modeled by a math referred as the boundary between disorder and stability.

In a practical sense, you can visualize a fractal. Imagine a tree and its roots. As fractal properties are seen in clouds, the same pathways appear in rivers. When tree branches extend from one to another, we scientists call this "fractal properties." Think of a tree's roots. Just like a tree has roots, fractal properties are witnessed in the human body. Consider the human nervous system: veins also "branch" off into distinct pathways, connecting organs to the heart and brain. Like a tree has roots, the *Triabrain* has roots, too, comprising the nervous system.

Image 3-8: NASA Image of the Lena River of how Chaos Fractal Mathematics is seen in nature. Credit: Courtesy of NASA

An awe-inspiring picture above, the Lena River is more than 2,800 miles (4,400 km) long and is the 11th largest river in the world (Administration). With respect to its configuration, the Lena Delta Reserve forms a chaotic mathematical fractal design. At each bend is a fractal that extends into multiple pathways. The Lena Delta Reserve is also the most extensively-protected wilderness area in Russia, serving as a refuge and breeding ground for many species of Siberian wildlife. This particular image was captured by *Landsat 7's* Enhanced Thematic Mapper plus (ETM+) sensor on July 27, 2000, where the actual color of the river is not as vivid. The river's natural design is accented by using shortwave infrared and red wavelengths, and a false-color was added to create the composite of this image.

As I mentioned earlier, an oyster's inner shell is similar to pathways leading Mars. In fact, fractal pathways visible in oysters have helped Jet Propulsion Laboratory scientists find super highways to Mars (Laboratory). The below image illustrates travel trajectories near Mars using Chaos Theory. These superhighways in Space allow rockets to travel faster to distant planets, so fuel will not run out. The slight change in position is a fractal. By finding this fractal, the direction chosen allows the space vehicle to move toward its intended destination. The slightest change in position in a point at a given time causes a major impact that continues far into the future. In short, fractals are the measurable geometry shapes from which Chaos Theory is based.

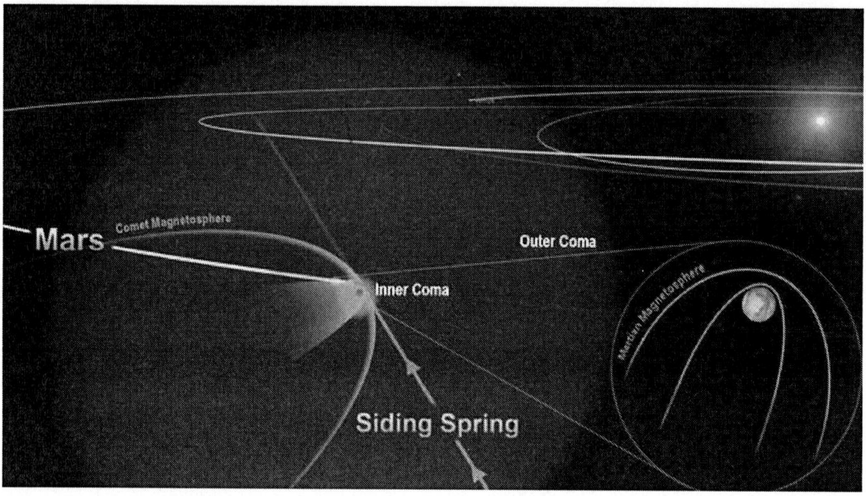

Image 3-9: Close Comet Flyby through Mars' Magnetic Field into Chaos
Credit: Courtesy of NASA

The boundary of a success radius, or death radius, is a pivotal fractal because the future hinges on the balance of one deciding moment. As you may recall, a fractal is a moment in time where an event is a precursor to decidedly intensive end results.

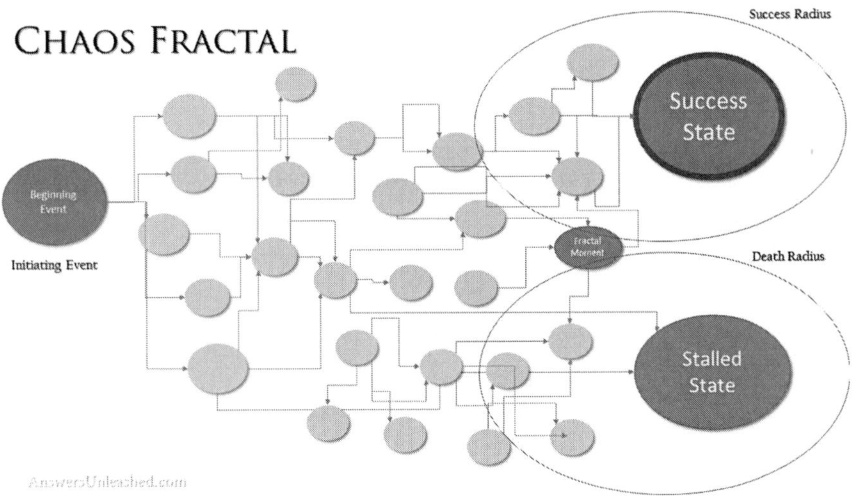

Image 3-10: Chaos Fractal on the Boundary of the Success and Stalled State, on the boundary of the success and death radii.

FRACTAL MOMENTS

Within the *Triabrain*, fractal properties represent your decision-making process. The brain constantly moves between stability and chaos through your pathways. There are also paths leading to instability and mental awareness. Either the pathway to mental stability already exists, or it must be formed. If the path must be created, chaos from the world will do one of three things for you in your fractal moment: It will attract chaotic situations to help you make a decision; permit people into your life to help you form a decision; or allow your body to experience internal pain to force a decision. In doing so, your brain either reshapes or stays in a traumatic/painful memory loop and fails. In real life, your mental decision-making process is your fractal moment.

Bruce's Unintentional Arson

Bruce has been trying to quit smoking cigarettes for a few years. When he sees the cigarette butts in his ashtray, it makes him feel worse. So, he decides to throw the used cigarettes out his window as he drives. One day, he is driving past a brush area that is suffering from a drought. Without thinking much about it, Bruce finishes his cigarette and contemplates using his ashtray. At the moment, he decides to throw out his cigarette butt. Against his better judgment, he flings the cigarette butt out the window, where it ignites dry brush next to the road. The natural wind traveling through the valley serves as an oxidizer to the brush. Next, the plant roots ignite. The fire spreads underground, spreading to nearby plants. Within a 20-minute time span, the fire has turned into a brush fire, threatening over 100 homes up the hill (LePoint).

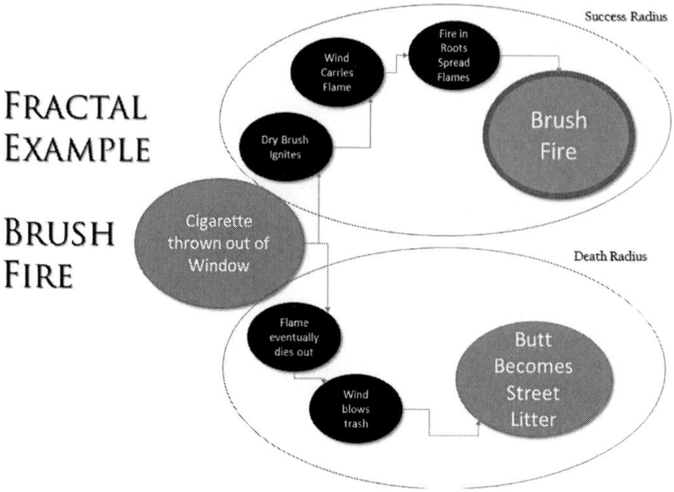

Image 3-11: A fractal moment example with a human decision

Fractal moments can be simple or complex. Allow me to reiterate this point. A fractal moment in your brain is your human decision. A simple example is when a student decides to attend a particular school. This decision will establish life-long friendships. Or, a more complex fractal moment is selecting a wife. This decision will create new lives if children are birthed. Everyone has these decision-making processes that will ultimately change the trajectory of their lives. Fractal moments create your future moments – independent of space and time. These fractal moments literally define the pathways to multiple futures existing simultaneously.

Image 3-12: Image from a driver as he passes a brush fire.

In the *Triabrain Theory of Relativity*, the role of the *Triabrain* is to use thoughts to convert energy from outside situations into energy used for personal growth. Every single situation in the universe provides energy. By using free will, thoughts can convert situational energy into beneficial energy. This new energy can be used in the brain, body, or directed outward into environments by means of your *Triabrain* energy field.

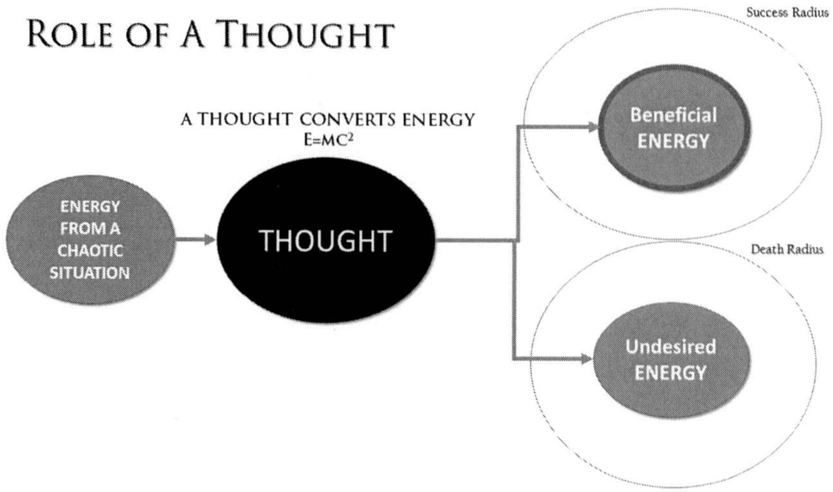

Image 3-13: Per Chaos Theory, the Role of a Thought is to convert energy through particle collisions and neuron synapsis.

When a person experiences chaos, free will uniquely define the direction. One of two situations appear: a person will choose beneficial or destructive thoughts based on life experiences. This is the **subconscious belief system**.[5] The role of this thought process is to convert energy from a chaotic situation into energy that is directed to growth. If the thought is beneficial, energy gets fully converted in the brain and released into the *Triabrain*, body, and environment. If it is a destructive thought, energy becomes trapped in the brain, body, and environment. Thus, a person goes into a mentally-, physically-, or environmentally-stalled state.

One pivotal business decision made by Country superstar, Dolly Parton best exemplifies how the subconscious belief system works (Bryer and Gibbs). In a *CNBC Meets* Interview with Tania Bryer, Dolly Parton stated that one time, Rock-n-Roll icon Elvis Presley, offered to cover her famous song, "I Will Always Love You." Parton was excited and ready to pursue his offer until she received a phone call from Elvis Presley's manager, Colonel Tom Parker. Prior to the scheduled recording date, Colonel Parker called saying, "Now, you know, Elvis don't record anything unless we get half the publishing," Parton told Bryer. Although a tough decision, Parton decided to pass since she had already spent time and money creating the track. She knew the "half" publishing fee would leave her company at a deficit. In faith,

[5] Subconscious Belief System is the area of thought that functions just below the threshold of awareness, where all experiences are stored as sensory data.

Parton decided to pass up what most people would have considered the "opportunity-of-a-lifetime."

She decided to keep her publishing rights and personally release the song in 1974. The singer-songwriter went on to earn estimated millions in royalties from the song — something that may not have occurred if Elvis performed it. Dolly Parton's original hit topped the country charts twice: once in 1974 and once again when it was re-released in 1982. Later, in 1992, the song skyrocketed to new heights following the infamous cover by Pop music legend, Whitney Houston. She performed the song as the title on *The Bodyguard* soundtrack. "I will Always Love You" zoomed to the top of the charts, going platinum in numerous markets worldwide. Parton's decision is now viewed as one of the most successful record moves in music history.

There are many other stories where a fractal moment changes the course of history.

Tim

Tim is a professional musician. After finishing his gig, he's invited to go out with friends. He is not sure if he should go or not. Tim feels tired and considers going home, or going out for a "little while." After much contemplation, Tim decides to go out. He searches for the bar's address online but cannot find the exact address. So, he goes to where he thinks the bar is located. Tim ventured into what turns out to be wrong the bar. While asking the bartender for the correct address, he meets a female bartender, who later becomes his wife. They would have never met if Tim had not chosen to go out and become lost in the process.

Auriel

While gazing at the Honda running the red light, Auriel's life flashed before her eyes. Auriel knew the car was about to hit the truck containing her and her infant daughter. She made a split decision. She could either remain where she was or veer her steering wheel toward the right. Auriel chose to veer toward the right. As the police officers made reports at the traffic accident scene, they noted the power in her choice. Had Auriel not turned the wheel right, her and her baby would have been dead.

Pamela

Pamela knew her daughter was smart. But, Pamela did not have access to quality education for her daughter. Nor, did she have a higher education or insight on the process of locating quality education. Poverty separated

Pamela from quality schools in areas outside of their assigned school district. Until one day, when she saw this flyer about CHOICES Magnet Schools. This program permitted students to be bussed to various schools as part of a diversity program. So, Pamela decided to attend the meeting to learn from a visiting principal how to enroll her daughter. Pamela followed the advice from this guest speaker.

One month later, Pamela's daughter was hit in the face by a 10-year-old gang member in the classroom. Her daughter received five layers of facial stitches, and nearly lost her left eye. In horror, Pamela demanded the boy be expelled. When he was not, she pulled her daughter out of school to protect her from future violence. Pamela was at her wit's end. Then, a miracle happened thanks to her CHOICES application. Three months later, Pamela received word in the mail that her daughter had been accepted into a gifted magnet school for future child prodigies. Because Pamela envisioned a brighter outcome for her daughter, one was created. Her daughter later became the world-renowned rocket scientist, Olympia LePoint.

Fractal Vortex Moments – When Two Chaotic Situations Unite

When two chaotic forces unite, a new form of reality emerges. Think of two black holes colliding. Einstein's theory was proved because of the impact of the two massive chaotic systems united and unleashed a new form of energy from their union. It was a gravitational wave, as mentioned in Chapter 2. When powers of two powerful forces unite, it forms what I call a Chaos Vortex. One form of chaos is powerful. But when it unites with another form of chaos, the force unleashed is explosive in nature. The combined power either promotes all things near it or destroys anything in its path. A new set of fractals called ***Fractal Vortex Moments***[6] exists within this force.

When two people are required to make a major decision that will change the course of their lives, they experience what I coin a "Chaotic Vortex," which leads to a Fractal Vortex Moment. Chaotic Vortex occurs when two major chaotic situations unite and one fractal changes both situations. The Fractal Moment (shared decision) during this time will create a new force that births a powerful change in those sharing the same Fractal. When there are two Fractal Moments, both people will become powerfully pulled in one direction. The force will present a seemingly uncontrollable interval of both

[6] Fractal Vortex Moments are part of the Triabrain Theory of Relativity, and represents when two individuals experience separate, chaotic situations, while sharing the same Fractal Moment.

discomfort and pleasure. As a result, making a decision is the only way to transform the powerful chaotic pathways.

The following is a real life story of two people who cared for each other in a "fractal vortex moment."

A Chaos Theory Mathematical Computer Simulation of a Chaos Vortex .
Credit: Courtesy of NASA

The Chaos Vortex between Ann and Robert

Ann (36) had not been in a relationship for seven years when she met Robert. Ann survived sexual trauma caused by her mother's poor choice in men. As a result, when Ann grew into an adult, she shied away from relationships to avoid making the same mistakes as her mother. Consequently, her sisters followed a similar path resulting in having children with men who later abandoned them. Fearful of making mistakes, Ann became a devout church-goer, who turned celibate and avoided relationships by throwing herself into her career. Although she earned multiple degrees and was building a successful career, Ann knew she had just scratched the surface of her potential. She knew she could become a celebrity and philanthropist if she worked a few more years to reach her goals. Ann also had another desire. She was in her late 30's and longed to be a wife and mother. Unfortunately, she had not cultivated relationship skills needed to attract a loving partner. Ann was afraid of being addicted to love like her family members.

Robert (40) was also afraid of being addicted, but his reasoning stemmed from a different set of circumstances. At an early age, Robert encountered a father who suffered addictions. Sadly, his mother did not pay attention to him during the times he needed nurturing the most. At the age of 13, he was sexually abused. To cope with his emotions, Robert threw himself into soccer. His efforts allowed him to become a professional soccer player and coach for Olympic hopefuls. Throughout his career endeavors, Robert turned off his emotions. He would sleep with women to fulfill a physical need. But deep down, Robert craved love and affection. He made himself believe that he did not need a woman until he met his financial retirement goals.

One day, Ann and Robert meet at a local restaurant bar. Ann walks to the restroom and on her return, she is greeted by Robert. Before leaving the restaurant with friends, Robert feels compelled to speak with Ann. He hands Ann his card and asks her to call him. They connect, but Ann soon realizes that Robert is a "player" and says that she and he are best suited as friends. Although many men came in her path, Robert is the only man Ann has been attracted to in seven years. At the same time, Robert is deeply is attracted to Ann in a way that he could not explain. She was not like the shorter blonde, women who he frequently pursued. Ann was tall, exotic and seemed to have a "swagger" that made Robert feel like a school boy when he tried to get his way. When they met in social circles, Robert would watch her all night. He would go out of his way to protect her from other men, even from himself at times. They would text message and communicate nearly every day for four years. The mutual physical and mental chemistry becomes unbearable between the two. Unconsciously, they become deeply drawn to one another. After four years of off-and on-again flirtations and impromptu rendezvous, the vortex fractal moment occurs.

During a night of passion, Ann (now 40) and Robert (now 44) sleep together. At this moment, the contraception fails. Ann and Robert are both in shock. Ann and Robert are not in a committed monogamous relationship. Ann realizes that she will become pregnant due to this encounter and questions her health. Having recently turned 40, Ann wonders if perhaps this event was the way for her to have a child. She also questions her choices and begins to feel unloved. Robert realizes that he is not ready to have children. He feels shame. He never wanted Ann to go through this experience. Robert reminds Ann of her work in the media and all her future plans when she freaks out. He also reiterates that he is not ready for marriage or children with anyone. Secretly, Robert can't image himself with anyone else other than Ann.

Robert and Ann are mutually attracted because they are mirror images of one another. Their combined decision at that moment will either lead to growth or to a repetitive cycle of chaos they both feared. More importantly, Ann's decision will affect not only her life but also determine Robert's future. At this moment, their chaos unite to unleash a chain of events that no one would expect.

(The conclusion of this story is revealed in Chapter 8)

BRAINBRINK

CHAPTER 4

BRAINBRINK:

WHEN CHAOS SEPARATES YOUR BRAIN

Is there a powerful, beneficial reason why you experience challenging life situations?

The answer is an unequivocal, "yes." Every stressful situation helps you reshape your brain faster and stronger than before. But you will understand this concept fully by reading this chapter, taking the self-test at the end of this chapter, and by reading the next chapter about the truth in why traumatic situations happen to you. Chaotic situations are far from pleasant. These stressful situations can bring you into a state of confusion or clarity. The role of a chaotic situation is to transform you into someone who thinks differently.

However, the process is typically not immediate. It takes time: the energy in the situation is sometimes trapped in our *Triabrains* through a myriad of dysfunction. Naturally, when you think of trauma, you think of severe situations like men and women who witness war. Or, you may consider survivors of The Holocaust. Perhaps, you think of people who survived natural disasters like plane crashes, floods, earthquakes or tornados. However, trauma is far more sophisticated. Trauma is painful memories you continually relive. Some examples include:

- Surgeries
- Dental Procedures
- Childhood Abuse
- Childhood Molestation
- Experiencing Severe Poverty
- An Emotionally Absent Parent
- Bullying in School
- War Victims and Veterans
- Car Crashes
- Physically- or Mentally-abusive Work Environments
- Physical Disciplinary Action in Schools

- Repeated Sports Injuries
- Rape Survivors
- Mugging Survivors
- Natural Disasters (e.g., earthquakes, floods, hurricanes)
- Riot Victims
- Incarceration
- Abandoned Mothers
- Competitive Acceptance
- Murders and Deaths
- Marital Affairs and Divorces
- Sexually Transmitted Disease
- Biological Pandemic Outbreaks
- Terrorists Attacks
- Financial Bankruptcy
- Sports Injuries
- Work Accidents
- Spousal Abuse
- Miscarriages / Abortions
- Job Layoff
- Evictions

In this chapter, you will see how traumatic memories separate your brain's sections into three disconnected hemispheres described as ***Brainbrink.*** You will also see how stressful emotions can create new chemical structures in the brain that serves to separate it. More importantly, you will discover how to determine which section of your *Triabrain* requires reconnecting.

TRAUMATIC MEMORIES ARE REROUTED IN A HIDDEN WAY

Your memories are a form of energy, usually stored in distributed brain networks including the cortex, and therefore can be readily accessed to remember an event consciously. When your energy remains trapped, it turns into a physical mass that can be either good for you, or extremely bad. In the *Northwestern Now* article, "How Traumatic Memories Hide in The Brain, And How to Retrieve Them" by Marla Paul, it explores how stress-related memories can sometimes be hidden and rerouted (Paul). For example, if someone does drugs or drinks alcohol to cope with a painful memory, the memory still exists, and the brain completely uses different molecular pathways and neuronal circuits to store the memory.

Unconscious fear-related memories can remain completely hidden from your conscious mind, yet they can still dramatically affect your everyday behavior and emotions. The research from Northwestern University identifies a specific brain mechanism that has the ability to hide traumatic memories in the brain—and also retrieve them.

Timothy

Timothy was a very neat and tidy person who enjoyed a clean apartment. He was a fitness model and loved cooking healthy meals. He was from Germany and strived to run an organized, efficient home. Timothy smoked but was trying to quit. He prided himself in cooking and maintaining a tranquil and quiet home. One day, he left food on the stove and forgot about it, while kissing his girlfriend. Upon hearing a loud noise from the kitchen, he realized the food was on fire. As Timothy tried to douse flames by pouring water on the grease fire, the ignited pot exploded in his face, burning the skin off. As a result, Timothy received third-degree burns.

His girlfriend jumped in and extinguished the fire, saving Timothy and his home. She then rushed Timothy to the hospital, where he stayed for a week, while a medical team determined if skin grafts were needed. Numerous people prayed for Timothy's recovery.

Timothy miraculously recovered, and his face healed. He even returned to work as a TV actor. But, every time he was at home, Timothy never felt settled. He stopped regularly cooking and began eating out. He went from maintaining a clean, orderly home to no longer having the strength to clean. Timothy would go days without vacuuming, dusting, or washing his dishes. Although he survived the event, unconsciously, Timothy felt horrible and uncomfortable in his home. He began smoking more cigarettes. Then, he started smoking marijuana. Subsequently, Timothy's unconscious, non-safe feeling transferred over into his lack of self-care. Little did he know: memories from the house fire still lurked in his brain.

Anytime you experience a painful memory, especially if the painful memory remains within your brain, it is considered Post Traumatic Stress Disorder (PTSD). There are neurological effects associated with how you store that memory in your system. According to *Dialogues in Clinical Neuroscience* article, "Traumatic stress: effects on the brain" by J. Douglas Bremner, MD, it reveals that Post Traumatic Stress Disorder has a scientific and biological effect on the brain (Bremner MD):

> PTSD is characterized by specific symptoms, including intrusive thoughts, hyperarousal, flashbacks, nightmares, and sleep disturbances, changes in memory and concentration, and startle responses. Symptoms of PTSD are hypothesized to represent the behavioral manifestation of stress-induced changes in brain structure and function. Stress results in acute and chronic changes in neurochemical systems and specific brain regions, which result in long-term

changes in brain "circuits," involved in the stress response (34-37). Brain regions that are felt to play an important role in PTSD include hippocampus, amygdala, and medial prefrontal cortex. Cortisol and norepinephrine are two neurochemical systems that are critical in the stress response. (Bremner MD, Traumatic Stress: effects on the brain).

Like a room caught on fire with smoke, your brain becomes an environment for hellish interactions. Douglas Bremner showed that glucocorticoid, corticotropin-releasing factor, adrenocorticotropin hormone; norepinephrine; heart rate; blood pressure; dopamine; benzodiazepine; glucocorticoid levels all create an environment for a toxic chemical reaction in your brain during your stress. Thereby these chemical reactions cause your overall brain structure to be vulnerable and sensitive. When the brain experiences a painful event, there is a sequence of hormonal effects that alter natural chemical processing. Furthermore, if your stress does not become resolved, your brain will still operate in a state that creates a firestorm. A quick summary of effects are as follows:

- **Norepinephrine hormone**, a neurotransmitter misfires inside and outside of your brain, near your spinal cord and within your abdomen, releasing excess hormones into your bloodstream, which leads to incorrect targeting and cell binding.
- **Cortisol** hormone of your adrenal gland begins secreting to release an excess of this hormone which throws your system into immune deficiencies.
- **The Hippocampus** on both sides of your brain fails to consolidate information from short-term and long-term memory. It also fails to reorganize the brain during your sleep.
- **Your Amygdala** fires and affects your memory, decision-making, and emotional reactions. You fail to recognize promptness. Your right amygdala hemisphere is associated with negative emotions doesn't talk to your left. Parts of your personal memory and how you felt during events is hidden. You think everything is a fight/flee/freeze type of chaotic situation and everything should give you pleasure.
- **Prefrontal Cortex** prevents your "executive mind" from working and understanding cause and effect logical events. You start being incapable of socially "controlling" your urges, and unable to decipher when to use resources to gain solution for pressing problems.
- **Striatum and the Basal Ganglia** go haywire with respect to your reward systems. During stress, the striatum creates mixed messages

which lead to a variety of disorders, most notably, depression and obsessive-compulsive disorder which can lead to addictions.

- **Dopamine** in the kidneys increases sodium excretion and urine output; in the pancreas, your insulin production reduces; your digestive system goes haywire, which reacts to the dopamine levels in your brain. Neuroscience Researcher Kent Berridge found that your facial features are linked to proper dopamine functions in the body.

PAINFUL MEMORIES' CHEMICAL REACTIONS FORM GLUE-LIKE TOXINS IN THE BRAIN

In the book, ***Switch On Your Brain,*** Caroline Leaf explores how your brain fails to reshape when negative thoughts are present in the brain (Leaf, 2015). She explains that chemical reactions formed from stressful situations will act like glue in the brain, and this chemical reaction will cement your brain tissue together. Leaf's insightful lectures and talks expound on the theory that once the stress is removed, your brain still has a signature dark mass associated with the chemical reactions released when recalling your memory. Therefore, when you experience toxic emotions, a dark tar-like mass formed in your brain blocks pathways. And, Leaf states that this "dark, tar-like matter" serves to impede natural brain function. She writes:

> "When you meditate on toxic thoughts such as fear, anxiety, unforgiveness, bitterness, anger, rage, resentment, self-hatred, guilt, condemnation and so forth, a toxic memory is being built that has a different type of chemical structure to a positive memory. It has a totally different electromagnetic field around it that looks heavy and dark. A toxic memory built from toxic thinking actually looks like a thorn tree... [These] grow like weeds and occupy the space in your brain with a dark, heavy Electro-magnetic field around it. It looks like a thorn tree," (Leaf, 2015, p. 9).

When you experience a painful situation, and it leaves painful memories in the physical form of brainbraink masses, your thoughts will struggle to recalibrate the energy running through your system. Your thoughts will either give you positive, solution-finding pathways, or create toxic masses. These masses will physically separate your *Triabrain*. This scenario is when your *Triabrain* disconnects.

Brainbraink is not just a trauma caused by emotion. It can be a trauma caused by the injury itself, with the emotion that follows. Brainbrink causes disconnecting neurotransmissions and synapsis. It is an observable mass seen in the human brain. Evidence of brainbrink is being discovered in various areas of science. Dark, brainbrink glue-like masses serve to impact brain tissue. According to the ***Triabrain Theory of Relativity***, this brainbrink mass sticks the brain together and prevents it from reshaping. Prolonged brainbrink exposure together with traumatic situations, including physical blows itself, can lead to symptoms of Chronic Traumatic Encephalopathy. Also known as C.T.E., this form of encephalopathy is a progressive degenerative brain disease. Currently, C.T.E. can only be definitively diagnosed after death in individuals with a history of multiple concussions and other forms of brain trauma (Wikipedia, Chronic Traumatic Encephalopathy, 2017).

As an example, symptoms of C.T.E. can present themselves immediately following a concussion or after a few hours and persist for months or even years after the injury. Once a concussion occurs, you are more susceptible to repeat occurrences. It is advised to seek medical treatment as soon as possible following even a mild head injury to minimize the risk of long-term brain damage.

Concussions are a major concern for anyone in sports like football, soccer, boxing or any other full contact sport. Dr. Ann McKee finds the scientific evidence of this disease in her new study: "***Clinicopathological Evaluation of Chronic Traumatic Encephalopathy in Players of American Football***" published in ***The Journal of the American Medical Association*** (McKee, Ann, M.D.; Jesse Mez, MD, MS; Daniel H. Daneshvar, MD, Ph.D; Patrick T. Kiernan, BA; Bobak Abdolmohammadi, BA; Victor E. Alvarez, MD; Bertrand R. Huber, MD, Ph.D; Michael L. Alosco, Ph.D; Todd M. Solomon, Ph.D; Christopher J. Nowins, 2017).

The July 25, 2017, ***New Your Times*** article, "110 N.F.L. Brains", by Joe Ward, Josh Williams and Sam Manchester, further reveals how the trauma of repetitive blows to the head trigger degeneration in brain tissue, including the build-up of an abnormal protein called "tau." To find the abnormal protein, thin pieces of tissue are dyed, and tau presents itself as these darker areas (Ward, Williams, & Manchester, 2017). The article references the findings of Dr. Ann McKee, a neuropathologist who examined the brains of 202 deceased football players. These findings were published in ***The Journal of the American Medical Association.***

> "Of the 202 players, 111 of them played in the N.F.L. — and 110 of those were found to have chronic traumatic encephalopathy, or C.T.E., the degenerative disease believed to be caused by repeated

blows to the head. C.T.E. causes a myriad of symptoms, including memory loss, confusion, depression, and dementia. The problems can arise years after the blows to the head have stopped."

The article continues to show images of the brain of individuals who experienced trauma:

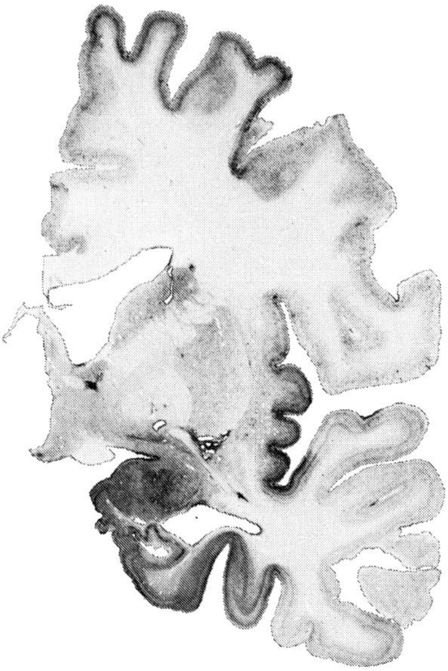

Image 4-1: The image above shows the results of dark, brain toxic masses at the bottom cross section. Image provided courtesy of Dr. Ann McKee.

"The image above is from the brain of Ronnie Caveness, a linebacker for the Houston Oilers and Kansas City Chiefs. In college, he helped the Arkansas Razorbacks go undefeated in 1964. One of his teammates was Jerry Jones, now the owner of the Dallas Cowboys. Jones has rejected the belief that there is a link between football and C.T.E."

– New York Times Article *"110 N.F.L. Brains" by Joe Ward, Josh Williams and Sam Manchester.*

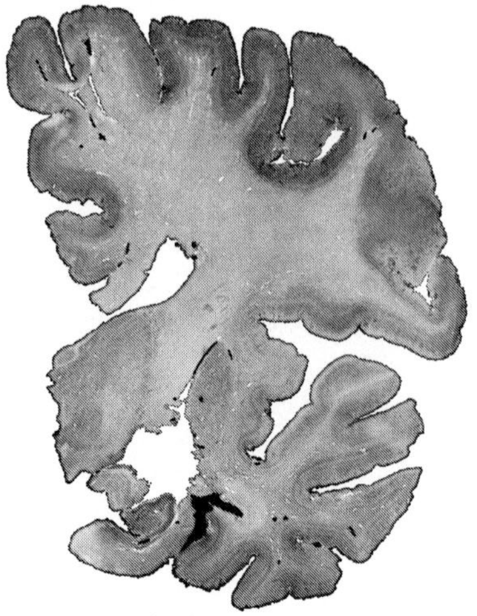

*Image 4-2: The image above shows the results of brainbrink which takes the form of severe **Chronic Traumatic Encephalopathy**. Image provided courtesy of Dr. Ann McKee.*

> "The image above is from the brain of Ollie Matson, who played 14 seasons in the N.F.L. — after winning two medals on the track at the 1952 Helsinki Games. He DIED in 2011 at age 80 after being mostly bedridden with dementia, his nephew told The Associated Press, adding that Matson hadn't spoken in four years."
>
> – New York Times Article *"110 N.F.L. Brains" by Joe Ward, Josh Williams and Sam Manchester.*

Dr. Ann McKee's research showed that C.T.E. affected multiple parts of the brain. C.T.E. often affects the superior frontal cortex, an area important for cognition and executive function, along with the prefrontal lobes in both left and right hemispheres. This part of the brain is responsible for the working memory, planning and abstract reasoning. The insula, a small region of the cerebral cortex located in both brain hemispheres, is also affected. This part of the brain is responsible for the regulation of important emotions, social perception, and self-awareness. And in almost all cases, the amygdala which processes emotional control, aggression and anxiety, was severely affected in both left and right hemispheres. C.T.E. frequently damages the mammillary bodies, an area that's important in memory.

FAITH TRIABRAIN DISCONNECTION

There is a normal function of the faith brain, as well as a dysfunctional function. Your faith brain's function is to connect the energy of your exterior situation into energy for your interior experience. But this natural function alters when painful memories arise. Dysfunctional thoughts no longer convert 100% of the chaos energy into the power that you need. As I mentioned earlier, thoughts can become trapped in the brain, body or outside in the energy field around you. The brainbrink masses in your brain cause this obstruction and are identified with black circles in the figure below. Chaos-induced toxic masses disconnect the faith sector of your *Triabrain*. And these masses can be found in your nervous system and attached to parts of your body. The masses disrupt connections between the left side of the brain, the right side of the brain, within the nervous system and these masses take the form of disruptive energy in your *Triabrain* field.

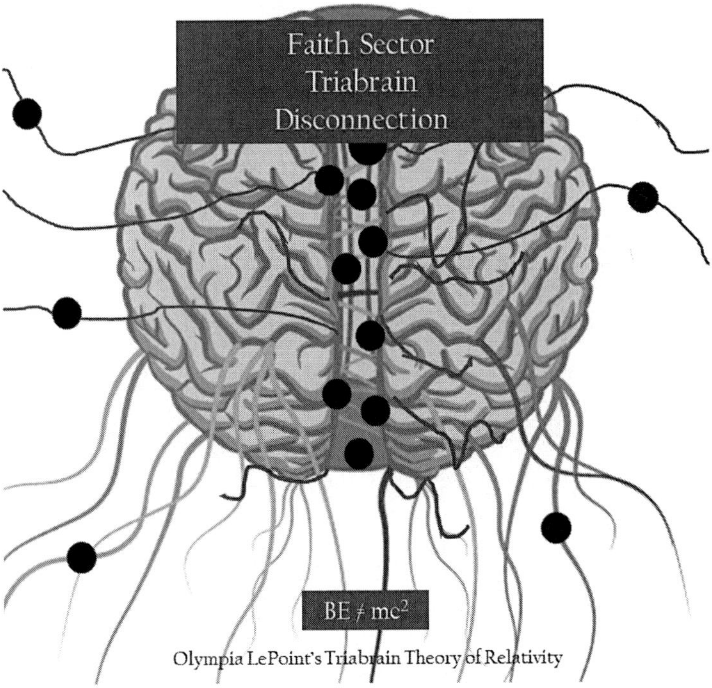

Image 4-3: Brainbrink Masses Causing A Faith Triabrain Disconnection

When painful memories exist, you fail to embrace visionary thinking or trust your natural intuition. Your spiritual awareness becomes mute. The past and present appear as one painful memory. Additionally, the present and future appear in your brain as a disappointment. Your faith sector still impacts other sections of the brain, body, and environment. But, pain from your life impacts others in a negative way. Your drive to thrive decreases and intentions becomes confused. A lack of confidence manifests. As an example, a person may experience extreme bodily pain periodically. Or, people may tell you that you unintentionally inflict pain on them. There are three major ways that a person will experience the faith brain disconnect.

1. Out of Body, Out of Faith

When you go through a traumatic experience, your memories will resurface in other areas of your life. Even when you do not remember the event itself, your body's nervous system remembers it for you. You will experience an uneasy feeling and will do anything to exit a situation. Moreover, during the process of exiting a situation, you may mentally "check out. " This means, you consciously shut down your awareness by literally escaping out of yourself due to a lack of hope. The process of mentally escaping is often referred to as "spacing out," "excessive random daydreaming" or seeing the world outside of your body.

Olivia

When Olivia was eight years old, she was molested by a family friend. At that moment, she jumped out of her body. And her conscious brain did not remember the event afterward. She then returned to her body and went through an extremely emotional period.

Because of the molestation, Olivia's body underwent internal turmoil. When she became sick with the flu, her body could no longer handle the additional stress created from the sickness. Additionally, Olivia's body could not endure any form of pain. Although Olivia had no memory of the rape, her nervous system was completely overwhelmed. During her sleep, Olivia had an out-of-body experience that scared her into falsely thinking something was wrong with her. Some people refer to this "out-of-body" experience as astral-traveling or astral projection.

While asleep, Olivia remembers getting up from the bed. She looked around and saw cookies on the table that she did not buy. Her sister bought them as Olivia slept. She reached down to pick up a cookie, and her hands seemed to pass through the cookie package. Olivia could not pick up the package. She was puzzled. Olivia looks around the room and sees her robe on the chair. She attempts to pick up her robe from the chair. Her hand could not pick it up.

Olivia then looked back at her bed. She saw herself lying down. Olivia gasps at the shock of this vision. Simultaneously in that gasping moment, her body in the bed gasps for air. She is instantaneously pulled back into her body. From that fractal moment on, Olivia remained afraid of that experience. She frequently questioned what happened to her, while conscious outside of her body. Some people call that an "out of body experience." For a period, Olivia walked in shame thinking something else was wrong with her.

Addiction is a form of "Out of the Body" faith brain disconnection. When someone has not dealt with painful memories, the faith brain's nervous system may disconnect from the brain to organ connections. Or, the faith brain disconnects you from the outside world as a way to cope with the lack of sensations or excessive sensations. Oftentimes, many attempt to self-regulate connections through various forms of addiction.

Substances fail to work since painful memories still run in your unconscious mind like a background app on your mobile device. You may do anything to regulate the shame or guilt feelings that you experience. Through compulsive behaviors, you are temporarily brought "out of your body." You may have a glass of wine or alcohol every night then follow it up with tons of coffee the next day to re-energize. Or, you may fall in love with men who share a sexual connection just to escape your reality. If you are a man, you may have sex with multiple women thinking you are a "ladies man" as a means of attempting to feel a rush. Others are addicted to work and stay for long hours, to avoid dealing with dysfunctional home situations. Many turn to drug substances that they hide from others. Such addictive cycles take place because your faith brain is stifled. Guilt or shame feelings become toxic chemical cycles causing you to be uncomfortable in your own body.

Lars

Lars was accustomed to being an athlete since the age of 13 when he was first recruited in football. At 13, he is recruited into an elite football program to make money for the family. Through football, Lars finds a way to escape his home life, while also placing value on always performing. When Lars 15, he is seduced by an older woman. At the same time, Lars is unaware that he is experiencing trauma by being placed in adult situations too early. He later travels the world as a football player and retires from sports in Los Angeles, California.

He works hard for everything he gains. Lars lands a high-paying job and becomes a workaholic. As the company goes under, Lars resorts to coaching football on several campuses to prevent financial ruin. However, he misses the performance part of the sports profession as a player. Eventually, Lars starts to feel uncomfortable with his position in life. To fill this void, Lars goes out on the weekends and has way too many drinks. Lars turns to alcohol almost nightly to cope.

2. Fearing the Future, Fearing the Past

This person fears that what they foresee will really happen, and will create their own mental prison. This jail repeatedly "plays" memories of the dreaded future in the person's head. He fears the future and can no longer pay attention to what is currently happening in the present. He overlooks things that are right in front of him. He is mentally stuck in time.

Or, this person may become stuck in the past and relives an event that eats away at his memory. He constantly fears that what he experienced will happen again, even though the situation is completely different. He cannot pay attention to the present because his senses simultaneously recall experiences that he could not control.

In both cases, he is accepting into his brain a fear energy which is outside of him. And this energy seeks to manipulate the mind's free will faith process. As a result, the future is created in a distorted manner. Subsequently, he forgets that he and God are co-authors of the future. So, he simply thinks that whatever he focuses on will solely happen.

Auriel

When Auriel was 30, she was in a severe car accident. As she entered the intersection at a green light, another vehicle ran the red light. Acting to protect her and her baby, she quickly veered her steering wheel to the right to minimize the potentially fatal impact. Auriel and the baby blacked out immediately after the accident. However, when she became conscious, she saw the wreckage and went into mental shock. Although she and her child could walk away from the accident alive and with a concussion, she still suffered physical discomfort every time she drove. Anytime Auriel would look to the left; adrenaline would run through her system, causing body and headaches. She also feared looking to her left and rotating the steering wheel to the right, as it would trigger trauma about the accident. As a result, Auriel was always tense while driving due to her fear of experiencing a similar accident.

3. Ignoring God (or a Higher Power), Promoting You

When you have an issue with the faith sections of your brain, you have an urge to overly self-promote without considering all the factors that made your situation possible. If you are a go-getter, but fail to understand that gratitude is just as powerful as self-promotion you, may fall into this category.

Executive Ronald

Ronald is a well-known business mogul. He always wanted to become a governmental leader. But when a leaked audio tape depicting him in a revolting situation hits the media, Ronald does anything possible to alter the truth. So, with his money, he hires the best publicity agents money could buy. Ronald finds people to spin his racist and misogynistic comments to "sound acceptable." In his mind, he is always right. Ronald even seeks the help of international firms in securing election votes. He wins.

But while in his governmental position, Ronald angers the people who supported him. And, he now finds himself conducting massive self-promotion, including rebranding his persona as the "savior," who's acquired problems that "everyone else" created. All the while doing so, Ronald negates the support of everyone who would have voted for his measures. He also goes into a political battle without most of his supporters. Ronald later faces riots and is removed from his leadership position as a result of a hostile takeover.

RIGHT TRIABRAIN DISCONNECTION

Have you ever experienced pure joy when deciding to take action on a plan? Or, on the flip side, have you experienced tremendously difficult trials, which left you questioning every immediate future decision? Have you ever been so determined to change your situation that you look for a viable solution? If so, you are using the right *Triabrain.*

The right *Triabrain* represents how your feelings affect your conscious and unconscious decision-making process. This *Triabrain* sector selects and interprets your experiences, and chooses a belief based on its experience. Future decision-making derives from feelings formed while understanding the event. The feeling response is a type of *Triabrain* thought designed to take energy and convert it to pleasure, which in turn is a sensation that affects the physiological systems (e.g., immune, endocrine, cardiovascular) of the body connected to the *Triabrain.* Neuroimaging studies of emotional self-regulation, psychotherapy, and doctor placebo effect studies are examples of how feelings influence automatic body reactions and future decision-making choices.

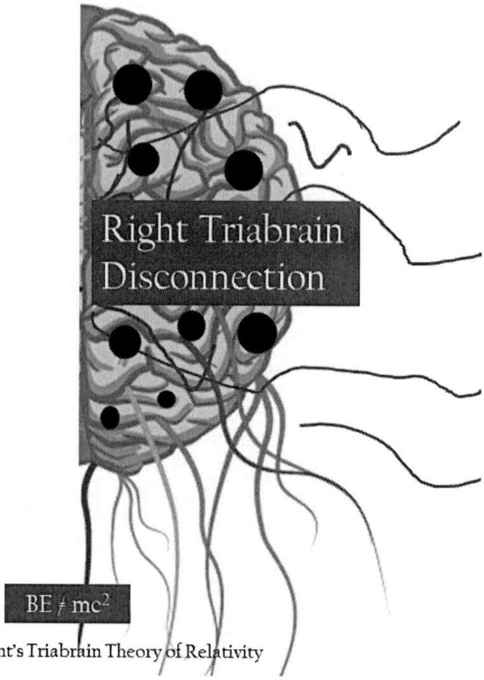

Image 4-4: Brainbrink Masses Causing A Right Triabrain Disconnection

However, when your right brain begins to disconnect from itself, your brain fails to convert emotions into feelings in the body. Emotions then affect the immune system and alter your relationships. Your emotions will confuse you and make you clueless on what makes you happy. You also begin trusting other people more than yourself. Or, you rely on logic to reinforce your toxic emotions. You may delay significant decisions until there is an extreme "vortex moment," which threatens your security. The cause of brainbrink is depicted by the black circles in the figure above. These chaos-induced masses separate the right side of the *Triabrain*. There are three primary examples where right-brain disconnections can occur.

1. Hiding in You, Only Seeking in Others

In this form of right-brain disconnection, you lose confidence over discerning your feelings about situations, people and your own decisions. In your eyes, it is easier to trust someone else's thoughts over your own. The justification for following the will of others: If you believe someone else's ideas and it backfires, it is better to blame someone else and not yourself. In this disconnection, you have experienced chaos where you learned to turn off your feelings because you were never able to move beyond your conflicting emotions successfully.

Shonia

Shonia is a successful real estate agent who wants to build a strong business. However, she always second guesses her feelings during certain situations. As a result, it clouds her decision-making process. Shonia turns to her friends for the simplest decisions. She even asks friends to choose her clothing. Shonia frequently asks non-experts for business networking advice. She easily befriends people who she feels are beneficial. This behavior makes Shonia feel good because she hides her feelings as she focuses on others. Shonia is experiencing what many would call "codependent" behavior. Her thoughts and feelings merge with someone else's, and she's no longer able to identify her own.

2. Needing Drama, Lacking Self- Romance

In some cases, when your right brain stalls, the creative, expressive side of your brain cannot express feelings or interpret situations in a healthy way. Instead of being able to express how you feel and what you see. You begin to expect everyone to know through osmosis how you feel and what you see by telepathy. You read far more into situations than what is healthy. Like a snowball effect, your issue becomes bigger than its actual size. As a result, explosive brain energy from your thoughts gets trapped in chaotic cycling emotions that seem to ravage your heart and body.

Antoinette

Antoinette is a strikingly beautiful woman. She is a single mom that struggles without a high school education. Antoinette had a job, but she lost it and now struggles to pay rent with part-time work. Her emotional fear of returning to school haunts her. She gets engaged to a man who financially helps. But, Antoinette questions his loyalty in their relationship due to certain actions. Instead of expressing concern about his inconsistent statements regarding his location, Antoinette withholds her emotions. As a result, Antoinette becomes quick-tempered and regularly argues with her fiancé. Instead of seeking help from friends to escape this toxic relationship, Antoinette receives help from one of her ex-boyfriends (not the baby's daddy). She creates unnecessary drama in her life because she does not know how to romance herself, invest in herself and contribute to her education.

3. Expecting A Let-Down, Not Re-Directing Power

In many cases, your right brain will stall in its decision-making process. You will stop talking to someone instead of speaking up for yourself. In some cases, you cannot calm yourself. And if you have a weak relationship with inner feelings, it's extremely challenging to change stressful situations. You fear to make any decision. For fear that your circumstance is "punishment" from God or a "Higher Power." More importantly, you believe this problematic situation is "meant to teach you a lesson." So, you feel that you must endure the situation, or need to flee it for hopefully something better. In both cases, your brain stalls in its ability to direct your power.

Maria

Maria had been working as a part-time professor for over ten years at a local community college. One year, the faculty supervisors changed. The new director made life difficult for Maria, so she started getting harassed. Soon, personal attacks began to affect her annual evaluations. Requirements were changed without Maria's knowledge, causing her to receive low-performing scores. She simply looked at the writing on the wall and thought her only recourse of action was to find another job quickly. Her situation changed once she began working with a life-coach. Maria discovered she could stand up to her supervisors, and communicate her expectations of having non-modified guidelines. Maria realized that her existence and ability to speak up empowers her situation, which made it shift in her favor.

LEFT TRIABRAIN DISCONNECTIONS

Have you ever had to investigate the facts before making a decision? Have you ever navigated your way through a situation by only using logic or resources to solve issues? If so, you were using your left *Triabrain.*

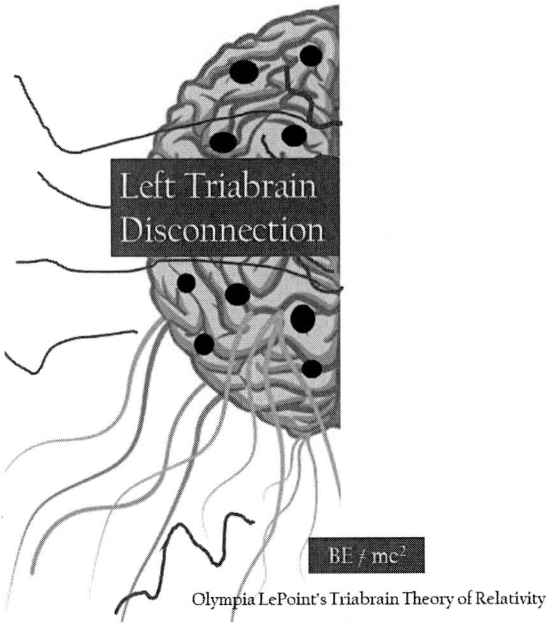

Image 4-5: Brainbrink Masses Cause Left Triabrain Disconnection

However, when there is a disconnection in your left *Triabrain*, you are no longer able to use your space, time, and resources in logical ways. You will find Science, Technology, Engineering and Mathematical (STEM) calculations difficult to understand. Your cause-effect thinking becomes hindered. Your left brain will no longer know how to make physical things out of nothing. You will have a tough time understanding what is real and what is a fantasy. You may spend your money or time where it runs out. You will have difficulty predicting cause-and-effect. This chaos separates the connection on the left side of the brain as seen with the dark masses above.

1. Rejecting Logic, Embracing Fantasy

In this left *Triabrain* disconnection, you have escaped rough situations, and you stumble in finding practical solutions and approaches. Instead of figuring out the available resources to change your position, you will turn to fantasy to avoid the strict process of problem-solving. In turn, artificial pleasure hormones release and serve as a childhood-like distraction.

Mario

Mario was a man who experienced a brain injury. He was in a car crash and the car overturned. When found, they discovered Mario suffered a brain injury. Mario survived and recovered. He was young, and the doctors said he still had his cognitive abilities. Mario even took classes at the local community college to become a chef. He was working toward a new career. Secretly, his logical reasoning was affected.

Soon after, Mario dated a woman he met in his culinary arts classes. They dated for nine years. He proposed to her but had no ring. He even desired to start a business with her. But, Mario never registered the company, nor found any clients. He saw himself as a business owner, but he still lived at home with his mother. And when Mario is strapped for cash, he was convinced that he was "sure" to win the mega lottery. Mario did not have the strength to follow through in completing physical tasks.

2. Subtracting Science, and Only Adding God

In this *Triabrain,* disconnected state, you may strictly rely on God and refuse to see the facts. Practical approaches will be lost. You will rely on God for "miracles" in your situation, without understanding that you have an important role in the practical transformation. You may think that prayer alone can change your situation. You may not believe the Earth is round and may not think that there is such a thing as biological evolution. You may wonder how God and science could be the same.

Alan

Alan is a strong, Christian man raised with an angry father. At the age of 21, he found the Lord, and his life forever changed. Alan found peace and joy in trusting the Lord for all his needs. However, he still had unresolved hidden emotional issues that he worked on eliminated through prayer and spiritual classes. However, secretly, Alan did not have courage in taking action. He always felt more comfortable hoping that miracles would happen organically without much work on his part. He did not have the full picture that great things also manifest with physical effort.

One day when Alan is at home, while he gets up to go to the bathroom at night, and he falls and hits his head. He wakes up and has a huge knot on his forehead. Alan lays down trusting God will heal him. He goes back to sleep. A few hours later, he awakens, and God tells him to call his church friend, Olivia. Alan calls her, and Olivia urges him to go to the Emergency Room immediately. He hesitates, but he truly knows that it is the right thing to do. Alan trusts Olivia and agrees to go to the Emergency Room. He gets dropped off at the hospital and diagnosed with a severe concussion. Alan is unable to work for two weeks. The doctors prescribe medical strategies to help Alan's recovery. However, Alan initially planned to work that same day had he not talked to Olivia.

3. Overlooking Resources, and Struggling for Scraps

In this *Triabrain* disconnect, you may believe that there is a lack of physical resources to help you. As a result, you will think there is no option except to take matters into your own hands through any means necessary. You are accustomed to being the BEST at everything so that others will know your worth. Instead of naturally allowing your logic to find resources that you need for innovation, you believe that anything exciting must be begged for, or secretly taken.

Soroya

Soroya is a beautiful woman. However, she never felt capable of earning a college degree. Soroya knew she was considered attractive by many. She would pride herself in her appearance and expect people to do things for her. Soroya wanted people to buy her food and pay her rent. She always overlooked her skills and abilities. Soroya was determined to take what others possessed because she never felt confident of her skills.

One day, she encounters a person equally beautiful, who was an author and successful in her career. She was so angry to be reminded that she had not created success for herself. The first chance she had, Soroya stabbed her friend in the back by trying to take the attention away from her friend to feel as if she had control over what resources can come to others. She always secretly thought there was not going to be enough success for her. She failed to see what she had in her own life and build on it.

For the following questions, select your response by the following criteria: 5 = strongly agree; 4 = sometimes agree; 3 = neutral; 2 = sometimes disagree; 1 = strongly disagree. The test is short.

FAITH BRAIN DISCONNECT SELF-TEST

1. When I envision myself doing something, I see myself doing it, as if I see myself in a movie. 5 4 3 2 1
2. When I was younger, I could see the future clearly before others could see it. Now, I try not to think about it too much because it brings anxiety. 5 4 3 2 1
3. I do not believe in God or a higher force at a place in the outcome of my life. 5 4 3 2 1
4. I experience physical accidents frequently. 5 4 3 2 1
6. When I think about things that I have done in the past, I regret many things I did or experienced. 5 4 3 2 1
6. I am annoyed when someone says that they "will pray" for me. 5 4 3 2 1
7. I daydream often. 5 4 3 2 1
8. Often, I am thinking about what happened a few days ago, or what's going to happen tomorrow. 5 4 3 2 1
9. I always can do anything I set my mind to without seeking outside guidance. 5 4 3 2 1
10. Parts of my memory from the past are missing from my brain and I do not know why. 5 4 3 2 1
11. I feel uncomfortable with people who say that they can predict the future. 5 4 3 2 1
12. I do not always agree with people having "extra sensory perception" or knowing things more than their five senses. 5 4 3 2 1
13. At times, I do not feel parts of my body. Fingertips or my stomach sometimes have no feelings. 5 4 3 2 1
14. My stomach ties up in knots when thinking about something that I have no control over. 5 4 3 2 1
15. I find myself doing endless research before I make a decision. 5 4 3 2 1

____

Add up Scores from 1, 4, 7, 10, 13.
"Out of Body, Out of Faith" **SCORE** ________

Add up Scores from 2, 5, 8, 11, 14.
"Fearing the Future,
Fearing the Past" **SCORE** ________

Add up Scores from 3, 6, 9, 12, 15.
"Ignoring God, Promoting You" **SCORE** ________

Circle your highest score of the three categories.

RIGHT BRAIN DISCONNECT SELF-TEST

16. I often ask others what they think about what I plan to wear. 5 4 3 2 1
17. In romantic relations, I always seem to find people that involve me in arguments. 5 4 3 2 1
18. I have changed jobs often within the last three years. 5 4 3 2 1
19. When there is a tough situation to handle, I always seek outside advice. 5 4 3 2 1
20. Pasion in relationships is far more exciting than dedication. 5 4 3 2 1
21. I hate when people flake in situations, and they have done it often lately. 5 4 3 2 1
22. When I have a dream that I do not understand, I ask if someone else has similar experiences. 5 4 3 2 1
23. I find myself bored often. And I wish I has more fun in my life. 5 4 3 2 1
24. It is tough for me to express how I feel about the opposite sex. 5 4 3 2 1
25. When I grew up, I had to find people to show me how to do things since my parents did not to show me. 5 4 3 2 1
26. I get angry when someone questions my decision. 5 4 3 2 1

27. I sometimes wonder if I am supposed to be in certain situations to learn a lesson. 5 4 3 2 1
28. I devote hours on emails and texts trying to analyze what someone is saying to me. 5 4 3 2 1
29. I hate when I ask a question, I do not get an answer, or a response. 5 4 3 2 1
30. Sometimes I question why certain situations happen to me. 5 4 3 2 1

Add up Scores from 16, 19, 22, 25, 28.
"Hiding in You, Only Seeking in Others" **SCORE** ________

Add up Scores from 17, 20, 23, 26, 29.
"Needing Drama, Lacking Self-Romance" **SCORE** ________

Add up Scores from 18, 21, 24, 27, 30.
"Expecting A Let-Down,
Not Directing Holy Power" **SCORE** ________

Circle your highest score of the three categories.

LEFT BRAIN DISCONNECT SELF-TEST

31. One day, I will win major prize in the lottery. 5 4 3 2 1
32. I feel that God will deliver me from all difficult situations. 5 4 3 2 1
33. I don't see why certain people gain recognition. 5 4 3 2 1
34. I stayed in a relationship because he/she would eventually fall in love with me. 5 4 3 2 1
35. The money invested into science research would be more useful in other areas. 5 4 3 2 1
36. I have stolen a woman from her man. (Or I have taken a man from a woman.) 5 4 3 2 1
37. I believe natural healing will cure all cancers. 5 4 3 2 1
38. I do not believe in taking medicine or going to the doctor often. 5 4 3 2 1
39. I shoplifted before in my youth. 5 4 3 2 1

40. If I am in a terrible situation at work, it will eventually resolve itself.	5	4	3	2	1
41. I question the origins of evolution.	5	4	3	2	1
42. I sometimes feel like I need to cheat to get ahead.	5	4	3	2	1
43. One day, I will get noticed by investors and will gain income for projects	5	4	3	2	1
44. Faith can overcome any difficult situation.	5	4	3	2	1
45. All the good men are married. (or Men must have money to attract a hot woman.)	5	4	3	2	1

Add up Scores from 31, 34, 37, 40, 43.
"Rejecting Logic, Embracing Fantasy" **SCORE** ________

Add up Scores from 32, 35, 38, 41, 44.
"Subtracting Science, Only Adding God" **SCORE** ________

Add up Scores from 33, 36, 39, 42, 45.
"Overlooking Resources, and
Struggling for Scraps" **SCORE** ________

Circle your highest score of the three categories.

The Truth

Chapter 5

The Truth

The Power in Your Triabrain Connections

"May the ***Force*** be with you."

We have all heard this saying before. Trilogies have been created from this concept of having a "force." Do not be fooled. There are forces that are for and against your success. This concept is not only in space movies but in your daily life. When you are in the process of accomplishing something HUGE that will change the course of your life, you will be tested by countless forces. Millions of thoughts will run through your head.

In the process of writing this book, for example, I encountered numerous obstacles. My sister had brain surgery and nearly died. One of my part-time teaching jobs went into question. Then, the days I was supposed to write, flat tires "mysteriously" appeared. Within the final stretch of writing this book, the hard drive crashed on my computer. Not once, but twice. Thankfully, I had a dream to back up the contents and additional information moments before it crashed. After repairs were made, there was a 12-hour electricity outage from a power plant explosion a few blocks from my home. I sat in the police station until 3 a.m. one morning to finish charging my cell phone with their emergency generators. Although tired with just four hours of sleep, I attempted to write. But I needed to buy replacement groceries first then my American Express card disappears then reappears three hours later. When I return to write, my "repaired" computer crashes for the second time. Money originally saved for a vacation transformed overnight into money required for buying the second computer. I did anything I could to finish writing Calculus midterms *AND* this book. All these events point to one major fact.

Without connected thinking, these negative situations are designed to tire, disappoint, distract, make you go crazy and give up. These negative forces will attempt to make you use your *own free will and* thoughts in a toxic way as a weapon against you. Consequently, you feel like turning around, going back, and no longer determined to finish your race.

Hold on! Stop! Don't give up! If there is one piece of advice I will give you, it is an important action. Keep moving forward! Don't turn back! The finish line is closer than you think!

Do not be fooled by people who want you to believe that life is always "bliss." No. Do not be fooled by people who say there is no Devil. No. You have an Enemy. This Enemy oversees destructive forces that attempt to trick you into using your power against you. His job is to make you depleted, disoriented, doubtful, weary, disappointed, depressed, and feel defeated. Know the truth. Chaos has two branches. One is for growth, nourished by God and the other is toxicity overseen by your Enemy. There are indeed dark, toxic forces the Enemy oversees that trigger your painful thoughts. Deep, painful memories you encounter as you break through barriers is a sophisticated, destructive distraction aimed at preventing you, a potential leader, from transforming your life.

These forces use traumatic situations as a way of creating painful memories in you, so you will begin to fear your own future. When you are tricked into using your free will and thoughts against yourself, then, obsess about a dreadful future, the Enemy wins. You *ACTUALLY* have the power to create your future. Not just one. More than one. *Both* exist at the same time. Don't be fooled and frustrated by this Enemy and his helpers. Instead of fearing chaos, you can gain God's help in using these forces to your benefit. Keep reading.

Yes, you read this correctly. You can use energy from destructive forces for your benefit if you recognize why chaos enters your life. Then, you will learn how to deal with chaos so you can unleash your brainpower force. Know these three facts. 1.) Traumatic experiences heal you from past experiences even if you are unconscious of what happened to you in the past. 2.) Chaotic situations allow you to redirect your power through your thoughts in a healthy direction toward your life purpose. 3.) Energy from chaotic situations is for you to use in transforming your life to 100% innovative growth. Such development can be used for healing your body, transforming relationships and changing your environments.

Anything you set your mind to accomplish will happen. This is your true power. This fact is *real.* You will discover more truth statements about how chaos empowers you in this chapter. You have an inner force that empowers you to change your life. It is your *Triabrain* force. The *Triabrain* is your three-sided brain power field, but most people are unaware of its power. When you discover and develop the faith of your brain with its intuition, you connect your brain together to unleash a powerful, force that changes your life, the lives around you and invents science breakthrough.

Not only does this side of the brain connect to unleash the power, but it also helps you unleash joy in overcoming your challenges. The art of overcoming, healing and innovation are based on your connections to the Source. Whenever you think chaos is happening to only you, think again. It is happening to everyone in order to create powerful connections. Rather than purposely avoiding chaos, you must learn to use chaos energy to connect your life. There are three main principles in converting chaos into your *Triabrain* connection.

The recipe for reshaping the brain through self-directed neuroplasticity depends on recognizing connections. God is in Chaos Theory, Einstein's Equation, and your human brain. They are all connected together. By using intuition and science, you can change the shape of your brain. Your thoughts will convert energy from situations into energy needed for selecting an emotion. Subsequently, this energy is used to convert emotions into feelings. New energy is then used to convert feelings (which are also a type of thought) into physical action. Energy from your action draws you closer to success. This process will change the inner makeup of your brain. If you embrace these three following truths, you will access the power of your brain that you have not actively used. Your brain's power will begin to unleash life-transforming connections.

TRUTH #1:
God is Part of Your Chaotic Equation

Now, many people often say to me, "Olympia, you are a scientist. How can you believe in God? I thought that science and God are separate."

In fact, there are many scientists out there who argue against a "God" force. These are individuals who only view life with science and facts, and seek to disprove a Higher Power that exists. Naysayers seek to disprove God and/or a "Godly influence." Nevertheless, everyone has a right to believe what is best for them. Throughout history, countless scientists believed God was the force behind every scientific discovery.

The discussion of God within Science is nothing new. For centuries, such discussions have been a long-lasting topic among scientists and religious leaders. In Ancient Greece, philosophers believed that science was a process to understand the natural laws behind creation. Mathematics was viewed as a perfect tool in understanding the "mind of the gods." From the 9th Century until the 12th Century's expansion of Islam, great developments in medicine, astronomy, and agriculture were believed to be the "Will of Allah." For many years, during the 12th Century's great learning movement in Europe, Christianity and science were proposed together. That is until a series of natural and political disasters spread fear.

During these events, imprisonment and death were the results of fear. For example, Nicolaus Copernicus (1473-1543), who proposed the Earth revolved around the sun, was in direct opposition to theology leaders. Later during the *Witch Trials*, Giordano Bruno (1548-1600) was burned at stake for agreeing with Copernicus and suggesting other stars have worlds revolving around them. (Note: Today, this logic seems insane, because NASA telescopes have proven planets revolve around suns. But this technology was not previously available.)

During that time, there was an effort to remove this fear. Many scientists-philosophers did as much as they could to spread eye-opening knowledge. World-renowned Catholics René Descartes (1596-1650), Robert Boyle (1627-1691), and John Ray (1627-1705) tried to reunite religious beliefs and scientific research. But their efforts made a very little dent into removing this fear. Physicists Michael Faraday (1791-1867), and Max Planck (1858-1947) attempted to demonstrate how evolution versus creationism was never debatable. Did you know a Roman Catholic priest, Georges Lemaître (1894-1966), was the first to propose *The Big Bang Theory*? Lemaître's work later inspired Albert Einstein (1879 -1955) to revise his famous theories of relativity. Don't be fooled: God has always been an integral part of Math and Science.

More importantly, God plays a pivotal role in the science of the brain. As described previously in the *Triabrain Theory of Relativity*, the role of thought is to convert energy from one situation to be used for another. Thoughts can remove and replace energy. God is the major connecting force which generates a fractal movement, allowing you to take the energy of a situation and use it for your benefit.

This point was driven home for me personally on a lunch date with a man named "Glenn." I was single and on a date with Glenn. He is a gorgeous green-eyed, dark haired, 6'5" nuclear chemist who possessed all the wonderful characteristics that most women would desire. He even flew planes. Glenn was wealthy and owned a house on the beach. He was very athletic and played volleyball weekly. This charming gentleman also had a great sense of style, and frequently wore trendy business suits on our dates. Most of all, Glenn's romantic pursuit was unquestionably directed to me. So, I was excited to spend time with him at lunch. We ate an amazing meal and had an excellent discussion until he voiced something revealing.

Image 5-1: Photo of the lunch dessert at the luxury hotel where the truth was explained.

Glenn said, "I do not believe in God."

I gasped inside and deeply swallowed.

Glenn continued, "I don't see how God can exist when such chaos goes on in the world. I don't know why God causes horrible things to happen."

Looking up, he saw my expression and continued, "Oh no! I see the expression on your face. Is not believing in God a deal-breaker for you?"

You see, I knew about Glenn's backstory and how chaos purposely worked together for his good. Although God did not cause his situation, Glenn was helped through it. Glenn's father was an alcoholic, who neglected Glenn and his brother. Yet, Glenn and his older brother became highly successful in life. His brother graduated from an Ivy-League school. Glenn became a nationally-recognized technology salesman, who expertly invested in start-up companies due to his success.

I explained to Glenn something very simple: God was embedded in Glenn's situation from the beginning. Although Glenn grew up with a dysfunctional, alcoholic father in the house, God did not cause those events. Rather, God helped Glenn use those events to his benefit. Glenn was given a gift. "Survivalist" skills learned as a child helped Glenn to become extremely successful. Not everyone could handle a severe situation of that sort, but Glenn prospered. As a result, Glenn learned how to read people effectively. From neglected experiences, Glenn learned both the negative and positive aspects of reading people.

However, Glenn focused on positive traits then converted his experiences into success. Every time his father was hot and cold toward him, Glenn turned that experience into the skill of reading his clients' moods. Glenn could decipher if customers were hot or cold toward his products. I further explained to Glenn that his father's inability to have the right faculties in situations empowered Glenn with the ability to determine if a customer had resources to pay for services sincerely. Because Glenn frequently witnessed his father's drunkenness, Glenn chose not to drink. Despite growing up in a dysfunctional home, Glenn received powerful gifts that contributed to his success. Not many people could handle a daunting situation, yet Glenn not only *survived* – he thrived! Glenn used free will and wise decision-making to change the direction of his life. That seemingly traumatic childhood circumstance was used to transform Glenn's life positively. More importantly, the energy from that situation continually assists Glenn as he finds additional ways to convert the toxicity of his childhood into tools needed for further success.

God is a connection. Love is being connected. Connection first starts in the mind, body, and soul specifically. Love is embodying the healthy connections you possess, as well as, developing those connections with others. This Godly connection guarantees how your brain connects its left side to its right. It is how your brain connects you to your body. It is how your brain-to-body connects you to others' thoughts and the universe. The connection is when you see or travel to, far distant planets. Most importantly, love is how you connect with God. The connection is knowing you are not alone. You are always connected. The connection is knowing that no matter what, you are connected to God – the energy source of all living things. Therefore, God connects you to the strength you need to overcome anything.

If there is one major concept to take from this book, know that God loves you, me and everyone. We are loved by God so much that he will always offer ways to escape the chaos. In my opinion, God and Science are the same. They form two sides of a 3-sided coin. God shows universal power in scientific principles as we humans discover scientific laws. Science is the evidence of spiritual laws that promote both eternal growth and death. Science is evidence that God exists.

GOD IS IN YOUR BRAIN AND IN THE TRIABRAIN THEORY OF RELATIVITY

*"God does not play **dice** with the universe." - Albert Einstein*

This quote is important for two reasons. First off, Albert Einstein believed that God was accessible to everyone. Secondly, the word "dice," expresses a world of tiny particles behind everything that's governed by total randomness. Einstein believed there was an underlying divine law of nature that could define particles, and make it possible to calculate both their speed and position. Plus, Einstein ascertained how everything in life is connected. This theory includes the way your brain connects to all matter in the universe.

More specifically, God is part of any given situation. God works through your *Triabrain* and the *Triabrain Theory of Relativity*. Within any chaotic situation, God provides the gift of human free will, your belief systems, and your natural intuitive guidance. God embeds himself into science, thereby giving you ways to unleash power from your brain. "Randomness" is simply how humans interpret situations without the use of their intuition.

In the last chapter, I clearly define how chemical reactions happen within the brain during chaotic situations. Anything outside of God during this chemical reaction is simply chaos manifesting in your brain and in life. Brain reshaping depends on acknowledging God in your brain and your perception of the world.

God in Your Speed of Light (Squared) = The Way You See The World

Within the *Triabrain Theory of Relativity* (which is based on Einstein's Theory of Relativity), people see the light differently based on where they are located in the universe. For example, imagine viewing the Santa Monica Mountains in Los Angeles, Calif. It would be different if you were to take a picture of those same mountains and post it to social media. Or, send it to a friend in the Ukraine. Your friend would see the same mountains in this picture while sitting in the Ukraine. Yet, your experiences would greatly contrast based on how the light hit your eyes. The way you experience the same object will be different based on where you are in time *and* space. You will never see the same things as your mother, your father, or your best friend, even if you are in the same home. Perception varies according to your location in the universe. Therefore, you will not see nor have the same experiences as your parents or best friend.

Furthermore, in Albert Einstein's Theory of General Relativity, he described how massive objects could tug on light, and even pull at the fabric of space-time. Simply put, strong gravitational fields from massive objects can act as lenses — warping, magnifying and redirecting light as it travels through the cosmos. Your brain is a miniature cosmos. Any of your massive toxic fear-formed brain structures can pull on the light in your brain. These structures tug on light and even pull the fabric of how you view space and time. Thus, your perception of life will appear distorted. In turn, fear and toxic emotions can warp your lenses (view of life) by magnifying and redirecting light as it travels through your brain.

To take this concept a bit further to your brain scientifically, the equation $BE = mc^2$ hinges on one major concept: how your brain energy changes based on the speed of your light and brain mass. Only one part of the equation carries information. It is the speed of light. In a vacuum space, the most efficient way energy can travel is through a straight line with the speed of light, which is 299, 792, 458 meters per second. Although some faster-than-light physical theories (like *The Big Bang Theory*, *Quantum Entanglement*, and *Negative Matter*) propose travel faster than the speed of light, these things cannot carry brain information. Nothing within you can travel faster than your "inner light." Nothing changes situations faster than enlightenment. This "brain light" is your "ah-ha" awareness that reshapes connections within your brain. The speed of light is God in your equation. In science, you call this light. In spirituality, this light is an "all-encompassing" Godly light. In energy healing work, this light initiates rebirth. Essentially, this light is a straight line pointing you toward success.

How Your Brain Works to Reshape Itself

Your brain creates millions of thoughts simultaneously. But only a select few are conscious. The following sequence is the chain of events that happen with just ONE thought. Again, this sequence represents a chaotic reshaping with only one thought. However, within your brain, this sequence occurs in multiple sections. The chain of brain events occurs in this sequence:

- **Step 1:** An event happens.
- **Step 2:** ***(Fractal Moment)*** – You decide to be impacted by the event (free will). Your faith creates at least two future events, but you will only physically reach one event in the future. (You physically cannot be in two places at once.)
- **Step 3:** Your thoughts about the situation converts the chaos energy to a new energy. You have multiple thoughts. You pick one main thought to move forward.

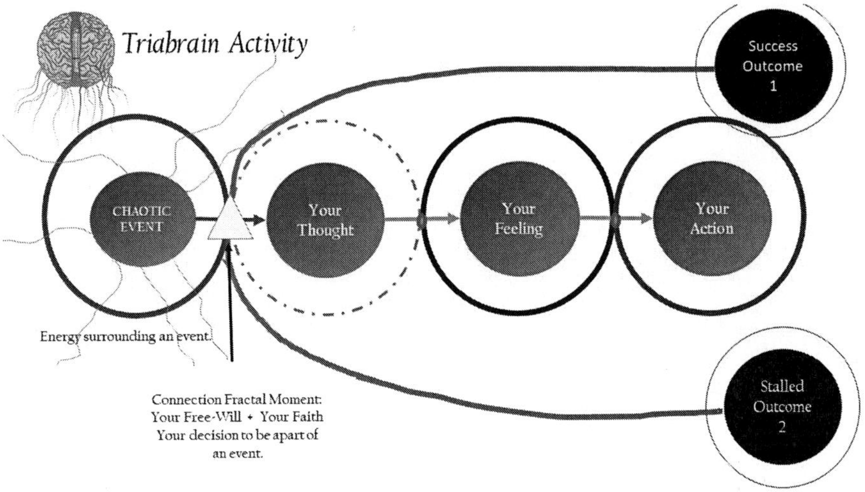

Image 5-2: Triabrain Theory of Relativity fractal moment of Free Will. Fractal Movement in the brain that connects the energy of an event with a person's life purpose is a decision-moment called free will. The choice creates two futures to exist simultaneously. You will go to one outcome, while someone else will be attracted to the other.

In the *Triabrain Theory of Relativity*, God is embedded in your connection to a chaotic event. A chaotic event releases potential energy. This energy is for your use. Think of a car bomb, earthquake, or tornado. Energy from each event is released into the environment. Even if you see the event through the TV, you can choose to use that energy. Your brain then ingests energy from the event through your free will and faith. Your free will and beliefs surrounding the event creates your fractal moment. This moment is when you decide if the event will help you move forward in growth, or pull you into a stalled state.

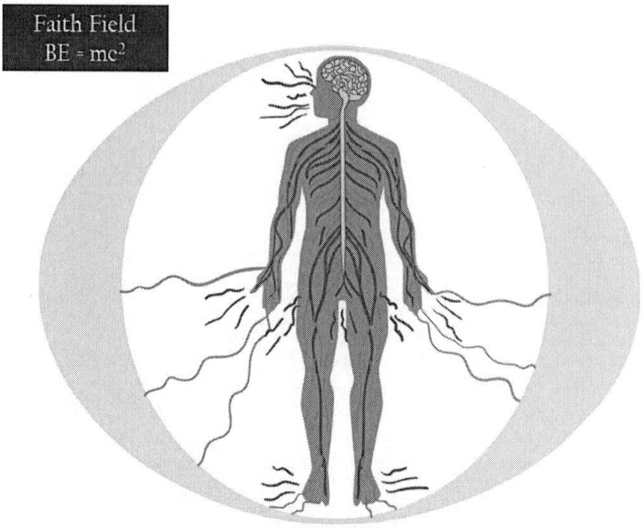

Image 5-3: Per the Triabrain Theory of Relativity, The Triabrain Field has a faith field which captures your beliefs surrounding all situations that impact you. This field is responsible for the first thought conversion process. Energy can be felt as an energy field around a person and through their hands.

To better explain this situation, consider an earthquake. Some people experience an earthquake, while others have not encountered this type of natural disaster. Now, think of what happens when all survivors of this earthquake choose to grow from that experience. This earthquake is designed to offer people a way to use that powerful earth-shaking energy in their individual lives. Some people will transform their lives using that energy. Others will "stall" and go into mental shock. It is a subconscious and conscious choosing power you have been given. No scientist has ever fully understood this process because Chaos Theory was not formally introduced until the late 1970's. In 2016, I developed the *Triabrain Theory of Relativity*, which expounds upon the Chaos Theory.

I sincerely believe our human gift of free will is a special ability from God that's embedded in Science.

Second, you have beliefs associated with events. Such beliefs are based on past experiences. If a man elected to the presidency is ignorant and ill-prepared, you can choose to believe the country is going into utter turmoil. And in this case, you will create suffering for yourself. Or, you can choose to believe the country will benefit overall as an individual awakens to his or her decision-making power. You are, in fact, creating two different futures for yourself based on your beliefs. Both outcomes exist simultaneously at the exact moment based on your belief about the situation. This means that you create two futures, but your free will chooses only one outcome based upon thoughts, feelings and future actions.

"Trust in the love of God and that all things will work together for your good." This belief is powerful. If you choose to have faith in a beneficial future during an extremely difficult situation, you are literally reshaping your brain to follow the path to reach a better future physically. When you fail to see the benefit in the most horrific situation, you create a reality of suffering. And, if you witness shocking actions in others, you suffer in that reality as well. In both situations, this time of suffering will seem like hell to you.

Vanna

Vanna was a woman married to a physically-and emotionally-abusive man. It all started when she was placed on bedrest while pregnant in efforts to reduce the risk of another miscarriage. During this time, Vanna was forced to quit her job and rely upon disability insurance until her baby arrived. When her baby was born, her husband was enraged about having the sole financial responsibility for their household. As a result, he took his anger out on her – first verbally. Eventually, the abuse became physical. Vanna was on a path of pure hell in her marriage and began praying – day and night for God's intervention. The energy from her situation was giving her energy to transform her circumstances.

One fractal moment changed this situation. Her husband prepared to hit her baby. At that moment, Vanna saw two futures that could exist: both she and her baby were hurt, or she could protect her child. At that moment, Vanna gained enough strength to see the priceless value of protecting her child. She gained a new thought (per her words): "Throw his ass out."

Vanna harnessed the energy for protection. So, she threw him out the house. She later filed for divorce. In efforts to get divorced, Vanna experienced financial bankruptcy and multiple challenges as she resumed a course toward the best successful path.

Two futures existed: Through her choice of free will – and belief that her baby was worth protecting, Vanna chose the future that would be most beneficial. Vanna is now divorced and experiencing a thriving career in property management, where she can take care of her son. Her baby has grown into a young boy and is well-protected. Another woman is now with her ex-husband, subsequently choosing the future that Vanna rejected. He and the new woman are repeating the cycle of abuse. On the other hand, Vanna broke free! She now has met a man who believes in protecting her and her son.

GOD IS PART OF YOUR FAITH BRAIN'S INTUITION

I remember driving down the street while talking on my hands-free mobile phone. Out of nowhere, I received the gut guidance to take my foot off the gas, and stop accelerating. Not even a moment later, I saw a white SUV run a red light and speed in front of my car. The SUV was literally just three feet away. Had I not removed my foot from the gas, I would have been a dead woman. But my gut instinct allowed me to listen to an inner voice for guidance. Intuition saved my life. God is guiding us all through our gift of intuition. In short, intuition is how your brain interprets light.

How Your Brain Works to Reshape Itself (continued)

- **Step 4:** You have a connected intuition that guides your thoughts, feelings, and actions, and places you near your physical outcome.

  During the entire sequence of events, there is a light that is recognized by your brain in the form of intuition. This light converts into intuition within the brain and serves to select the best thoughts, feelings, and actions. Combined, this intuition creates an energetic path that will result in your efficiency. Your efforts are directed close to your success radius, so you are pulled into success. And in turn, you succeed in your future outcome.

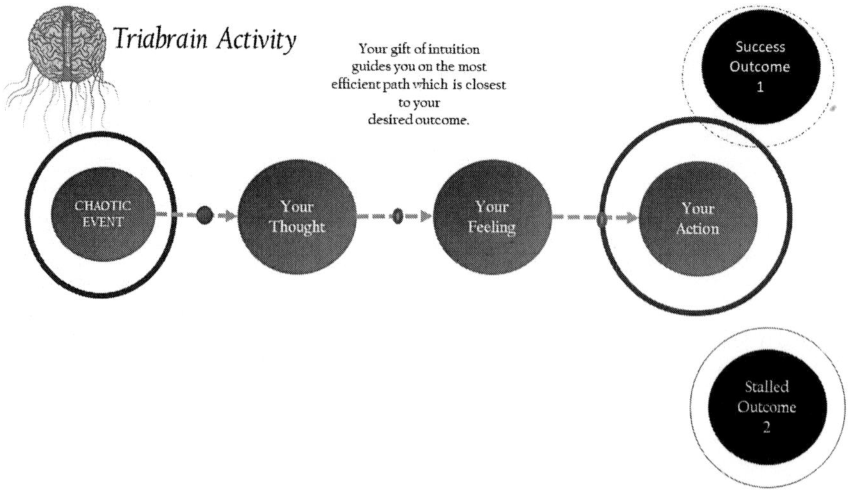

Image 5-4: Triabrain Theory of Relativity of Intuition. The center line is your intuition. It is the way your brain interprets light. It acts as a target. It guides your thoughts, feelings, and actions. The result is that your actions become close to the success convergence, so you are pulled into success.

Imagine going through a corn field maze. You would completely become trapped if you did not have a bird's eye view of your location. With a bird's eye view, you can move through the maze to find the light at the end of the tunnel. However, when you are in the maze alone, you will find yourself making incorrect turns. Most likely, you will get lost several times while moving in the maze. Just imagine if you heard the voice from a helicopter pilot directing you toward the end of the maze. That person would be able to guide you in avoiding all the dead ends and lead you out of the maze before sundown. This Guide can see things impossible for you to view. God has the bird's eye view. And he (or she) is like the man in the helicopter. Your intuition is the way that God communicates with you as you encounter the chaos of transformation in your brain (and life). It is the mental way that you understand light, and it's the most direct, efficient way for you to transform energy. You pick up intuitive signals through the faith sector of the *Triabrain*.

Dr. Doreen Virtue writes about this natural way to listen to your intuition in her book ***Divine Guidance***. (Virtue & Bunick, 1998) In it, she writes about four major ways that a person can receive and feel guidance in the form of thoughts, gut feelings, visions, and pictures, or by sound. But in order to receive this guidance, Dr. Virtue says we must be willing to have conversations with God and commit to building an ongoing relationship. This relationship is built on the desire to recognize and decipher between light and truth in all things. This relationship is also established by agreeing to recognize there are beneficial and non-beneficial paths that exist within chaos. In the next chapter, you will see one major way to build intuition through constructing a relationship with God. Also, you will see how to develop your intuition.

Charlene

Charlene did not feel like giving a presentation at the campus. She volunteered on her day off. She thought about calling in and saying that she could not make it. But, she had an overwhelming feeling that it was beneficial for her to attend. Charlene followed her gut feeling. When she held the workshop, she met a fellow employee who started a book publishing business. After talking to her workshop attendee, they connected and are now working on creating fresh, new workshops for students in her department. Charlene is also working with her new friend on writing her first book.

TRUTH #2: Your Power is Found in Choosing Positive Chaotic Relationships

When you really desire something that you have never experienced, watch who will enter your life. There will be three types of people. One type will be exceptionally knowledgeable and possess the ability to mentor you. These people are designed to point you in the direction to use your energy for accomplishing your true desire. Another type will be brought into your life to reinforce old ways of thinking further. These people are stuck in the same situation as you. They desire more as well but have not personally made the decision to take additional action in their own lives. And, the third type will mirror you, demonstrating strengths and weaknesses you possess. They will also point out things you aren't doing in your life. All three types of people are designed to help in your decision to take action toward reshaping your brain and life. They do this by forming a relationship where you begin an honest relationship with yourself. These people are helping you transform negative emotions into positive feelings so you can efficiently make the best brain shift.

How Your Brain Works to Reshape Itself (Continued)

- **Step 5:** ***(Fractal Moment)*** - An opportunity to turn emotions into powerful feelings. Energy from your thoughts provides the opportunity to dissolve toxic brain mass formed from past emotions.
- **Step 6:** Energy from past emotions surface. The new, emerging emotions attract similar energy to you. These are in the form of relationships with people who have (or are) experiencing the same emotion. You select one main emotion to be transformed into new feeling sensors in the Triabrain's nervous system. This new, emerging feeling gives the energy to take action.

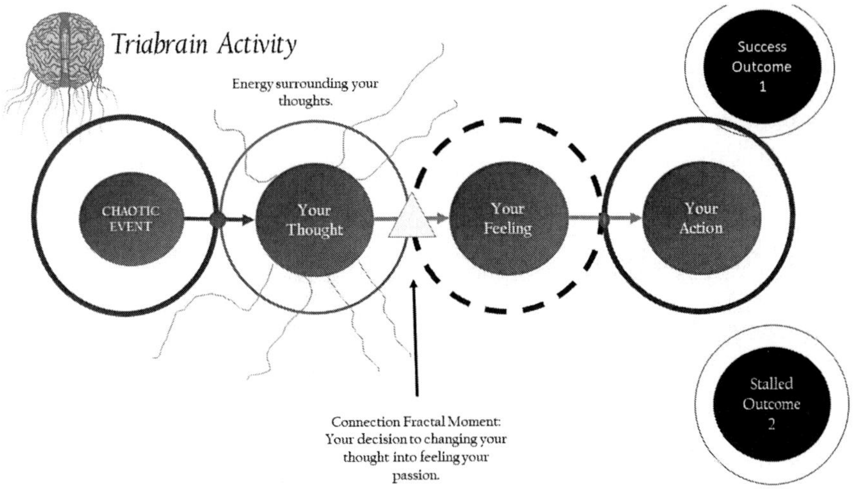

Image 5-5: Triabrain Theory of Relativity during Fractal Moment of Decision. Fractal Movement in the brain connects the energy from thought to a person's desire to pursue a passion. The choice creates three types of relationships, a constructive, potentially destructive or reflective one.

In the *Triabrain Theory of Relativity*, the main way to transform emotions into feelings is through relationships. And through your *Triabrain* waves, you will attract people to you based on what you are trying to accomplish. Your thoughts will convert chaos energy to emotion. This emotion will be a honing device for people to help or hurt you. Triabrain waves will then be sent to others to help you transform emotions into feelings that will guide in making beneficial decisions. The fractal moment is in your decision to transform toxic emotion into a healthy feeling and relationship within yourself. And you do this by ***fractal attraction***. In this fractal moment, you attract others to you in order to decipher which relationships are most beneficial. This fractal moment serves to offer your brain energy for reshaping. At this moment, your awareness to convert a toxic emotion into a feeling will turn on your prefrontal cortex, making you more capable of carrying out wise decisions. Additionally, the relationship sector of your right brain also helps develop a deeper relationship with yourself and the special orientation in how you fit in the world.

Your Energy = The Way You Feel in The World

Within the *Triabrain Theory of Relativity*, people feel energy differently based on where they are situated in the universe. Imagine yourself sitting directly next to a warm fire. Your skin will feel hot. Now suppose you are on the other side of the room from the fire. You will mainly use your other senses, like sight or smell, to determine its heat intensity. Your relationship to the fire will determine how much heat you absorb, and give off. You will never feel the same intensity as others within the fire's close proximity because your perception will be different. Because your past experiences are unique to you, sensational thoughts also convert your emotions into tailored feelings. This experience gives you a deeper relationship with your own situation.

Attraction is not just sexual. Partnerships are not strictly professional. Relationships are not just emotional. Rather, two people meeting can be brain-transformational. As the brain seeks answers to change a specific situation, it sends out brain waves. This is like Einstein's gravitational waves that he found when two black holes collided in 2016. This brain energy is designed to attract people who are willing to help you reshape your brain. However, most people are unaware of these signals and do not know what their brains exude. When other individuals approach, they may not be able to determine which people will help the situation or make the problem worse. You can clearly choose the best brain attractions for heathy brain reshaping-shifts.

The *Triabrian Theory of Relativity* explains that just like gravitational waves can pierce through all matter, you have brain waves that also penetrate through all matter. These waves also penetrate through space and time which are felt by other humans. When facing an issue that requires a resolution, your brain sends internal and external "S.O.S." signals for help. People receive these signals through body language and through an unconscious type of "knowing." It is your desire part of the brain that is firing. As a result, people will approach you, but not all are helpers. Some are sent to test the brain's reshaping capability. And you will be tested in deciphering the best type of people to create a connection. You will be tested within deciding how close emotionally and physically you are to be with them. The brain reshapes through making the decision on who to have regularly in your life. Healing relationships connect you faster to the solution that you desire. They also help you have a deeper relationship with yourself.

Your Soul Family, are those tuned into your frequency. You sense a strong connection beyond blood or race; you're connected by energy and vibration. Through quantum communication, they intuitively answer your silent call and show up bringing unconditional love and support at the perfect times. You share unspoken levels of understanding...they just get you and what you are about. For those people, be thankful...they are your reminders from the universe that on the deepest level of our existence, "We are one."

– Kianu Starr

Blake

Blake was in school to become a computer scientist, but he failed his Calculus class. On the border of giving up, he contemplated leaving his field of study for something easier. But he knew that he owed it to himself to see what he could do with his brain. Following a promise to himself, Blake decided to go back to school where he retook the Calculus class. On the first day, he met Sue. He immediately takes a liking to Sue. She was extremely fast at mathematics, and they often studied together. He admired her ability to solve problems and master Calculus. Sue showed Blake how to view situations in ways that would point to solutions instead of problems. Blake realized that Sue was a woman he wanted in his life for the "long haul." He proposed. Sue said, "yes." Sue and Blake have been married for 35 years and gave birth to a son. Blake has successfully retired from a career in cyber security for the U.S. Government. Their son was a student in my Calculus class.

The second type of people you will attract are those with mirror troubles but have not fully made their decision to transform. Nevertheless, these individuals are in your life to help you make a decision. For any area where you are wavering, these people are meant to help you make a choice, so you can move forward.

Often these people are puzzled when you no longer make similar choices. Some will become annoyed if you share your progress. They secretly admire you, yet they feel threatened as they see you taking action to change your circumstances. They wish they had the same courage. Many reactions to you may be supportive at one moment, then vindictive the next. They are supportive when you have their same struggles. But, they become unsupportive when you make different decisions. They are not working on self-improvement or inner growth at the same rate. Surprisingly enough, these individuals, in turn, are your greatest helpers. They point you in the direction, NOT TO TAKE! More importantly, these people are some of the best helpers in your fractal moments. They help you choose the opposite path.

Krystal

Krystal had an older sister, Katelin, who was great in university studies. Krystal would often go to her sister for tutoring. During a series of events, Katelin experiences a traumatic incident and begins turning to men for reassurance. In doing so, Katelin misses her college classes and eventually drops out of school. Krystal sees her sister and begs that she returns. But Katelin is headstrong.

Krystal continues to earn advanced degrees. But at family reunions, Katelin will go out of her way to be rude to Krystal. Unfortunately, Krystal's success reminds Katelin of her failure to be courageous and continue her university studies. Meanwhile, Krystal views Katelin as a role model. In doing so, Krystal simply does the complete opposite: she's guided toward completing her higher education.

And the third type of people that you will attract is a mirror image of yourself. You will encounter them at any time and place. You will meet people who experience the same emotion as you, but their issue pertains to different circumstances. On assignment, these people enter your life for a short period of time. They have the exact same emotion that you need to transform within you. These people are meant to show you the true aspects about yourself and how your decisions can change your brainpower.

Susan

Susan was a university professor experiencing marital problems. Each day, she dreaded returning home to her alcoholic husband. Every time Susan went home, she felt like she was walking on egg shells. Susan knew her marriage was falling apart. However she feared to leave and to establish her own life. She was overwhelmed at the thought of finding an apartment and separating herself from the man who she had known for 15 years. But at the same time, she could not complete any of her teaching assignments while at home. Susan knew something had to change.

One day at school, she noticed a student named Jack who had been missing from the class lectures. Jack returned after being absent for nearly two weeks straight. Susan was accustomed to dropping students from the class in such cases. However, intuition told her to pull aside Jack and find out if he was okay. When Susan spoke to Jack outside class, she discovered he lived at home with an alcoholic father, who made his life a living hell. Jack could not study at home nor complete any of his class assignments. He found himself crying and ashamed to admit that he could not do his homework. So, Jack thought it was easier to skip class. Immediately, Susan saw a reflection of herself.

Susan suggested Jack attend on-campus counseling for his trauma. Jack agreed. He went and later had the courage to move out of his drunken father's home. Jack's story also helped Susan see that she too, needed to attend counseling. Susan gained enough courage to divorce her husband and is now feeling peace living on her own.

All groups are designed to show you positive and negative aspects of yourself, so you can transform toxic emotions into healthy feelings.

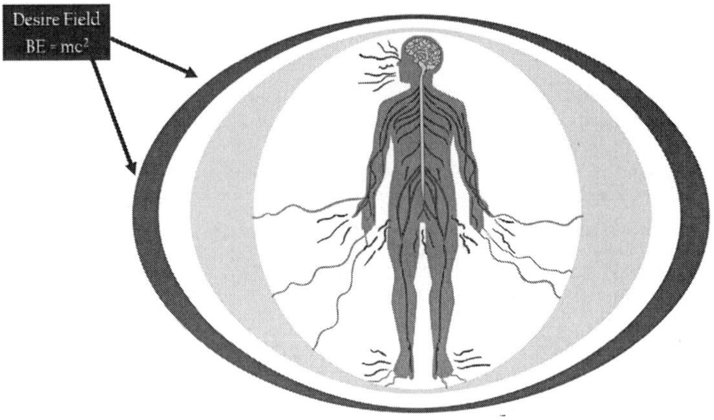

Image 5-6: Per the Triabrain Theory of Relativity, The Triabrain Field has a spiritual base field, then the desired layer which sends your thoughts and feelings to others through your Triabrain waves. People become attracted to you due to your desire energy in your field.

Backstory of Fractal Attraction

Olympia LePoint's Theory of Brain Wave Fractal Attraction came one day while attending an evening event. She was approached several times in one evening. However, this evening was peculiar. She noticed that everyone who approached her desired to start their own businesses. And just three years earlier, she had accomplished the same goal.

Then, a few months later a similar event occurred at a different location. She was looking for a personal trainer. Everyone she met at a restaurant had recently found trainers. Ironically, just a few weeks prior, she made a decision to pursue physical training.

When this series of events repeated multiple times with other situations, Olympia discovered that these events were not random. Rather, there was a hidden brain wave working. People's brains were signaling for help to solve their issues. And they were attracting people who had the information they needed.

TRUTH #3: Your Physical Resources Help You Transform Your Chaotic Environments

Science, time and physical space rebuild brain mass which leads to the innovation outside of you. By clearing out physical situations and allowing scientific principles to play out, you can literally rebuild the brain's mass. The connections formed in building this mass is used to connect your brain to your body, and your entire being to the universe. In forming these connections, you transform your space, time, and personal environments. This breakthrough leads to innovative science, technology, engineering, or mathematical (STEM) discoveries. This concept is explained by *Triabrain Theory of Relativity*.

How Your Brain Works to Reshape Itself (Continued)

- **Step 7:** ***(Fractal Moment)*** - You make the decision to take action from a feeling.
- **Step 8:** Your desire moves you to take several physical steps in using your internal and external resources to change a physical situation.
- **Step 9:** ***(Fractal Moment)*** - The energy from your action draws you closer to a success radius, where you are "pulled" into success. Here, you gain the energy to continue growth and reshape your brain. Physical movement happens in your brain. You change the exterior world simultaneously through your action.

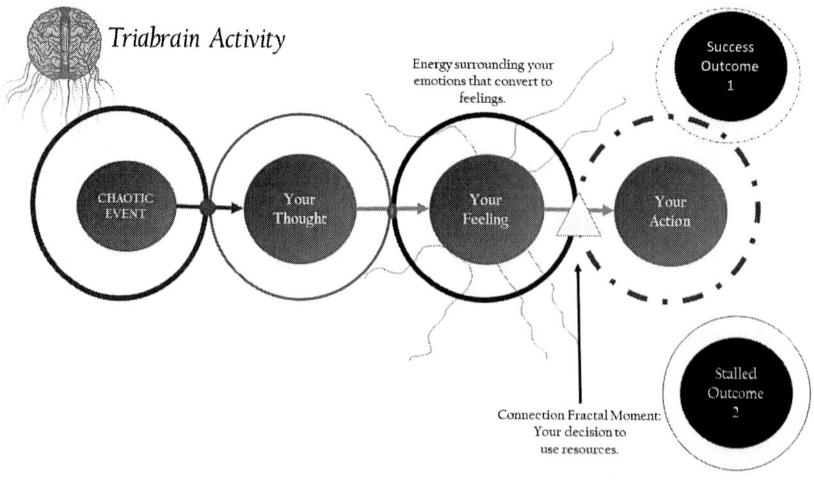

Image 5-7: Triabrain Theory of Relativity fractal moment of Science. A Fractal Moment in the brain connects energy from a feeling to an end result. The decision to take action creates a close proximity to a future outcome which is either success or failure.

You Conduct Energy to Change Physical Situations

First, the energy within your body alone can shift your brain and outside environment through conductivity. Per the definition in science, conductivity is the degree to which a specified material conducts electricity. It is calculated as the ratio of the current density in the material to the electric field that causes the flow of current. It is the reciprocal of the resistivity. Conductivity is the rate at which heat passes through a specified material.

Your *Triabrain* has an energy field that flows energy into and out of you. And, it is charged by hand, eye, foot and other bodily movements. This energy helps you heal yourself. In life, everything is based on energy. Einstein stated this fact. To illustrate, do a little test.

1. Rub your hand together for 1 minute straight. Now separate your hands. But keep the palms of your hands 3-4 inches apart.
2. Feel the pulsating energy inside of your hands? This is your *Triabrain's* energy. It comes from you.
3. The energy will tingle. It will feel warm. In some cases, you may even see this energy swirling around like clear steam between your hands.
4. You do not imagine things. This is your *Triabrain* energy.

Your Mass = The Way You Create Physical Things in This World

Within the *Triabrain Theory of Relativity*, people build things differently based on a number of resources (accessible energy and light). Your space in the universe is unique to your being. And, you have the energy in your being to change outcomes by simply being present. When your personal brain space is altered and reorganized, you gain a higher capacity to build new mass. When toxic emotions are dissolved in the brain, there is new room for new brain mass to be created within the available space. Imagine filling up a new balloon with water and stretching it out until the balloon nearly pops.

Now, if you were to remove the water, the balloon capacity would be greater since the balloon would be stretched. The balloon would have a higher capacity to hold more matter than when it was fresh and new. Your brain is identical. The more toxic emotions you experience in life, the greater capacity that you have for innovation. As you remove dark toxic mass from your brain, the more space, your brain has to reshape. In reshaping, it will be able to hold highly-technical and even groundbreaking ways to build new things in the universe. Plus, the new neurons formed in your cranial capacity will recreate identical pathways to solutions outside of yourself. Consider how the oyster's sand particle path mimics the path to Mars (as described in Chapter 3). Your new brain pathways result in your outer environmental change.

Per the *Triabrain Theory of Relativity*, *Triabrain* energy is designed to connect parts of your body mass through physical movement. Your body's natural movements conduct energy. Minerals and water in your body help this electrical energy to flow inside and out of you. This energy connection requires the right bodily pressures and temperature environment to reconnect your brain to your body fully. In turn, your entire being is connected to the outside world. This energy is something you are naturally born with as a baby. But through trauma, we unconsciously give this power away. Remember the energy felt by rubbing your hands together? This energy source is renewable and re-programmable with your thoughts 24 hours-a-day, 7 days-a-week. With this *Triabrain* energy, you can change physical situations.

For just one example, your movement generates friction. The act of rubbing hands together (or other parts of your body together) connects both sides of your brain. When you rub your hands together: energy exits and re-enters your body through your hands. Even when you innocently rub against another person, energy is exchanged. Almost every single cell in your body has some percentage of water molecules (or liquid) energy that conducts throughout your entire body. However, rubbing hands is not the only way to create energy. Walking conducts energy. Sex conducts extreme, intensified beneficial or destructive energy. Daily, any sweat gland that brushes against air conducts energy. Air that you inhale helps you conduct energy. This energy builds what is known as the *Triabrain* field. Water molecules inside of you transfer energy electrically. This is your *Triabrain* power that connects you to the outside world through energy transfer. This brain energy is sent throughout the entire body to reconnect itself and you to the outside world through your physical movement. Consider Michael Phelps, Serena Williams, and Nadia Comaneci: they have mastered unleashing their *Triabrain* power in sports.

Brian

Brian was adopted as an infant. He never knew his biological parents, nor did he know his DNA. He was a person with a dark olive complexion and was adopted by a Jewish couple. He always desired to feel connected, but never felt connected to his caring, adopted parents. So, to feel his connection to the world, Brian would run outside at night, where he enjoyed feeling the air against his skin. Each time he ran, his speed increased. New insight came to Brian with each breath. With each movement, he sensed a connection to Mother Nature, and he felt like a loved child of the Earth.

While running regularly, Brian became a world-record distance runner. He later coached students who became Olympic Gold medal winners in Cross Country.

Chaos Theory mathematics explains how energy travels not only in the sky but also through your brain and the human body. This energy is represented by sine and cosine functions in Mathematics. Energy flows through the human body, in circular, swirling motions, up-and-down, left-and-right. This swirling is similar to the NASA jet fuel image seen in Chapter 3. As energy travels from your brain, it connects to outside sources. Consider how smoke swirls from burning objects. Your brain sends out energy and receives energy in circular swirling motions as well. And this circular, swirling motion comprises your entire *Triabrain* field that changes physical situations. Indigenous medicine doctors refer to this as your "aura." Chinese medicine will call this your "Chi."

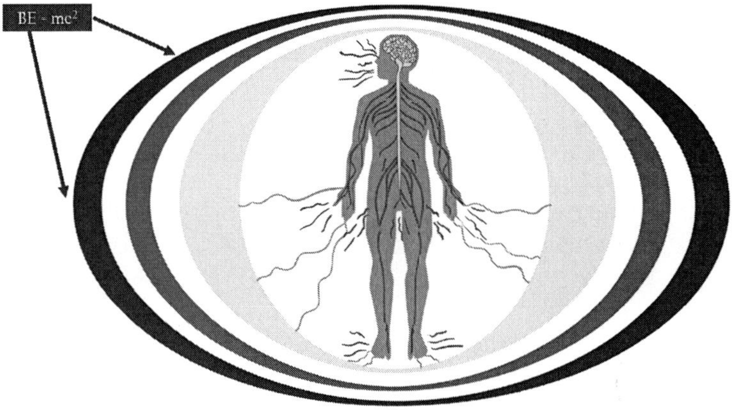

Image 5-8: The Triabrain Field conducts energy through your movement and water molecules in your system. It can be partially recharged with thoughts, desires, and friction between hands, feet, skin rubbing and bodily movement. Your presence alone changes outcomes.

Chaos Connects Your Skull and Body to Give You More Internal Energy

Secondly, your body alignments are a way to convert chaos energy into the beneficial energy required for action. Through realigning your skull joints to body and movement, you gain more internal energy to change physical situations. Chaos Theory explains these connections in your head to your body.

In the skull where the brain is housed, there are joints mirroring every part of the bodily structure. In 2013, kinesiologist Joel Crandall discovered this mirror imaging in the body through a therapy coined the *VOILA Method*. Joel Crandall appeared on my radio show, *Answers Unleashed,* on Episode 3, where he spoke about the *VOILA Method.* VOILA – Vector of Indication, Los Angeles. As the body moves, the skull joints are supposed to move in conjunction with bodily muscles like Olympic synchronized swimmers. But when this conjunction is off, or not moving in a mathematical relationship, it affects the temperature and pressure system of the entire body. This off-nominal state throws other parts of the body in over-compensation mode.

On the show, Joel Crandall explained there are parts of our body that are supposed to work in coordination with others like in a beautiful dance. There are parts of our body that mimic other parts of the system. These are just a few examples:

- Your hip bones and facial bones are identical, per Chaos Theory math. One bone type is just a smaller version of the other. If your hips are locked, that means your cranial bones are not moving when breathing. If your hips are locked, that means your cheek bones (which are the miniature hip bone structures) are not moving when breathing
- The bridge of your nose, per Chaos Theory, is like the esophagus
- As per movement: When you inhale, your skull lobes have specific opening functions, which synchronize the air valve movement within your diaphragm

After I experienced the extensive process of realigning my cranial joints with Joel Crandall's *VOILA Method*, I regained full flexibility of motion. Plus, the entire mathematical symmetry in my face changed, as viewed in the attached image. My right cheek is rotated back toward my ear; my nose is slimmer; my jaw and smile are balanced; my forehead is lifted, my eyebrows have more of an arch; the entire face is narrower; eyes are whiter, and neck muscles are more pronounced.

Image 5-9: Per the Triabrain Theory of Relativity, healing methods such as the VOILA Method are used to create organized connections in the brain and skull which translates itself into higher physical healing capacity.

My right cheek rotated back helped my lower hips move in dancing. My nose became aligned at the very top, and this made it slimmer, straighter, and stopped digestive discomfort and allergies. My balanced jaw helped my shoulders have a full range of motion while driving and twisting. My lifted forehead changed the air pressure system in my body, allowing me to raise out of a seated position and climb stairs without pain. My neck muscles became more pronounced, which permitted my abdominal core muscles to fire, allowing me to lift heavier objects and sit up straighter. These are just the physical changes. But there was another deep, interior organ-nerve-tissue-energy change that happened inside of my body. As a result, the entire way I processed and perceived the world shifted which allowed creativity and more innovative energy to flow through me.

New Triabrain Pathways = New Life Pathways

As your brain changes its shape into new pathways, you create new pathways in your life. This concept is frequently manifested within STEM Innovation. Chaotic environments must be transformed. When you arrange the interior of your brain, your exterior situations change to reflect the change inside of your head. This new reflection propels you faster to your desired result.

*I was fascinated by Joel who was a guest on my talk show, **Answers Unleashed**. Joel was 8 years-old when he fell down a hill and received* *a concussion. After that, he had long-term issues with his eye sight, and his middle school reading began to suffer. He found a way to compensate by enjoying science that did not require the same type of long reading. He was always active in sports, and he played collegiate football. However, while attending college, Joel suffered another concussion during football practice. This injury physically complicated Joel's academic progress.*

Joel majored in Kinesiology and became a kinesiologist for decades after graduating college. He continued with his career, until, he found himself experiencing pain while treating his clients. In working to heal his own brain from past physical trauma, Joel found himself becoming a scientific innovator using his education and intuition. To add, Joel gained the ability to read faster, while his vision shifted to have prolonged focus. He soon mastered his new method of self-treatment and regained the focus to write. Joel later created the VOILA METHOD and is writing his first book. He now travels extensively, sharing methods to remove pain permanently. Joel travels around the world and teaches massage therapist, ophthalmologists, neurologists, moms and anyone who wants to help themselves recover from pain. The new room in his brain converted to a physical book. And the new pathways in his brain translated into his world travels.

Logic and science also will naturally change your brain's shape. As I wrote in my first book, ***Mathaphobia***, when a person learns math and science, a person must turn off the fear response in the brain. In doing so, the frontal brain lobes re-fire and reshape the prefrontal cortex. When Science, Technology, Engineering or Mathematics (STEM) is studied and mastered, brain toxins are naturally dissolved in the brain. Fear no longer fires from the brain's amygdala. As the brain finds solutions to problems, the solutions are applied from one area to a completely new area of life.

Joy

Joy Mangano (Mangano, 2017) is an American inventor and entrepreneur known for inventions such as the self-wringing Miracle Mop. The 2015 film ***Joy*** *was loosely based on her life. Joy became an inventor when red wine glasses were dropped, and she severely cut her hands wringing out the mop when cleaning. One day, she had a dream about a new product for a "self-ringing mop," but she did not know any math or science to create engineering products. As she learned the science of product construction, she gained the ability to use engineering molds for additional household inventions. Today, Joy is the president of Ingenious Designs,*

LLC, and appears regularly on HSN, the US television shopping channel. Joy Mangano is also the author of "INVENTING JOY," and has made multi-billions from her decision to study science on her own.

As you can see, there are people who have mastered unleashing the power of their *Triabrain*. Some use faith and see the world with new eyes. Many rely on their intuition. Some learn to transform chaotic emotions. Other individuals master internal energy and create external change. Each has used their brain's power in awe-inspiring ways. They have transformed their lives. In the next Chapters, you will learn how to master flowing God's power through your *Triabrain*. You will learn how to reconnect your faith brain. You will learn what originally disconnected you from your intuition. You will begin to feel pleasant feelings again and reconnect your right brain. Lastly, you will learn how to reconnect your left brain with its powerful, solution-finding logic using physical exercises. The following chapters will help you unleash the change that you wish to see in your life. Hold on… You are about to be blown way because the force will come through you!

Unleashing Your Faith Brain Power

Chapter 6

Unleashing Your Faith Brain Power

The Power in Embodying Faith

Five hours earlier, the brain surgeon looked at me in my eyes and delivered a powerful divine message saying, "Your mother will survive."

The waiting room's cold walls and sterile air did not predict the miracle we were about to witness. As we were waiting for our mother to have brain surgery, friends from my church came to the hospital to offer support. My pastor, Jeff Fischer, and his wife Lisa were there, along with my friends Peter, Dey, Rathy, Nathaniel, and Joji. We all were part of the same small church group, who prayed for each other and the people in our lives.

I was so thankful to have their support. It felt good knowing my church family was by my side. Although I'm usually the rock for my family, this time, I needed to cling to a rock. My friends were there to help me stay afloat during this chaotic storm. We sat there for 11 hours. All of us were in sorrow. Yet, Lisa whose gift is faith constantly reminded us of God's promises.

To pass the time, we talked about church and social events. We talked about the weather. We talked about anything and everything other than the terrible situation that my sisters and I were facing. During the time, Nathaniel and Rathy were platonic friends. However, I could always sense the chemistry between the two. And during all the chaos, I forgot to have filters in my words. I accidentally said, "When are the two of you getting married?"

The truth seemed to fly out of my mouth. And I caught what I said as they both looked puzzled. Then, I quickly backtracked by saying, "When do you both think is the ideal time to marry other people?" They both shrugged with an "I don't know motion," and went back to talking. Most importantly, I remember Lisa's words.

Lisa reminded us, "God is a good God." Meaning, God was always going to take care and provide for the people who sincerely honored Him. At one point, Pastor Jeff had everyone pray together. Lisa prayed out loud, "Lord, make the bleeding in Pamela's brain stop. Let God guide the Surgeon's hands so Pamela can survive the surgery. And, let there be a full recovery."

This faith brought peace that surpassed my understanding.

Five hours after constantly repositioning ourselves on the cold plastic waiting room chairs, one of the neurosurgeons come out of the room. He tells us, "Your mother has suffered a severe blow to the head. It is an injury-induced stroke. And we were able to stop the bleeding. Right now, she is in a medically-induced coma. We are going to keep her in the ICU and monitor her throughout the night. We are hoping the brain swelling goes down. We do not know if she will survive the night. But we are hoping she does."

My heart feels a glimmer of hope.

The doctor continues to say, "There is another thing. During the surgery, the other surgeons and I saw your mother has two broken vertebrae. And, if she survives the night, she may not be able to walk."

My heart sinks.

I lost feeling in my feet. I no longer feel my knees. I find myself falling backward without feeling any of my lower body. Peter catches me as I stand directly in front of him and his wife. I wondered how on Earth I could handle this situation.

The doctor continued, "We do not know the extent of the injuries yet. We will have a better idea tomorrow when we take x-rays. But the good news is that she made it through the surgery. I suggest you go home and get some rest and come back tomorrow morning."

At that point, I felt so lost.

Then Lisa said something I will always remember, "Olympia, God answered our prayers. Pamela made it through the surgery. The doctors stopped the bleeding. God will answer every one of our prayers."

I looked up. And there was something in me that finally woke to up how God is so good, merciful, loving and always looking out for the best interest of every person on this Earth. For the first time, I consciously experienced how God loved me, and God loved my mother. God loved us so much that He would allow my mother to survive the surgery. Despite the risk of the final outcome, I decided to place my faith in God's plan. This time, I knew without a shadow of a doubt, God would answer EVERY one of our prayers. Now and in the future.

Pastor Jeff suggested we gather in a circle to pray. During praying, I remember this energy of faith coming over me, where I prayed for my mother and family as I had never prayed before. The look on Pastor Jeff's face was of amazement. He saw strength come through me that I never thought I had owned. Our combined prayers were lifted up to God for the details of the situation to work out in a way that would forever change the course everyone's lives.

That night Auriel and I went home and returned to the hospital the next day. Our mother made it through the night. When I asked for x-rays to be taken of my mother's vertebrae, the doctors came back a few hours later with the results. One surgeon said, "We have taken several x-rays. There is absolutely no sign of any broken vertebrae. We do not know what happened from last night to this morning. But, we do know that her back is fine."

A miracle happened overnight.

That moment, I realized God's UNFAILING power.

The following months were extremely challenging. I remember seeing Mom's faith as she relearned how to walk, talk, and eat again. There were nights when cracked teeth shot pain throughout her system. Emergency Room visits became a frequent necessity. There were times where I saw how much effort my mother placed into her traumatic brain therapy. Every time I watched Mom overcome her odds, I gained strength in my life by watching her embody faith. She made her mind up to heal, despite the challenges she would face fully.

From that experience, faith exploded into a power that could not be contained. My friends and I witnessed its impact. Pastor Jeff and Lisa's church grew. Peter became a pastor with his wife Dey in a city across the country. Rathy and Nathaniel are now happily married with beautiful children. And my mother is alive today. Faith is contagious.

Power comes when you make a decision.

FAITH TRIABRAIN BLUEPRINT FOR RECONNECTION (FTBR)

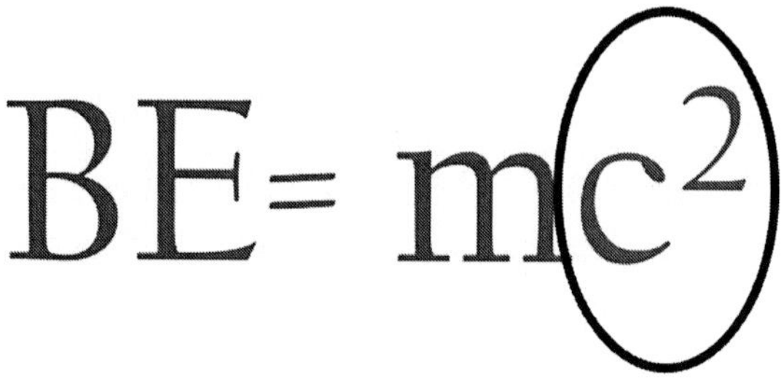

Image 6-1: The Triabrain Theory of Relativity focuses on the speed of your brain light within neuron connections and brain synapses.

There is a healthy function of your faith brain. The faith brain's function is to connect the energy of an exterior situation through your faith-based thoughts into an outcome. At the same time, faith-thoughts connect to emotions that are transformed into feelings. These feelings will promote interior and exterior experiences of your body.

Faith-based thought converts the energy from the situation into the energy you need to transform your life. When you are aware of your thoughts, neuroscience researchers call it ***mindfulness*** or mental awareness. Your faith brain sector has a non-measurable direct impact upon everyone and everything around you through your faith brain field. Other brains, bodies, matter and the physical world are also impacted by your thoughts. Your faith brain sector also oversees your intuitive observations and visionary capabilities. Plus, your will and intention connect you to a chaotic experience that your faith-thoughts convert.

You influence the state of the physical world in an extended way through your faith brain. It is not confined to a specific location in space, nor a specific period of time. Your faith brain can simultaneously view the past, present, and future in one continual instantaneous thought. This part of your *Triabrain* influences scientific observations and controlled experiments that you conduct. Overall, this part of your *Triabrain* connects all humans to the "bigger picture," where no logical boundaries exist. Your faith sector is what allows prayers to work, through a magnetic *Triabrain* energy field as described in the next chapter. Your *Triabrain* proves to you the validity of a future before any evidence of it exists.

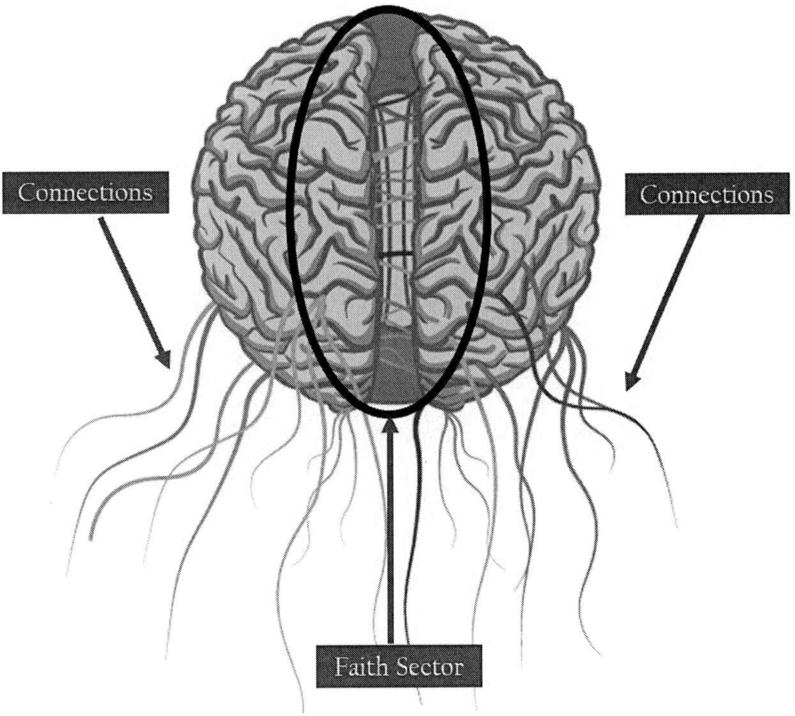

Image 6-2: The Connections of The Faith Brain

In Chapter 4 you took the self-test to help you determine how your faith brain was disconnected. The following parts give a summary of how each brainbrink can be reversed. If your primary score was *"Out of Body, Out of Faith,"* then you would want to pay close attention to the first *Triabrain* reconnection principle in this section: "*Re-embody yourself, life and actions by embodying faith.*" If your primary score in Chapter 4 was, *"Fearing the Future, Fearing the Past,"* you would benefit from reading the second reconnection principle, "See the beauty and opportunity that exists in *Every* situation." If your top score was, "Ignoring God (or a Higher Power), Promoting You," then be prepared to see things in a new light using your intuition within the third reconnection principle, "Accept God's guidance by committing to use your natural *Triabrain* Power's intuition." The chart below lays out your plan of action. But first, it is important to understand why your *Triabrain* disconnected in the first place.

Brainbrink Disconnection Toxic Emotions	Triabrain Reconnection Principle (Faith Triabrain Blueprint)	Score Index (Results from the Self-Test in Chapter 4)
1. Out of Body, Out of Faith	1. Re-embody yourself, life, and actions by embodying faith.	• Primary focus if your score is 20 and up. • Secondary priority if your score is 15 -19. • Third priority if your score is 0-14.
2. Fearing the Future, Fearing the Past	2. See the Beauty and Opportunity that exists in *Every* situation.	• Primary focus if your score is 20 and up. • Secondary priority if your score is 15 -19. • Third priority if your score is 0-14.
3. Ignoring God (or a Higher Power), Promoting You	3. Accept God's guidance by committing to use your natural *Triabrain* Power's intuition.	• Primary focus if your score is 20 and up. • Secondary priority if your score is 15 -19. • Third priority if your score is 0-14.

Why on Earth does the faith Triabrain disconnect?

To reconnect the faith brain, you must know how it was initially disconnected. According to the *Triabrain Theory of Relativity*, a person forms their view of reality from the ages of 4 through 9. A child can develop in an environment where God is never mentioned, or the child grew in an environment where God is the center. It's irrelevant if a child comes from a home of Christians, Muslims, atheists, Buddhists or any other spiritual environment. The spiritual impact is the same.

Between the ages of 4-9, a child makes a conscious decision to accept or reject that there is a higher order to this world. This child also decides if a universal power exists. More importantly, the child acknowledges whether this Higher Power cares for him. However, during this same period, everyone on Earth will encounter a situation which questions his faith. It can be neglect, divorce, molestation, life-changing accident, genetic impairment, abandonment, a parent's addiction, or a physical injury, where God "appears missing." Consequently, the child loses inner peace. Because of this experience, his internal being feels torn apart. As a result, the child will literally and physically see the world differently. The light (or absence of accurate senses) alters the way he sees the world. This is the point when darkness enters his vision. Darkness prevents "seeing the full picture." For example, you may park your car in a parking lot and return to a lot covered in fog. Your car is still in the same location, but your vision is impaired. Darkness is your brain's fog after experiencing one of the faith-changing situations above.

Ways to Reconnect the Faith Brain

You can take your brain power back once you understand that you are not completely in control of anything except making decisions in your life. You are never supposed to know how EVERYTHING will work together. You will never know why "good things" happen, and why "bad" things exist. You will never have all the answers in life. Your brain connections cannot handle the full power within the universe. If you try to know why God allows things to happen and why he doesn't, you further traumatize your present living experience.

God lives within you and is embedded within every atom and molecule in your body. Transformation power is activated by your faith. Although you are not 100% fully knowledgeable like God, you can have ownership over your power in life through your *Triabrain*. The great news is that that you can seek God's guidance within you. In doing so, God-conscious thoughts move in you, work through you to transform you. From this new insight, you see the big picture and find your car in the foggy parking lot!

Your role is to trust that everything in your life happens for a reason, but be practical at the same time. If you accept that there is a much greater force governing your life, you make up your mind to own your brain power. In doing so, you join an army of people who will change the landscape of this Earth. You're pulled in to success. To start the process, you can embrace these three steps:

1. Forgive yourself for turning away (or being angry at God or a Higher Power) at a pivotal time in your life.
2. Decide to build a relationship with a Higher Power today. Go back in time at that every moment, as well as the present moment by asking your Higher Power how to see a certain situation clearly.
3. Acknowledge in your adulthood that your intuitive gifts can be developed and used to help you.

When you take practical steps to understand that a Higher Power is the force behind reshaping your mind, your brain transformation equation will include your Higher Power existing both inside and outside of you. When you are aligned with this Almighty efficient brain light, it doesn't matter if you are male or female, young or elderly, rich or poor, prepared or dysfunctional, you can give birth to great ideas at any age. You become an innovator.

∞ Forgiving Exercise ∞

Allocate at least one hour for this exercise.

1. Find several sheets of paper. Sit in a quiet space, with both feet firmly planted.
2. Think back to a time (or series of times) where you lost faith in God's protection and care over your life.
3. Write a letter to God sharing how you honestly still feel about what you experienced. Release all of your thoughts and emotions. No human will see this paper except you. Let everything out onto this sheet of paper. (This process may take several sheets of paper.)
4. Now, breathe deeply 10 times, preferably through your nose.
5. Review the letter. Look at the letter. Feel the letter with all its energy. Give everything that you just wrote to God by imagining a white light that's completely burning through the letter and all of its pages.
6. Now, on new sheets of paper, write a letter to your past self. Tell your past self all the beneficial skills and outcomes you wish you knew when the event occurred. Share important life lessons that you wish you could tell your former self.
7. Forgive your former self for taking actions when you did not listen to your interior guidance. Forgive yourself for turning away from a Higher Power and taking alternate paths when you felt a need to "take measures into your own hands."
8. Now, make a commitment between you and your former self to start working together from this day on to receive unconditional love and truth in your life. Decide to be open to the ways you'll be shown how much you are loved. Ask the Creator for the strength to see your opportunities in situations. Ask the Creator to provide you with the strength to follow wisdom from the inner most core of yourself (past-future-and-current self).
9. Keep these sheets of paper for another powerful exercise in the last chapter of this book.

RECONNECTION #1:
Re-embody yourself, life, and actions by embodying faith.

In order to change your life, you must first decide to feel the Higher Power inside of you. Many religions often suggest the Almighty is outside of you, yet controlling everything that happens. This concept is simply not true. A Higher Power resides inside of you, just as much as science shows that this force exists outside of you. Success is a Godly attribute. Love is a Godly attribute. You are a Godly attribute. If you will accept "It," the Creator is embodied within you.

You and the Creator are designed to partner together to change all chaotic situations here on Earth and in the Universe. God helps you reshape your memories associated with those moments in order to give you peace. When you see the truth in a situation, the memory transforms from terror to fact. There is only one way for this healing to happen. It is for you to allow the Power to come to you through your thoughts. Embodying the Power means that you are willing to align your thoughts, feelings, and actions with a powerful life force that can move through you to change lives.

Lifting Your Life Up in Prayer

Before you attempt to bring anything new into your life, it is important that you make an offering. Now we ***are not*** talking about slaughtered animals or blood sacrifices! No! An offering simply means that you offer your life to become part of a major plan that will positively impact you and others. You do this through prayer to the Creator. This action is how you reconnect with the Power and activate this force within your being. The goal in praying is to establish a healthy relationship with the Creator as an adult.

In short, prayer is a direct communication with God. The process governs how things will play out and be witnessed here on Earth. Prayer may be done privately and individually. Or, it may be done together in a group. Prayer is a type of thought that immediately connects a chaotic situation to you in a beneficial way. So, you can co-define your path with God in advance of your success.

Specifically, prayer connects your free will to your conscious and hidden thoughts to be aligned on a pathway to success in chaos. Remember, there are two paths in chaos: success or stalled state. God's response to you is given through your intuition because God exists within you as well as outside of you. Some begin and end their day with prayer. Others pray for guidance only as situations arise. Prayers can even be answered in dream form as you will see in the next chapter.

Prayers may be recited from memory, read from a book of prayers, or even spontaneously composed as the words come to mind. There is no specific way to pray. As there are countless languages on Earth, there are numerous ways to communicate with the Almighty. Prayers may be said aloud, chanted, or sung. Prayers may even accompany musical sounds. Most often, prayers happen silently and mentally.

Some see prayers answered immediately. Others witness changes a few days later. Many see answers years later. Nevertheless, all prayers are answered, although some may believe their prayers haven't been answered. This is a false perception. Every prayer is answered, but answers may not be in the form that you would expect. More importantly, the response may not be what you desire, but it is in your best interest. There can be many different answers to prayer, just as there are many ways to pray. Prayer is like talking to a friend daily to update them on your life. With any friend, you would want to hear what they think or how they would react in certain situations. And, what they would do if they were in your shoes.

∞ Offering Prayer Exercise ∞

God, thank You, for being in my life, and showing me that You are here for me. I come to You and give You my life. Align me with what You see as the best path for my life. Give me guidance as situations arise. Allow me to understand the unique ways in which You communicate with me directly.

Give me strength and wisdom to follow Your guidance. And give me the strength to make the internal changes to harness the power that You will unleash. I promise that I will, to the best of my ability, use these gifts wisely.

The great news is that science now is proving how powerful prayer is in reshaping your brain. In the book, *The Metaphysical Mind: Probing the Biology of Philosophical Thought,* by Dr. Andrew Newberg, findings are revealed on what happens when people pray (Newberg A. B., 2013). Newberg is a neuroscientist and pioneer in the field of neurotheology, which is the neurological study of religious and spiritual experiences. In the 1990s, Newberg began his work in this field by scanning what happens in people's brains when they meditate. Interestingly, meditation is a spiritual practice that is relatively easy to monitor (Newberg A. B., 2014).

Newberg viewed nearly 150 brain scans, including those of Buddhists, nuns, atheists, Pentecostals speaking in tongues, and Brazilian mediums channeling spiritual messages through handwriting. Newberg says, "Practices that involve concentrating on something over and over again, either through prayer or a mantra-based meditation, tend to activate the frontal lobes, the areas chiefly responsible for directing attention, modulating behavior, and expressing language."

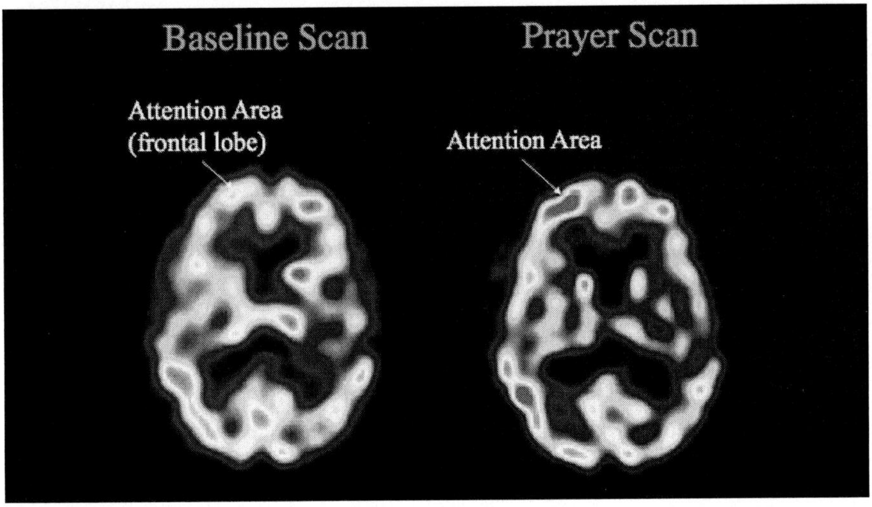

Image 6-3: Image from two brain scans depicts how prayer activates the frontal brain lobes that are responsible for executive thinking. Photo courtesy of Dr. Andrew Newberg/The Atlantic

One major way to embody faith is through prayer. Prayer is regular communication with the Creator and a divine kingdom that promotes growth for you and all people and things in your world. It triggers your frontal lobes to fire regularly. As you recall in Chapter 4, this part of the brain is responsible for the creation and problem-solving. Prayer is honest communication with a divine Creator which in turn triggers innovative thinking in you!

Specifically, prayer to embody the Creator is unlike any other prayer. It is a prayer asking for the *Triabrain* power to be unleashed from within. Some refer to this force as the Holy Spirit. Regardless of how you view God or the universe, if you allow God to embody every bit of your brain DNA, you will have the ability to unleash your inner power. But, you must be specific when you pray. The following prayer is designed to internally pull you along the successful path of growth in the chaotic mapping.

∞ Reclaiming Yourself Prayer ∞

God, I am asking You to embody me. Please purify me, God. Mold me, fill me with You and use me. Transform me from the inside out. God, give me the strength to handle this powerful transformation. Help me always to choose Your ways and make me become aware of who I truly am in You.

Grounding Yourself in Faith

"Being beside yourself" is not just a saying. It is what happens to you once you are impacted by chaos. Imagine a glass of water on a table when it is jarred by a physical bump. The water will slightly spill out of the glass onto the table. In science, we call this "displacement." The glass is not as full as before due to a shock. When you experience stressful situations, shock energy from chaos will displace your energy. In this respect, you are the glass. You can learn to become half-empty, or half-full.

The shock will literally cause your *Triabrain* power to be displaced and slightly removed from the inner alignment. You are like the glass when jolted. But, you can realign your energy and return it to its original place. This energy powers your brain and can be replaced when you turn to the Source for help. The following exercise was introduced to me through Sean Wolf, Founder of the *Body Restoration Clinic* in California. I added a few more components to this exercise to help you recognize how to embody God during stressful situations.

Sometimes, traumatic shock can last for a while. Therefore you must learn to "ground yourself" before you start to move forward. Grounding is basically shaking off your daily troubles, so you can be completely focused on the present situation. If you are hyperactive and exhibit nervous energy, then you can't sit still and relax. Thus, you are not grounded in faith. If you feel restless and have trouble sleeping, you are not grounded. If you are often overwhelmed, you are not rooted. If you are feeling emotional and experiencing self-hatred, self-empathy (like Job) or feeling dizzy and spaced out, you are not centered. If you are experiencing forgetfulness, you are "beside yourself." The following prayer and exercise will help you return to your original state by embodying God.

∞ Reclaiming Yourself Exercise ∞

1. Rub your hands together. For 10 seconds. Then pull your hands apart from 2-3 inches. Feel the energy between your hands. It may tingle. This is Triabrain energy that's available to you as first introduced in Chapter 5. You can feel it through your hands. You can use this energy to reprogram your thoughts.
2. Look at the energy between your hands and think or say: "Inside of my body: full awareness, calmness, alignment, and love in my path. Embodying God's love, God's physical form of faith, able to handle all situations."
3. Now, place your hands on your head. Then, remove your hands and look them. Palms should be facing your face. Crisscross your hands in front of your face in a sweeping hand motion in front of your eyes. Sweep hands in a windshield-type of overlapping motion toward your neck, chest, back, knees and ankles. Then, takes your hands and swipe them a couple of inches under the soles of both feet. Next, perform the same cross, sweeping motion toward the back of your legs, back, and neck.
4. Now, with palms facing upward, take your hands, and imagine pulling this energy from your feet to the top of your head. Your palms meet 2-3 inches above your head.
5. Repeat this process every day, twice a day, for 30 days and notice how much your awareness increases.

**It is imperative that you do not use the word "I" while programming the energy between your hands. "I" is focused on the ego, which may attempt to draw power from within versus drawing power from the Source.

I must share with you a special note: You must allow the Creator to guide you if you expect to be successful in rebalancing your brain. You embody faith by letting go of your need to control situations. This is the act of embodying faith or "letting go and letting God." Many across the world consider this action as allowing Jesus Christ to point the way. No matter what spirituality you accept, the Creator has designed a specific path for you.

There are two more highlights to discuss in this chapter. Oftentimes, when a person cannot control reality, she will find many ways to escape it. She would rather escape reality than becoming frustrated by seemingly uncontrollable circumstances. People are addicted to alcohol, drugs, work, sex, gambling, relationships, and a host of other false remedies. She is escaping her power in directing the force of chaos. In doing so, she is also escaping the equally-powerful ***natural*** pleasures available to her. Ultimately, her life becomes an endless cycle of attempts to escape reality.

According to the *Triabrian Theory of Relativity*, your intuition alone can serve as your "GPS" that relocates the pleasure senses within your brain. Your intuition becomes the force for reconnecting and rewiring the striatum to the prefrontal cortex. All this is done by asking for, and focusing on embodying the loving energy to be brought to you. This will be seen in Chapter 8.

Removing Distractions (Addictions) and Replacing Them with Awareness

A major way to return to your meaningful life is to remove major addictions and distractions. You can be addicted to simple things. You may need coffee every day. Daily dessert and sugar fixes are "must-haves." You may need bread or pasta with each meal. You believe working overtime every day is the only way to feel important. You crave a glass of wine or Scotch at the end of the day to help you "unwind." You find partying with your friends every weekend is the only solution to "take the edge off." You may feel the need to pick up women to help boost your masculinity. Or, you may "shop 'till you drop." These are all distractions.

Fortunately, the key to building your faith brain connection is by embodying the Almighty and its loving faith inside of your brain and body. This means that you must remove distractions that allow brainbrink to grow within you. Removing distractions help remove the trauma-based brainbrink masses from your body. As you recall, brainbrink and brainbrink masses are discussed in Chapter 4. In the exercises described in future sections, you will begin to remove distractions. Oftentimes, I have seen this removal of addictions triggering bodily *inflammation* release.

Johann Hari in his Global *TEDx Talk*, "Everything you think you know about addiction is wrong," filmed June 2015, suggests that to fight addiction truly, a person must embody loving connections within themselves to overcome addiction (Hari, 2015). The writer and journalist discuss the real causes of addiction — involving everything from cocaine to smartphones and explores ways to overcome addiction seemingly deadly distractions. Johann Hari has witnessed our current methods fail first-hand, as he watched loved ones struggle to manage their addictions. Hari wondered why society treats addicts poorly — and if there's a better solution. As the author of, "*The First and Last Days of the War on Drugs*," Hari began to see how God (as the first step in Alcohol Anonymous) and loving human connections served in rewiring the brain to overcome addictions (Hari J. E., 2015).

Further claims have been made regarding fighting addiction with the connection. Research Psychiatrist and UCLA Neuroscience professor, Dr. Jeffrey Schwartz, discovered how thoughts and decisions change brain chemistry (Schwartz, 2015). The medical doctor explains the Neuroscience of habit – a sequence of actions that is treated by the brain as a single unit of behavior—can destroy a person's decisions making capacities. As a specialist, as related to obsessive compulsion, author Jeffrey Schwartz asserts that with compulsive addiction studies, habits destroy the goal seeking and rewards centers of the brain. Habits will have a life of their own. And the goals established by the prefrontal cortex are no longer an important function of the frontal brain, and habitual behavior takes over.

In his talk, "The neuroscience of habit," Dr. Schwartz explores how bad habits and unhealthy thinking take control of thoughts. Over a long period of time, habits turn the sensory motor cortex off, leaving the brain to operate from body circuits alone. And the striatum is run basically from a set of base physical movements unbeknownst to humans. The part of the brain that deals with decision-making go dormant. An active representation is like a person who smokes cigarettes. He may not even be aware that he lights a cigarette and has flames burning inches from his face until after the cigarette has been smoked.

The striatum, which sits at the core of the brain on each side, acts like an automatic transmission in an automobile. It "takes over" the gearing of the cortex, and runs it automatically. When the circuits adapt, they create "Go make habits." However, when circuits are not operating correctly, the circuits operate in an addictive circuitry. Dopamine is released during the addictive action and signals "pleasure" to the brain even if pain immediately follows. This has been witnessed in studies with lab rats. Behaviors become out of control because the brain is "running on automatic." Unless there is a way for a person to become aware and reframe his thought process regarding habits, a habit does not change and can become an addiction. Consequently, this addictive brain function turns off a person's decision-making capabilities.

Unless a person is willing to change his automatic drive, and replace it with a new operation to reframe his thinking, there is no way to overcome a person's deceptive brain.

Now, part of the *Triabrain Theory of Relativity* is that a person can embody faith and love as a new "automatic reprogramming," connecting the prefrontal cortex and striatum together through the ***Pleasure Principle***. (Exercises can be found in Chapter 8). When you seek to embody love and faith in lieu of a habit, this action rewires how brain pathways are formed per Chaos Theory principles. In this process, there are new pathways that reconnect the striatum and prefrontal cortex together to turn back on the brain's decision –making processes.

Jake

Jake's mother had just passed away, and he needed prayer over the internal turmoil he was facing. In the interim, Jake picked up his chewing tobacco habit and returned to heavy drinking. Each time he felt alone, he would chew tobacco or drink. Each moment of loneliness became harder to endure. To pass the time, Jake thought of joining his friend's book club, where they read spiritual-based books. While at the meeting, he confessed that he struggled with addictions. Jake then asked for prayer.

One of his friends led the prayer. She prayed that addiction would be removed from Jake and that he be embodied by God in the addictions' place. She also prayed that his decisions would be based from Godly-love. At that moment, Jake chose to believe that he could feel God. Then, he felt "heaviness" released from his shoulder area. Jake says he also felt freedom. Following this spiritual encounter, Jake has never felt a need to touch alcohol or cigarettes. Jake later began to receive counseling for his grief. Within a few months, Jake's life began turning around, and he saw the world in a more loving and connected way. Incidentally, Jake is now finding love in his life.

∞ Removing Addictions Prayer ∞

God, I ask you to help me remove the addictions from my brain, and give me the strength to remove brainbrink masses formed from years of addiction. Provide me with resources to get help and new passionate experiences to take the place of addiction. Reconnect my striatum and prefrontal cortex with my brain circuitry. Connect me with new people that can inspire me to transform into a healthier lifestyle. Allow my friends who are willing to beat their addictions to grow with me in the process.

∞ CANCEL CLEAR DELETE EXERCISE ∞

1. Whenever you receive stressful thoughts, you must cancel, clear and delete them.
2. Imagine a fly that you swat away: You can do the same with unwanted thoughts.
3. Imagine creating a bubble-like *Triabrain* boundary around you: Consider "flicking" away negative thought away from you like a fly
4. Simply think, "Cancel, clear and delete."
5. Focus on more peaceful thoughts.

Creating God Circles Around You

Embodying faith literally is creating a Higher Power circle around you which provides second-, third-, and fourth chances at life. One of the best examples of this principle is shared in the story of Leah. In short, when you embody faith, you take on a strength that is unexplainable. This Higher Power circle can be consciously formed and can help shield you from excessive harm. The circle is a natural function of your *Triabrain*. At birth, we are provided with a shield that surrounds us. When we experience fear, we unknowingly remove this shield, which makes us susceptible to injury. Both as a shield and bridge of connection, the Higher Power circle helps protect us as we choose the future we desire. The Higher Power circle connects our body with the outside world as well as creates a boundary between us and chaos. Sometimes embodying faith is having faith in a completely different future than what's expected at that moment. To create this Higher Power circle, you must envision yourself in the desired life that you claim.

Leah

Leah was a dear friend from high school. One day on Facebook, she shared a post that brought tears of gratitude to my eyes. We knew Leah had experienced a near-fatal car accident. So, all of our high school friends were thankful once we heard of Leah's fate. After calling her a week following the accident, Leah shared her miraculous story. I learned how Leah embodied faith and walked away from a near-death accident.

She was on the freeway traveling 55-60 mph when she glanced at the billboard for a second then saw there was a sudden stop. She pressed on the brake, but her car skidded. Her car went out of control when she tried to stop the momentum. Instead of hitting the cars in front of her, Leah swerved to the right to avoid the collision.

The next thing she knew, the car was spinning, and everything was flying inside the car as air bags deployed. Leah was screaming and panicked. She let go of the wheel, while the car overturned several times. At that moment, Leah didn't know if she would survive.

As the car overturned, Leah curled in a ball with her hands covering her face. She pleaded, "Oh my God! Please save me..." She thought of her two kids, and her late sister Catherine. As Leah spoke these words, she felt an invisible shield surrounding her as she bounced against it while the car overturned. The car suddenly stopped and landed on its wheels. Everything shattered. Leah was covered in broken glass from the windshield. The car door wouldn't open until Good Samaritans came to her rescue and removed the door. They held Leah while she calmed down. A firetruck and empty ambulance entering the freeway on the opposite side of the road saw her accident. They turned around to help rescue efforts. Leah immediately received help and was transported to the nearest hospital. At the hospital, Emergency Room doctors confirmed Leah didn't sustain any life-threatening injuries. Leah later posted this image on Facebook.

Image 6-4: Images of Leah's wrecked vehicle during her near-death experience. Photo Courtesy of Leah's Facebook post.

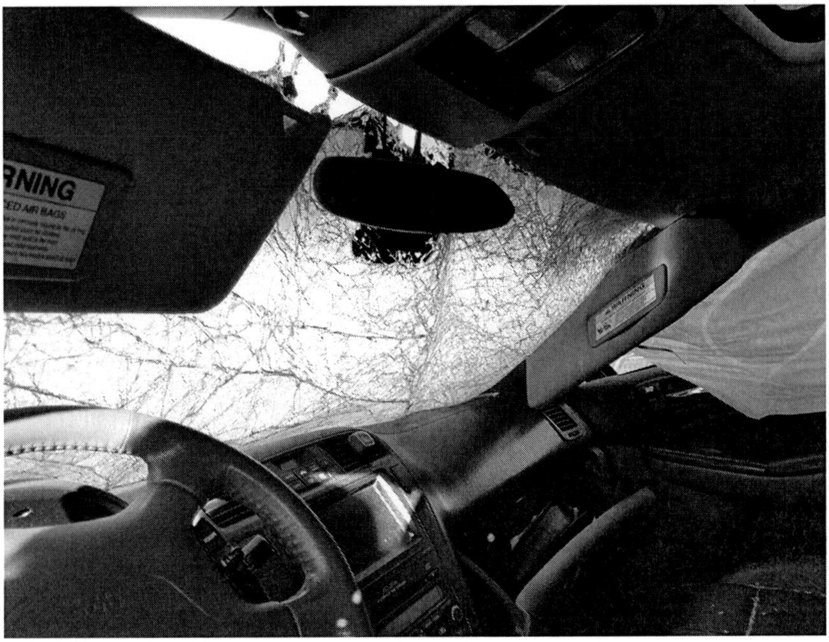

Image 6-5: Images of Leah's wrecked vehicle during her near-death experience. Photo Courtesy of Leah's Facebook post.

Whatever you imagine can actually come true. If Leah believed she would die, that faith would have propelled her to death. Thankfully, she screamed out for a future where she could still be with her children. I am a firm believer that our "imagination" is not really an imagination. I say this because I saw rocket scientists create huge engines based on what they "imagined."

You have power in chaotic situations if you are aware that you have it. You can envision yourself positively impacting a chain of events by your mere existence. This connected thought process is the most powerful when a person acts with integrity. With an intention to be true to the purpose of your existence, you can reshape your *Triabrain* in every place where you physically stand.

In addition, sometimes you can imagine having more power than you currently possess. Through the power of imagination, you can create a Higher Power circle around you to build your ***Triabrain*** into harnessing more power for lively connections. Here is a simple, yet fun exercise that makes you feel like a superhero!

∞ Higher Power Super-Circles ∞

Okay, this exercise will make you feel like a superhero!

1. Stand on the ground where there is grass or dirt so you can feel connected to the earth and the power that exudes into the sky.
2. Rub your hands together.
3. Imagine how lightning travels from the ground through a tree connecting to the sky.
4. Think of a slow-moving, lightning bolt, traveling through your feet, legs, and into your chest.
5. Imagine this energy moving into your arms.
6. Now, with your palms down to the ground, rotate your body in a full circle. Imagine slow-moving lightning traveling through you, via the ground. This is "internal energy" that travels through the Earth into your body. Imagine lightning traveling through your hands and scorching a circle of faith into the ground around you.
7. Draw the circle completely around you with palms down.
8. Now, in a "Wonder Woman-like" fashion, face your palms outward and turn around once like the superhero when she transforms.
9. Next with palms up to the sky, turn around in a circle and extend your palms out to the sky. Transport this energy from the ground back to the Higher Power and universe with your palms out. This energy will be at your disposal anytime.
10. Now, feel the same lightning energy moving through your body and branching off into your hands. Imagine a holy armour of faith surrounding you. Connect the lightning energy moving through you to the exterior of your hands. This is energy that extends outwardly beyond your body to create an invisible shield.
    - Place your hands around your waist. Envision a giant belt buckled around your waist, helping you to remain truthful.
    - Place one hand on your chest and the other on your back. Imagine a breastplate of integrity covering you.
    - Using the energy from the ground, touch your feet to feel your quick-moving feet, that's fitted with the readiness of peace.
    - Imagine yourself being a warrior with a shield of faith that transforms chaos. Touch the crown of your head as you imagine a helmet destined for success.

- Lastly, imagine the lightning energy coming through your hands in a "Thor-like" fashion, to create an invisible sword that only you and God can see. Imagine the slow-moving lighting coming through the sword and anywhere it is pointed. Truthful words about the past, present or future will be directed or received.

11. At the beginning of the day, envision this Higher Power circle around you and on you. You will be amazed by how much your life will transform if you perform these exercises daily.

RECONNECTION #2:
See the beauty and opportunity that exists in every situation.

When you stop expecting the worst, you no longer attract it. When you see a terrorist attack in a country, expect to see the courageous men and women who work endless hours to provide. When you see a tsunami that pours water onto a city, look for the rescue agencies that are willing to provide clothing and food to the victims. When a person witnesses a crime, look for the heroines who will stand and testify to remove killers from the streets. Where was God in that situation?" The truth is that God has always been embedded in every situation. However, you may not have have recognized his work firsthand.

Don't be fooled by evil forces that lie, cheat and try to steal your beautiful future. These situations are designed to pull the rug from under your feet. Let' just say that you were given a choice of two bags. One bag had a diamond ring in it. The other bag contained a rotten tooth. Both bags weighed the same. By opening both bags, you can choose the bag that you prefer. Would you choose the tooth? Or, would you choose the ring?

You have the option to keep wearing the ring, or holding the decomposing tooth all day. In life, we are presented forces that give us the option of looking at the outcomes as either diamonds or damaged goods. Nevertheless, both forces exist. Evil forces will try to sell you the rotten tooth and take your money in the process. Beneficial forces will give you a diamond ring at no cost because your gratitude alone spreads to others like wildfire. If you do not take the time to witness the benefits of your situation, you will forever focus on a path that is limiting your free-will, as described in Chapter 5.

You program your brain based on seeing as much "light" in the given situation. And, you program your brain based on how you embrace your purpose. By seeing your power in a situation, you are reversing brain DNA from the brainbrink effects.

Seeing In New Light

Have you ever noticed something out of the corner of your eye? Well, this is part of your *Triabrain* peripheral vision. It is the way you interpret light. This is your unique perception. When you see things in the world outside of your normal gaze, you are experiencing higher brain function. Imagine for years; you've placed your trash can on the right side of your desk. Then, one day, you place your trash can on your left side. The shift in your repetitive gaze creates higher brain function. I learned this phenomena first-hand while working to help restore parts of my mother's peripheral vision.

Your peripheral vision occurs outside the very center of your gaze. To be more accurate, let's consider a "Tick-Tack-Toe"-like a grid. Just like the grid has nine, squared quadrants, you, too, have nine major quadrants in your brain's eyesight. Each quadrant sends information to your brain on how you see the world. Even individuals who are blind still have ways to interpret light. This vision grid forms your perception.

My mother was given this simple exercise where the soft ball hung from the ceiling. As the ball swings around, she touched different parts of the ball based on where the colored push pins were inserted on its surface. The ball's movement began connecting Mom's brain to her hand movements to her abdominal movements. My mother's accident showed me that your eyes could adjust at any time in life. Muscles from the eyes connect to muscles in our diagram that create balance.

I participated in the same exercises as Mom, and my vision increased. It improved both me and my mother's balance. Essentially, your eye movements connect with your core movements in helping you see the world differently.

Working with one of the early pioneers of vision therapy, Dr. Carl Garbus, founder of *Family Vision Care Optometry Neuro Vision Rehabilitation* in Valencia, Calif., was able to determine how a person regains the ability to process light in the optical nerves. Enhanced muscles lead to restored brain function. In Dr. Garbus' rehabilitation vision therapy, he connects physical therapy for the eyes and the brain, which is a highly-effective, non-surgical treatment. His innovative therapy addresses common visual problems such as lazy eye, crossed eyes, double vision, convergence insufficiency, as well as certain reading and learning disabilities. Patients who have been told, "it's too late," or "you'll have to learn to live with it" have benefited from vision therapy. In the case of learning disabilities, vision therapy is specifically directed toward resolving visual problems which interfere with reading, learning, and educational instruction. Optometrists do not claim that vision therapy is a direct treatment for learning disabilities. However, I have witnessed that eye movement exercises allow a person to regain, and in some cases, restore better fields of vision, plus improve brain function.

Like any good lesson in chaos, important messages repeat themselves to you in new places. While attending an energy workshop led by Sean Wolf in Northern Calif., I received a "recurring message" regarding the importance of Rapid Eye Movement also known as REM, which is prevalent during sleep. REM is a chaotic way in which the eyes move side-to-side rapidly within closed eyelids. During sleep, REM is a phenomenon which can be monitored and measured by a technique called electro-oculography (EOG). Eye motion is not constant but intermittent.

Although scientists are not exactly sure what the purpose of REM serves, there is a consensus among scientists that eye movement may relate to internal visual image processing associated with brain wave spikes within regions of the brain associated with vision and the cerebral cortex.

Sleep is not needed to create REM. You can do it while awake. In both experiences with Dr. Carl Garbus and Sean Wolf, I witnessed how hand movements in front of the face create higher brain processing and synthesis of light. By retraining how you literally see the world, you change brain function. The following application incorporates some of the exercises my mother used to regain parts of her vision.

∞ SEEING YOUR NEW LIGHT EXERCISE ∞

Image 6-6: Olympia LePoint performing the Seeing Your New Light Exercise as the tip of her fingers meet the top of her eyes.

1. Stand up or sit down. Perform this exercise in whichever position is most comfortable. If you are seated, make sure the soles of your feet comfortably touch the floor. Sit up straight.
2. Take each arm and extend it on each side of you. Arms should be parallel to the floor.
3. Now, take both of your arms and wave them in front of your face like windshield wipers on a car. Make sure that the tips of your fingers move directly in front of your eyes. Your hands should be approximately 8-10 inches away from your face.
4. Alternate your hands while waiving, to that your right hand is closest to you. Then your left hand is closest to you.
5. Smile as you perform this motion. You will release endorphins which help break down the fear-based cortisol flow in your brain. Also, notice how much lighter the world seems.
6. Repeat this process in 3 sets around 90 times total every day, for the next 30 days.

The Power of Affirmations

When I was 5 years-old, I would watch a TV show called *Fame*. It was a TV series that ran from 1982 to 1987, where a talented group of teenagers attended the fictional New York City High School for the Performing Arts. In actuality, the TV show also loosely-based on the Fiorello H. LaGuardia High School of Music & Art and Performing Arts (Allen, 1982-1987). Dancers, musician, singers, and actors trained at this school on the TV show. I regularly watched the show and aspired to be a future performer. The opening theme song, *Fame*, was originally sung by Irene Cara, who played Coco Hernandez in the film version. The song was re-recorded by Erica Gimpel, who starred in the TV version of Coco. Here are a few lyrics to the opening theme song, *Fame*:

I'm gonna live forever
I'm gonna learn how to fly
I'm gonna make it to heaven
Baby, remember my name!

Baby, look at me
And, tell me what you see
You ain't seen the best of me yet.
Give me time,

I'll make you forget the rest.
I got more in me,
And you can set it free
I can catch the moon in my hand
Don't you know who I am?

Remember my name. Fame!
I'm gonna live forever
I'm gonna learn how to fly--high!

I feel it comin' together
People will see me and cry. Fame!
I'm gonna make it to heaven
Light up the sky like a flame. Fame!
I'm gonna live forever
Baby, remember my name
Remember, remember, remember, remember,
Remember,...

At the tender age of 5, I told myself that the world would eventually know my name. Yet, I didn't fully comprehend what I meant. When I was 8, I told myself I would be a rocket scientist. Both declarations ***actually*** happened through a *Triabrain* process called *affirmations.*

Affirmation is an intention placed into action through speech. When we verbally affirm our dreams and ambitions, we are instantly empowered with a deep sense of reassurance that our wishful words will become a reality (Harra, 2013).

Imagine if every statement that came out of your mouth was actually happening in real life. You would truly watch your words, wouldn't you? Instead of saying, she's never going to date me; you would say, "She is going out with me this weekend."

- Instead of saying, "I'll never get that promotion," you would say, "Oh yes! Soon I'll be the CEO of this company."
- Instead of claiming, "It looks as if I won't ever have children," you would say, "One day, I will have a beautiful and healthy son."
- Instead of believing, "He's a player, and he's not going to care about my feelings," you would say, "I am only attracting men in my life who care about me and stay in my life."
- Instead of saying, "I'll never get enough funds to create my own invention," you would say, "I am going to work on my invention. I will find honest investors who believe in innovation."

Think of yourself as a powerful, good wizard and affirmations are the spells that come out of your mouth. You can create anything that is verbalized. The role of affirmations in the brain is exactly this function. These positive words program your *Triabrain* into creating how you program your neurons to fire.

The question is: Do you believe in what you are telling yourself?

According to Dr. Sophie Henshaw in the article, "Why Positive Affirmations Don't Work," positive "self-talk" does not always work (Henshaw, 2015). She writes:

> "The reason positive affirmations don't work is that they target the conscious level of your mind, but not the unconscious. If what you are trying to affirm is incongruent with a deeply held negative belief, then all that results are an inner struggle. This interior conflict causes massive energy to diverge split in the body and creates massive tension in the body. The end result is that the negative belief becomes stronger as it fights for survival and what you really desire fails to manifest. You don't believe this new reality could be true for you."

Based on a groundbreaking study exploring declarative versus self-talk, Henshaw considers the beneficial impact of asking questions versus making positive declarations (Senay, Albarracin, & Noguchi, 2010). In order to realign your beliefs, so you do not have inner turmoil, you must acknowledge the reality that you no longer desire for yourself with the one that you truly desire. The act of choosing a new reality in conjunction with departing from an old one aligns your subconscious with your conscious mind. This process reconnects in a positive belief system about yourself. So, you see yourself with an outcome differently.

Affirmations will work only if you believe it will work – because energy responds to free will, beliefs, thoughts and your desire. If your thought is, "I can buy a Maserati," but your fear is, "I could never get enough money to buy one," then your thought won't work. By starting with simple things which are the ***TRUTH***, you can build up in increments and avoid self-imposed limitations.

You can create your own affirmations. The recipe is simple. You must replace brainbrink thoughts with new, connecting thoughts that show your intention. That is, you have the opportunity to change the belief system that surrounds your reality. To do this, you can make statements that are true, and not false.

Suppose that you are a poor public speaker, and you believe this to be factual. If you try affirmative declarations by saying, "I am delivering a great presentation that inspires my audience today," you will create inner conflict with yourself when you give a presentation, and it fails to communicate your point. The entire rest of the day and even month ahead will be stressful for you because you deeply did not believe that you could give an excellent talk.

Affirmation is saying words out loud and choosing to believe what you are saying. For example, if you have blue hair, you won't say, "I am blonde." This is not an affirmation. This is a flat out lie. Rather, an affirmation is the following: (1.) States a fact that occurred in your past; (2.) Acknowledges that the event was in the past; (3.) Takes a new oath about your proposed action for the present and future. An appropriate affirmation would be, "Before I had blue hair that is the past. I am now enjoying blonde hair styles in which I will eventually wear." Consider the additional examples.

A bad lie is posing as an affirmation: I can buy a Maserati.

The truthful affirmation: Before I drove economical cars. That is the past. I am now building lucrative skills to own a Maserati.

A bad lie is posing as an affirmation: I will give a killer presentation.

The truthful affirmation: Before I gave terrible talks where the audience did not pay attention. That was the past. I am now learning the skills I need to keep the audience captivated on my every word.

A bad lie is posing as an affirmation: I will have a boyfriend after this date.

The truthful affirmation: Before men would not call back after the first date. THAT was the past. I am now enjoying my own company and attracting responsible men with the same interests who want to be an active part of my life.

In short, you can use affirmations to see yourself in situations differently. You do this by turning away from the past and consciously selecting your desired future.

RECONNECTION #3: Accept the Creator's Guidance by Committing to Using Your Intuition.

Have you ever opened a book midsection and found the answer you were seeking? Have you ever wished for an event to happen, and it actually does? Have you ever had a dream that came true? Have you ever sat next to someone and realized they were in pain? Ever turn down a new street later to determine that you avoided an accident. If so, this was not a coincidence. You were experiencing a form of intuition.

Intuition is a guiding *Triabrain* system that provides insight into situations before any evidence of it is given. Everyone has it. It is like listening to your favorite music and hearing a message especially for you. Or, have you intuitively thought deeply about a friend, and then you run into her. Intuition comes in many forms and presents itself in people differently. And it is a natural part of your faith brain awareness. Intuition guides you toward a successful path when you do not have the facts to make solid decisions. Intuition pulls you into the success state without even trying. The next chapter explains more in detail about intuition to a great, expansive extent. So, I will leave that chapter for you to understand the mechanics of how intuition works.

First, you must acknowledge that your intuition exists. The brain naturally offers answers through your intuition. This "sixth sense" is located in your *Triabrain*'s faith sector. It is felt through your entire body and expresses itself in your *Triabrain* field. It's like a Global Positioning System (GPS), but it is powered by God. Consider this your "God-Positioning System." When a car is on the road, a driver may use a GPS system to find out how to reach a certain destination. Intuition will tell you how to reach your intended destination in the quickest way and will also help you avoid traffic jams. Your instinct will give you an estimate of how long it will take, as well as insight regarding alternative routes to your destination. Intuition helps you find your way in towns you've had never visited. When a person learns to embrace their gift of intuition, she avoids delays and travels faster to her end goal.

As you build your intuition every day, the same pathways in your brain (through Chaos Theory) will find paths to your resources in real life. Imagine closing your eyes and trying to guess the color of a man's shirt as he walks through the room. Imagine flipping a coin and predicting if it will be heads or tails. Or, imagine what a friend may be thinking on the other side of town. Could you look at an engine and have it talk to you? Imagine placing your hand on someone's arm and knowing their feelings. These are examples of using your intuition.

Developing Your Intuition Daily

Secondly, you must commit to developing your intuition and follow it. Your dreams reveal circumstances. When you touch someone, your touch will expose information. When contemplating a decision, a peaceful voice will provide insight. These are a few examples of methods to understand light as a way to translate chaotic energy into a successful path. Intuition is not just a "woman's discernment," it is also a male gut instinct. It was a baby's natural jolt. It is what we humans have been given to synthesizing energy and "stay on course." Intuition will help at that fractal moment where success or failure could equally result.

Your intuition is just as powerful as your logic and personal expression. It guides you in contributing and ensuring that your life makes a difference. Your exterior connections are built as you follow intuitive guidance. Western cultures do not give intuition as much credit as it deserves. Your Higher Power is the one who guides you through intuition. Even if you do not believe in a Higher Power, you are still given this gift to contribute to the world. Intuition is a means to connect you to the resources required to accomplish tasks in practical ways.

Dennis

Having worked in corporate America, you come across a variety of co-workers. However, Dennis left an indelible footprint on my heart. Looking back, I distinctly recall seeing Dennis demonstrate extreme intuitive gifts. Dennis used intuition in practical ways. He was one of the wisest and most patient men I have ever known. Dennis is a mentor who taught me how to inspect over 1,000 welds, 50 fuel and oxidizer lines, and six different sequences of pneumatic pressures simultaneously in my head. Yes, Dennis was a gift from God. He showed me how to look at every single possible situation that could happen in the future while retracing over 4,000 failures that could create problems. Dennis taught me how to see events before they happened in one visual shot.

I was like his "Daniel-san" in "Karate Kid." Dennis assigned tasks where I would evaluate over 200 engine tests and know every failure that happened in each. He assigned me Failure Mode Analysis to review which had over seven volumes of data. He trained my brain to retain everything intuitively. There was no way any human would remember all that information. Yet, Dennis showed me how to look at the engine as a living creature. In doing so, there was energy attached to its creation. And the science was the evidence of its power. He showed me how to analyze all 3,000 safety concerns simultaneously within Mission Control during the countdown. There were only two of us in that ROSC room who could do this skill. And we were the only two responsible for contacting everyone in case a Contingency Plan was needed (e.g., a plan would be implemented if the Space Shuttle Exploded). As a result, we were vital to the success of each program. Intuition allowed us to be faster than a computer. From the bottom of my heart, I thank you, Dennis.

Like the GPS, your intuition is your personal GPS required for life. It will also tell you how to accomplish your goal in the most efficient and safest way. Intuition provides direction for exiting the chaotic maze. However, most people do not know how to tap into their God Positioning System, so they fail to use this informative brain tool regularly. As through sight, sound, feelings and knowledge, information pops-up into the brain through a *Triabrain Magnetic field* as described in the next chapter.

Trusting God = Divorcing Yourself from the Outcome

The practice of building your intuition is founded on one simple fact. It is divorcing "self" from a specific outcome. You have no idea how your intuition or actions will impact the future. It can change at any time. This is God's prerogative. When you divorce yourself from trying to 100% know the future, you have faith that a Godly outcome will manifest itself through a universal force. This is the meaning of trusting your intuition. God is the one who gives you intuition, so you don't have to maintain control of your environment.

Most need help tapping into their intuition. When intuition functions, countless feel highly confident because they no longer second-guess internal directions that are naturally provided. If you need to learn more about your intuition, this book offers a plethora of helpful material. I wrote the entire next chapter for you to become more knowledgeable about your gifts. The role of intuition is to provide insight on how to remain on your own beneficial life path, as well as serve humanity in honorable ways. It is my hope that you truly enjoy the next chapter.

∞ Prayer for Receiving Intuitive Guidance ∞

God, I know that You always want the best for me. And I know You desire for me to choose the best for myself as well. I come to You and ask for guidance in the form of intuition. Please provide me with the knowledge that is higher than what I can physically see, hear, touch, taste, smell or know.

I realize there is more that exists than what meets my eyes. And, I cannot understand all things that are beneficial or not with solely my own current knowledge. You know what I cannot see and currently cannot understand.

I request the ability to be aligned with the universal success flow and receive your guidance. Please let me know, without a shadow of a doubt, that any intuitive message is from You, and no one else. In turn, I will agree to accept this guidance and move with this wisdom in all areas of my life. I choose to have faith that this early wisdom will later be confirmed by facts and science.

∞ Intuition Exercise∞

1. Upon waking up, do not get up. (Or, you can perform this exercise at the end of the day.) Rather, just lay in bed for a good 10 minutes – breathing deeply. Inhale and exhale as deeply as possible. Allow the air to reach your diaphragm area, if possible.
2. Don't think about anything for 10 minutes straight. Simply lay there and "feel" the inside of your body.
3. When you first start this exercise, you most likely will not be able to remain motionless for 10 minutes without allowing your mind to overflow with a random thought. But, as time progresses, you will be able to do this exercise for 10 minutes straight.

Know the Type of Intuition that You Use the Most

Third, you must know how you personally receive intuitive guidance. There are numerous ways to receive information. In the book, ***Divine Guidance***, author Doreen Virtue helps you understand how intuition is communication for obtaining the Creator's beneficial direction. In fact, ***Divine Guidance*** does a fabulous job describing how we typically gain heavenly information. In short, the Creator is communicating your importance on this Earth. As you build intuition, you gain a deeper connection with a universal success flow. In addition, you are equipped in using your thoughts to heal your brain and contribute to society using these gifts in powerful ways.

With my talk show guests on ***Answers Unleashed***, I heard empowering stories from people who use their intuition. From that experience, I compiled a list that may be helpful for you. When you use your intuition, I have noticed that there are roughly seven different ways people contribute to society using intuition that helps transform lives. These are the core techniques:

1. **Transformers**: Desire to help transform lives (e.g., comedians, educators, pastors, coaches, and psychologists)

2 **Overcomers**: Designed to overcome any physical, spiritual, or emotional situation, while embedding their faith in people who watch them (e.g., athletes, singers, dancers, and those healed from seemingly debilitative circumstances.)
3. **Protectors**: Strongly desire to protect what exists (e.g., police officers, politicians, civil rights workers, and judges)
4. **Innovators**: Seek to create people, situations, computer codes, and various inventions that transform how people on Earth live (e.g., parents, inventors, and software developers).
5. **Builders**: Yearn to grow whatever has been planted (e.g., construction workers, engineers, foster parents, and mentors)
6. **Organizers**: Crave to improve the world by rearranging its structures, and making it organized (e.g. lawyers, legislatures and those in the medical field)
7. **Connectors/Bonders**: Connect infrastructures to harmonize, or make sense of pre-existing systems (e.g., scientists, mathematicians)

You are alive for numerous powerful reasons. Intuition guides you in making the best decisions for yourself and others in a strategic effort to help you remain alive and thriving. The next chapter will help you use your intuition in various areas. You will learn how to interpret your dream for personal direction. You will learn about the mechanics of intuition and how it works. You will also read about experiences that very few people discuss. Your *Triabrain* is more powerful than you know. The next chapter will show you the power of your faith brain.

BUILDING YOUR INTUITION

CHAPTER 7

BUILDING YOUR INTUITION

THE GPS TO YOUR SUCCESS

"It will not be said, 'See, here it is!' or, 'There it is!'
For the holy nation of God is in you."

- Luke 17:21
The Bible, (New Life Version (NLV))

When I was younger, I watched the 1976 movie ***Carrie*** *(Monash, 1976), by science fiction horror author Stephen King. It was a movie about a girl named Carrie (played by American actress Sissy Spacek) who had a form of intuition known as telekinesis. Carrie's intuition led her to have the ability to move physical objects in the air and see the energy that was invisible to most people. Unfortunately, Carrie did not understand what she was experiencing, so she turned to her mother, Margaret (played by American stage and screen actress Piper Laurie) for help. Margaret was an ultra-conservative religious Christian woman who did not understand Carrie's amazing ability. Margaret shunned her daughter and called her a "witch" because she was fearful of Carrie's gift of intuition.*

This fear led to Margaret physically abusing Carrie. Among the many horrific acts, Carrie was stuffed in a closet and forced to live in a confined space until she went to school. At school, Carrie thoroughly enjoyed her freedom. Until one day when Carrie started her menstrual cycle at school. She was uninformed about the female reproductive system. So, she reached out to her schoolmates to show them that she was bleeding. Instead of receiving support, Carrie is now shunned by her peers for exposing her blood in the women's locker room. Carrie thought she was dying because her mother never taught her about how periods are a natural part of biology.

In reality, Carrie experienced sincere Godly gifts but never was told how to develop and direct these intuitive abilities. Thus, she was never taught how to embrace her power. Instead, Carrie was tricked into shame. This toxic emotion regarding using her abilities intensified as other people's fears increased. The chaotic cycle repeats in her life until there's a fractal vortex moment. Carrie is brought to the breaking point when her classmates fraudulently vote her into winning "Prom Queen," where they pull a horrifying prank on her. A couple of students drop pigs' blood over Carrie's beautiful white prom dress as she is being crowned. Most students were appalled by the prank. However, a small number of students laughed and mocked Carrie. In Carrie's mind, all her classmates teased and laughed at her.

People can only endure so much trauma before it 100% distorts their intuition. This chaotic event was the "third charm, " and it turns Carrie's powers fully "ON." But due to repeated childhood trauma, this teen's intuition goes haywire, and she does the unthinkable. Carrie uses per metaphysical brain abilities to lock all the doors and set the gym on fire. She kills everyone attending the Prom. (This is truly a horror movie!). In the end, Carrie loses control of her powers and dies at home with her mother.

I was 13 years old when I saw this film. It was 13 years after it had been created, and was mortified!!! At an early age, I experienced things that science could not explain. Other friends experienced the same phenomena. We were all kids and knew the brain had unlimited magnetic abilities. I was sad because I wished someone could have told Carrie that she was okay. She was a human girl who had natural abilities of the brain. The true horror in the film is the fact that no one showed Carrie how to use her powers in an intuitive way for success. If someone would have taught her about the mechanics of what she was experiencing, perhaps she would have been able to make better choices. Carrie could have harnessed the power to change her life and move out of her crazy mother's home. She could have lived in the real-world cultivating her abilities!

When chaos happens in your life, it can sometimes bring out intensive brainpower. And, if you do not know how to use your intuition in a Godly way to direct what is coming from your *Triabrain* connections, you may feel as if you are crazy. In reality, you are not. The chaotic situation is crazy, not you. Yes, you are sane.

I personally know this experience first-hand. The sight of my mother's head cracked open after her accident left me with intensive experiences that

I could not scientifically explain. I happen to be a person who follows the teaching of Christ as a Christian. And, I have witnessed what many people call "miracles" through embodying faith and following personal intuition. As a result, this chapter is dedicated to building your personal intuition, so you can direct the power that will emerge from your brain in an honorable way.

Per science, energy never dies. It simply transforms, forever. It transforms into light. It transforms back into energy. Then, the energy is transformed by your thoughts into a new energy. This energy transforms emotions into feelings. Then, feelings cycle back into energy again to produce action. This movement transforms into mass. Mass transforms back into energy. It is all a chaotic cycle. Moreover, situational energy transforms back into a new form of energy that is transformed by thoughts. This repetitive cycle is depicted by sine and cosine mathematical waves. Some are experts at interpreting and applying these mathematical waves in practical ways through a process called *intuition*. The result is often referred to as *metaphysics*.

The History of Intuition and Metaphysics

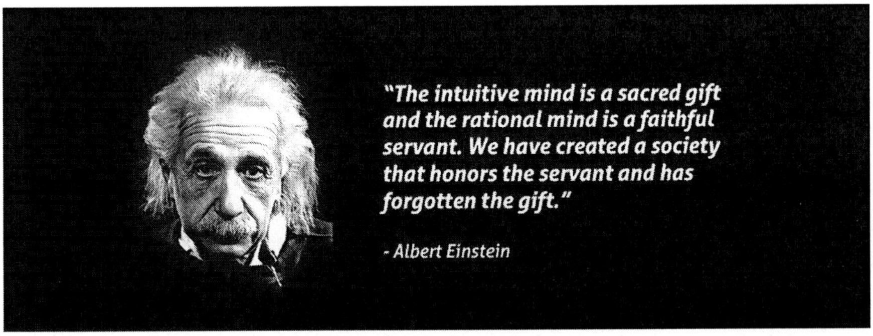

Image 7-1: The Intuitive mind is a sacred gift and the rational mind a faithful servant we have created a society that honors the servant and has forgotten the gift. -Albert Einstein.

Have you ever encountered a situation that you could not logically explain? Did it baffle you? If so, you were experiencing a metaphysical phenomenon. *Metaphysics* explains the existence of physical occurrences that are not yet proven scientifically. It is an age-old study which is a branch of philosophy exploring the fundamental nature of reality. The word *Metaphysics* means "over and beyond physical explanation." At universities, this study falls under "Contemporary Analytical Philosophy." (Wikipedia, 2017) Metaphysics seeks to answer two basic questions: *What is there? What is it like?* Prior to the modern history of science, metaphysics is known as natural philosophy and was originally part of science. Centuries ago, the term "science" (Latin scientia) simply meant "knowledge." However, through time, the scientific method transformed natural philosophy into an empirical activity based solely on experiments, unlike the rest of philosophy. By the end of the 18th century, the word "science" was segregated to distinguish experiments from philosophy. Thereafter, metaphysics separated from science.

Intuition is the ability to understand something immediately, without the need for conscious reasoning. The word intuition comes from the Latin verb *interim* translated as "consider." This mental process is just as important as science. It is just as important as psychology. It is the connection between you and the unseen spiritual-energy world which very much exists. Intuition lifts the veil between the two worlds. Scientists and psychologists are still discovering ways to prove the mechanics of how intuition exists plus measure its cycles consistently. Personally, I am a firm believer that intuition helps you know things, so you can be directed on a beneficial life path. Any use of this gift outside of a beneficial life path is not intuition, nor does it provide Godly-peace.

Intuition is a type of brain magnetism. Per the *Triabrain Theory of Relativity*, intuition is considered a spiritual, emotional and physical energy phenomenon that happens based on brain magnetic fields. These magnetic fields are how particles travel both in a specific direction and a magnitude within the brain. An electric charge and a twist of elementary brain particles act on other currents and magnetic movements which give rise to intuition. These particles can be both interior and exterior to the human body.

A ***Triabrain Magnetic Field*** is like a cylindrical magnet with its axis of symmetry down the center of the faith sector of the *Triabrain*, where the left and right brain connect. The brain's magnetic field is represented by magnetic field lines, which show the direction of the field at different points. Please note that the drawing is in two dimensions. In three dimensions, the forces will come out of the page and form spheres of magnetism.

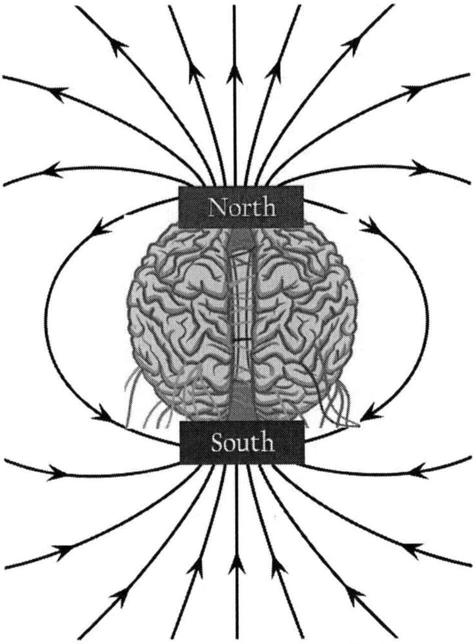

Image 7-2: A Triabrain Magnetic Field is like a cylindrical magnet with its axis of symmetry down the center of the faith sector which aligns with the human spine.

Don't be fooled. Every person on this planet has intuition. You have intuition too. However, some choose to ignore it. At a very early age, you may be a person who has learned to hush your experiences due to fear of being "crazy." Or, you may not know what you are experiencing, so you fearfully shut down your brainpower. Some of you fully embrace your intuition and change the course of your lives by accepting this divine guidance. A deep intuition within you connects your brain to itself and every bodily organ in your system to your brain. These connections exude a magnetic force which provides insight through intuition. It guides you when you do not have the logical answers. Intuition is powered by a *Traibrain magnetic field* that has been given to you as a gift. Its purpose is to help you navigate through chaos. Its Global Position Systems (GPS) navigates you, and your loved ones, on a path toward success. Chances are you are not accustomed to recognizing this internal guidance.

You are not alone. There are MANY people on this Earth who exhibit metaphysical abilities and are skilled at frequently using their intuitive gifts. These individuals help events transpire. However, society fears what cannot be explained. Sometimes, modern-day science pegs intuitive individuals as fictitious *X-Men* characters, instead of encouraging the use of this natural brain ability. The formal study of intuition still requires integration in psychological and physical sciences.

If individuals share their intuitive experiences, often they are considered "off their rocker!" For intuition is not a mainstream consideration within the current psychological and neuroscience definitions. Due to this gap in understanding, highly-intuitive individuals may be diagnosed with depression or having a mental disorder. As a result, they may falsely believe that their life is not worth living. Even worse, they may feel as if "something is wrong with them." One such example is documented on the *ABC News* segment, "Native Youth Killing Themselves," which explores mental illness and its rise in American-Indian communities (ABC News Go, 2005).

Indigenous Teen Suicides

According to the ABC News Segment aired June 30, 2005, and titled, "Native Youth Killing Themselves," American-Indian teens are more than twice as likely as other teens to kill themselves. Statistics show older Native teens and young adults, 15 to 24 years old, are three times as likely to kill themselves. A study published last year in Trends in Indian Health stated that suicide had become a community problem as "suicide clusters" occur.

According to the April 8, 2017, Washington Post article, "Anti-suicide bill moves forward in Montana Legislature," this crisis continued at an alarming rate in 2017, where anti-suicide crusaders fought to have a bill that demanded the state provide more resources to combat the problem. "This issue is happening in epidemic proportions. It's been quite alarming, and the problems I heard were pretty intense," Windy Boy said. (Calvin, 2017)

As a person who is Native American, I can speak with the authority that intuitive gifts have always been part of the culture within numerous indigenous communities. It is a way of life. Understanding God, energy, chaotic forces and spiritual influences are interwoven into the fabric of respecting life. It is the way that you honor the space in which you live. People who experience life in more than the traditional five senses deserve to know that their world, with intuitive gifts, is also mentally healthy.

Unfortunately, countless intuitive individuals are placed on antipsychotic medications and told that what they're hearing, seeing, watching or experiencing is delusional. As a result, embarrassment creeps up on them, and they are afraid to share their over-and-beyond physical experiences. This fear leads to toxic thinking and intensified emotions during chaotic situations. Godly intuition becomes warped and misdirected. In this case, intuition "shuts-off" and the energy goes astray to promote "crazy things." In the classic movie, *Firestarter* (Capra Jr & Schumacher, 1984), American actress Drew Barrymore plays Charlie, a young girl who develops pyrokinetic abilities and is stalked by "The Shop," government agency intent upon possessing Charlie and her abilities. With the intuitive ability to start fires at will, Charlie learns to hone her talent. Comic book and film hero, the *Incredible Hulk* "aka" David Banner transforms into a huge, "muscular green monster" whenever extremely stressed or angered (Parriot, Johnson, & Corea, 1977-1982). He aimlessly travels the world in search for a cure or way to control his super human strength. Sadly, many intuitive people often go insane when they DO NOT acknowledge their intuition. When people are taught to fear their natural intuition, they are guided off their success path.

However, when individuals are guided on how to use their intuitive gifts within society, beneficial fractal moments occur as with the case of Dr. John Nash.

Nobel Prize Winning Mathematician John Nash

Consider the late Princeton University mathematician and Nobel Prize winner Dr. John Nash, whose life was the subject of the film "A Beautiful Mind." (Grazer & Howard, 2001) The late Nash was depicted as a person who was diagnosed with the Paranoid Schizophrenia. For his entire life, he had "imaginary" people come to him. They would sit in his lectures and tell him things. He often would burst into conversations with these people who were not "real" in front of other students who questioned his mental state. In efforts to cope with this experience, Dr. Nash enrolled in psychiatric treatment and was prescribed anti-psychotic drugs, which led to his inability to perform his genius mathematics. When he decided to remove his Schizophrenic medication with the supervision of his medical doctors, something amazing occurred. He learned the ability to discern his reality versus another person's reality. He developed his extraordinary senses which led to winning the Nobel Memorial Prize in Economics for his innovative work on game theory.

I wholeheartedly believe that intuition is another form of genius. Do not misunderstand me: there are such things as mental disorders, where *anti-psychotic drugs* are completely necessary. But there is also a need for psychiatric treatment to include intuition in its understanding and application of how the brain functions. Once a person discerns how to live in the real-world with their intuitive abilities, individuals will contribute to society in extraordinary, healing ways. One such example is *Nobel Prize* winner John Nash. Many intuitive people are not crazy. Rather, they are simply using a higher brain capacity. They are experiencing additional brain connections that science has not learned to universally measure.

There is an opportunity to witness how your *Triabrain* works. You can honor your gifts and other individual's free will in the process. The following three practices will guide you in developing your own intuition and feel comfortable in its use. This chapter is presented in three parts. The first section shares how to interpret your dreams. The next section explains the types of intuition that exist. The last section provides practical tips on how to communicate your intuition in a non-threatening, peaceful way.

INTUITION PRACTICE #1: Interpreting Your Triabrain Dreams

I personally did not understand the power of dreams until my mother's accident. In a dream on that occurred several hours following her accident, I was shown this white-colored, thick substance that looked like large amounts of "snot" from a human nose. Sorry to be gross, but that is how it appeared. Several individuals were holding this slimy substance in their hands and explaining to me the importance of this gel-like matter. At first, my gut instinct was to wonder in the dream, "*What is this???*

This substance was shown to grow later. As it grew, it formed into a white mucus-like mass that seemed to have human tissue connecting brain cells together. In my dream, I was informed that this matter was the "connecting substance." This thick, "white slime" grew into my mother's brain tissue. I woke up and thought the dream was truly peculiar. After talking to doctors the next morning, I learned that there is similar colored white tissue that grows in the brain. As it grows, it reconnects brain tissue. I was in awe over this dream's profound message. I was further amazed because I did not know this neuroscience knowledge at the time of the dream.

Oftentimes, messages are delivered to you through dreams. God answers prayers even in the middle of the night. Your dreams are a way for you to know the impact of your current decisions, and the decisions you have yet to make. It is like your GPS when you sleep. There is no longer a need to turn back to your old ways when you pay attention to your dreams. Frequently, dreams may be forgotten, or they may be frightening. Some dreams may seem confusing. Others may seem quite entertaining!

First, it is important to get enough sleep. Neurologically, dreams often happen during Rapid Eye Movement (REM) sleep typically within the seventh- and the eighth hour of rest. REM is activated by secretion of the neurotransmitter acetylcholine, inhibited by the neurotransmitter serotonin, and this effect is (Garrity & MacMillan, 2017) principally generated in the pons region of the brainstem. It has been observed that people who tend to spend more time than usual in REM sleep have just encountered situations where new learning is being "downloaded" into the brain. This time is critical because the brain attempts to find solutions and connect ideas (Staff, 2017).

Your dream is simply a communication method to help you stay on your path toward a success-based future. And these dreams are designed to help in the reorientation of the optic nerve and optic chasm by integrating the pictures seen by the brain. Plus, your dreams are designed to help you gain a better idea of how you can change your thinking surrounding certain real-life circumstances. When you change your thoughts, you change your brain energy.

Dreams can be experienced in many different forms. There are informational dreams, which tell you the immediate future. Dreams can be nightmares that serve to help release subconscious fears in the night. This fear removes *brainbrink* dark trauma-toxins that glue the brain together, as discussed in chapter 4. Dreams have a specific purpose. They are designed to cause an "awakening" in your conscious, non-sleeping hours. There is never, ever, a reason to fear a dream. Your dreams are meant to help you handle life. As a result, it is important to know the following facts about your dreams.

You are Every Character in Your Dream

Have you ever dreamt that you were Wonder Woman or Superman? Have you ever run from a mass murderer trying to kill you in a dream? Well if so, you were viewing a reflective quality about yourself in that person. There is no good or bad. Dreams provide a way to be aware. Due to the chaotic nature of energy, the brain will use images of people to help you witness mirror qualities within yourself. As you witness the characteristics of a serial killer in your dream, for example, you are witnessing a characteristic in yourself. This person will do anything that may be considered underhanded. If you see yourself as a super hero, what are your non-realistic tendencies?

With each person, you are witnessing your own thoughts that are contributing to your current life situation. When you resolve or enhance that characteristic in real life, you resolve or enhance a certain real-life situation.

Patricia

In nursery rhymes, there was a huge egg-like character called Humpty Dumpty who had a big fall. And all the king's men (the experts) could not put Humpty Dumpty together again.

Patricia had a reoccurring dream for more than 20 years about Humpty Dumpty and her adopted father, Chad. Patricia was adopted at the age of nine months and was raised by a family member who became her adopted father. The trauma she faced while being separated from her mother at nine months caused a deep psychological wound that she could not remember. She always felt her safety was in jeopardy.

In Patricia's reoccurring dreams, she dreamt of Humpty Dumpty about to fall (although the fall never occurred). Later in the dream, Patricia and Chad were on a see saw, rocking on the edge of a skyscraper. As he came close to her side to be with her, Patricia felt herself about to fall off the building.

Patricia always woke up before death. In real life, Chad's character was the representation of Patricia. She was Humpty Dumpty. As a child, she felt unsafe (hence the see-saw about to cause death). Patricia constantly feared falling apart and not having someone to "put her back together." She wanted to authentically love herself, but trauma separated her from embracing a loving childhood.

The happy ending came when Patricia reached her mid 60's. She finally decided to seek counseling and trauma therapy. Today, Patricia is learning to integrate each character in her dreams, so she can feel safe and loved through her own pleasures. The dreams have now stopped.

Your Dreams Deliver One Primary Message

Most of us live in the hustle and bustle of real life. We write books, go to work, take care of children, and pay bills. There are countless responsibilities we are tasked to complete. As a result, we may ignore timely messages. And, the only way to deliver the timely message is when you are asleep. Dreams are "SOS" messages given to you when you are incapable of receiving a certain message while you are awake. These dreams give you the opportunity to change old habits that contribute to stressful, life situations. When you change your actions, based on a new feeling presented in your dream, you are pulled into your success radius.

Henry

Henry always wanted to be a news reporter since his childhood. Yet, he struggled with being punctual to all events in his life. During his 30's, Henry found a way to support his dream by creating a name for himself as an online expert. He hired a publicist to help promote him on TV. With the publicist's help, Henry appeared on serval TV News programs. He was proud of himself because he was punctual to all but two of the tapings. Henry enjoyed appearing on one particular TV News program; however, his favorite station did not call him back for a third appearance. This non-call back disappointed Henry, because he loved the atmosphere at that studio. He hoped to become a regular news reporter at that station.

While dreaming one night, Henry experienced being selected to appear on this national talk show. He was scheduled for two separate episodes that were filmed back-to-back. In the dream, he steps out of the studio for a break, and returns two minutes too late! Cameras were rolling, and the doors were locked. Henry could not renter while they were ON AIR. He pounded on the door. And the set producer explained to Henry that because he was late, the producers could not include him in the taping. Henry was crushed. He had hoped to appear on both national shows.

In the dream, Henry asked the set producer if he could appear on another show. The producer responded with a, "Don't call us. We'll call you," remark, which is a standard phrase used in Hollywood to brush people off. Essentially, Henry missed his opportunity due to his lack of time management.

When Henry awoke, he was thankful that the experience was a dream. And he recognized the main message. If he wants to accomplish goals, then he must learn to be punctual. From that moment on, Henry set in his heart to arrive early for all events. He knew that his change in action would create new opportunities. Henry embraced the messages of the dream. He is now hopeful for new opportunities.

Your Dreams Answer Questions and Provide Guidance

Have you ever wondered where you lost your keys? Or, have you questioned which class to take next? Have you ever contemplated if you should marry a certain person? Dreams offer answers to your pressing questions. Dreams access your subconscious memory and unlock the subconscious knowledge needed to reach a successful path. When a dream gives you direction, take it! Consider it clear guidance to help you avoid a "stalled state," while pursuing a successful route. Take the advice that was given. Take action that same day and the following weeks to come.

Suzanne

Suzanne continually wondered if she should go with a particular book publishing company for her next book. Before she went to sleep one night, she prayed for answers regarding this dilemma. In the dream, Suzanne saw that she would not have a good relationship with the publishing company. And, it was best for her to continue shopping for the most beneficial deals.

When Suzanne awoke, she took the advice of her dream. She declined the offer from the publishing company. Later, she made an astonishing discovery from her fellow peers regarding this particular publishing company. It was revealed that the publishers were being sued for plagiarizing authors. Thankfully, Suzanne listened to the guidance of her dream.

Some Dreams Are Meant to Invoke Fear(s)

Your dreams serve to convert a toxic emotion into a feeling that will allow you to break old habits. In the dreaming process, you are sometimes presented with dreams that will scare the living hell out of you! These dreams are designed to help you reshape your brain. In the fear response, emotions are presented for a purposeful reason. When you sleep, the dream's fearful situation creates an energy that stimulates the reduction of your brain's toxic brainbrink masses to shrink in size. If you ignore the dream's message, the brainbrink stays the same size or grows. In this case, you are not taking the opportunity to address beliefs that no longer serve to help you. If you pay attention to the dream's message while awake, you can break down brainbrink masses. The peace you feel while awakening triggers the release of endorphins which break down brainbrink masses. Additionally, brainbrink masses further decrease in size when you recognize the significant message in the dream.

More importantly, when you meet people in real life, their souls agree to be part of your dream to help you realize the relationship with yourself. Celebrities often appear in dreams. This is the spiritual role they have assumed as celebrities. These individuals not only help you in real life but also assist in your dreams. I am a firm believer that spirits allow the use of their images in your dreams to bring awareness of the importance in changing your perception.

Cathy

Cathy had a fear of fire. One night, Cathy dreamt that her mother was set on fire after her mother went to view a location that she was warned not to visit. In the dream, Cathy screamed for the help while putting the flames out on her mother. She woke up before the end of the dream.

When Cathy woke up, she realized that she could have changed the sequence of the dreams. She could've put out the flames on her mother and overcome her fear. And sometimes, it is best to not venture into areas where there is a danger. Also, the dream showed Cathy that she must do anything to keep the mother – her real mother and the mother inside of her - alive. She had the chance to nurture herself in all situations. She also realized that her mother loved her so much that she appeared in her dream to help teach her a lesson.

Dreams Reveal Significant Future and Past Events

When you dream, your brain is free from time constraints. Your past, present, and future are all processed with clarity. Due to the Chaos Theory having a periodic sequence, your brain will attempt to show you patterns from the past. Your brain will make sense of a hidden memory. Your intuition, or muscle test, will determine if this dream event *truly occurred*. Or, the test will show you if it is your imagination. If the event truly occurred, you will experience a déjà vu feeling in your nervous system. The dream will often reoccur as well.

Zena

Zena woke up one morning with a horrific dream of being sexually abused by her father. The dream left her disturbed and haunted by the visions throughout the day. At this point in her life, Zena was also battling alcohol addiction. While attempting to find clarity, Zena called her mother to tell her about the nightmare. Due to this dream, Zena's mother was forced to inform her daughter of their traumatic past. It was revealed that when Zena was 4, she was sexually abused by her father. That dreadful action later led to divorce. Fortunately, this dream helped Zena know a hidden, yet traumatic truth which jump-started her healing from alcoholism.

If you dream of the future, it is to show you how changing one situation in a sequence of events will alter the outcome. It is important to look at the sequence of events that happened in the dream. This is a forewarning to show how events are occurring in a specific order, create the outcome. In most cases, if one event within the sequence is changed, then the outcome will change altogether.

Frank

Frank's dream was truly vivid. As he drove on the freeway in the middle lane, he saw the following:

1. *The car in front of him in the left lane had a tire blowout.*
2. *The car swerved into his lane.*
3. *Frank had trouble breaking in enough time.*
4. *In the dream, he hit the other car.*

Frank anxiously awoke. He recognized that the dream was telling him two things. Be aware of cars traveling to his left. Keep a safe distance from cars ahead. Three days later, Frank and his girlfriend were traveling on the freeway. Like his dream, the car in front of him blew a tire and swerved into his lane. Frank slams on his brakes. However, unlike his dream, Frank goes into the right lane. His move avoids the car that swerved into his lane. Fortunately, Frank altered the chain of events in his dream. He and his girlfriend were safe.

In Eastern and Buddhist spiritual philosophies, past lives are sometimes thought to be revealed through dreams. If you believe in past lives as a part of your spiritual practices, you can understand the dynamics of past lives and learn from them. These dynamics are often presented in a "dream form." In such cases, there is an overall theme and important message regarding your present lifetime. This message helps you change your beliefs so you can transform your perception, emotional state, and current habits.

From a spiritual approach, past lives are a way of understanding current life themes and struggles. It is said that general Cosmic Law protects individuals with past-life forgetfulness. But for the fortunate few who can remember a past life, it is said these people have a second chance at a new life. Dysfunctional habits that you cultivated in past lives are meant to be corrected. By understanding bad habits, you can comprehend why your current physical, mental, and emotional makeup exists within this life. As a result, you can change the sequence of events from a past life, apply it to your present life, and gain a better outcome.

Victoria

Victoria was a feminine-looking woman with a masculine personality. She loved cars, trucks, and sports. Victoria felt most comfortable being around men. She thought of herself as being a "bad-ass chick." In fact, she preferred conversations with men over women.

But, Victoria struggled to find romance with a man who did not see her as "one of the boys." So, she found a dating coach. Her coach advised Victoria to emphasize her feminine qualities. However, this direction made Victoria uneasy. For some reason, she had a fear of being a woman. In working with her dating coach, Victoria's consciousness began to shift. Her dreams brought clarity.

In Victoria's dreams, she was the only woman on a pirate ship. She was uneducated and took a grueling job on the ship. The number "1580" kept surfacing in Victoria's head at the end of each dream. In another dream, Victoria saw herself distrusting other women and escaping on a sailing ship with men to stay safe. The men were business people shipping antique Spanish furniture from continent-to-continent. On the ship, Victoria found herself being forced to act like the men. She hated the masculine role she assumed for survival. Each day, Victoria yearned to be on land, where could express her "girly-girl" side by wearing dresses. She also desired to marry a man who saw her as a powerful woman.

When Victoria had the same dream a fourth time, she decided to look at world events in the year 1580. Her mouth dropped when discovering that 1580 was the height of the Witch Trials in Europe. Over 100,000 women were falsely being accused of being a "witch." As she found Internet pictures of pirate ships in 1580, she began experiencing flashbacks of times spent on a ship. At that moment, Victoria realized she was a woman escaping persecution initiated by other females during the witch hunt. She thought the dream represented freedom in her current life. Upon realizing her past life of persecution, Victoria decided to consider her present circumstances as a second chance to embrace the freedom and safety of being a woman.

Dreams Communicate Messages from the Deceased

Oftentimes, deceased loved ones who have transitioned to the other side can, and do, visit us in our dreams. These types of dreams are frequently referred to as "visitation dreams," and they can provide us with great comfort. I personally had this dream when my dear friend Kerri died. She told me that she made it safely to heaven after her death. Countless people have these types of dreams. There is no scientific explanation. Rather, your role is to simply appreciate the visit. Sometimes, you will be visited by people who you may not personally know. Nevertheless, everyone will come to you in peace.

"Miss P"

Miss P made the decision to change careers. She was a Hollywood Stylist who decided to follow in her mentor's footsteps by becoming a natural medicine practitioner. Although she experienced doubt after her mentor passed away, Miss P went to school for her certifications. But, she still lacked confidence in pursuing her passion until she had a significant dream.

Miss P dreamt of the late Coretta Scott King, who died in 2006. Coretta Scott King was an American author, activist, civil rights leader, and the wife of Dr. Martin Luther King, Jr. Coretta Scott King helped lead the Civil Rights Movement and became a health and natural medicine advocate for underserved communities later in life.

In Miss P's dream, Coretta Scott King informed her that she had help from heaven in her new career. Although Miss P never knew the Civil Rights leader, Mrs. King desired to help Miss P through intuitive guidance. This direction would help Miss P gain insight on the natural medicine knowledge that Mrs. King learned in her lifetime. The transfer of knowledge was also designed to preserve natural medicine innovation through humanity. Miss P is now starting her new profession, one-step at a time, with more confidence.

Waking Up from Dreams

If you retain a dream in your memory, don't keep it like "old mail." You are to write it down and delete whatever takes up space. When you repeatedly attempt to recall a dream, you use more memory in your brain. Think of a computer with multiple software applications simultaneously running. The processing speed slows down due to information overload. But, when you close an application, your computer runs faster.

Your brain operates in the same way. If you try to remember your entire dream, you will run out of memory storage. You are only designed to keep what you need and let the rest go. So, instead of using your brain energy to remember, use it to capture the message. The following exercise will help you capture the information from the dream, and open other pathways for your brain to retain more information throughout the day.

∞ Capturing Your Dreams Exercise ∞

1. Buy a journal from your local bookstore. Pick a color or design that brings you joy. Find your favorite pen and attach it to the journal.
2. Place this journal directly next to your bed at night.
3. Go to sleep. If you should have any type of dream, whatsoever, write it down. Just write down the main parts as you remember them.
4. Ask God to show you information on how you can change your thinking based on the type of information that was revealed over the next 7 days.
5. Identify the people in the dream. How does each person represent a side of your personality?
6. What emotion did you have in the dream? How did you feel when you awoke?
7. What transformations can you make in your waking hours based on the dream's message?
8. What is the overall message of your dream?
9. Commit to making any changes based on your new insight.

INTUITION PRACTICE #2: Building the Intuition You Most Commonly Use

In the previous section, you read about how many people can interpret their dreams and gain timely messages. However, there are times when you will gain timely messages when wide awake. This section of the chapter explains the intuitive abilities that you can master in your waking hours. Although I can write an entire book on *Triabrain* extra sensory perception, I will start with just this section. Additional information on this topic is available by visiting, AnswersUnleashed.com.

Every extra sensory gift starts with the word *Triabrain* below because it symbolizes using this intuitive ability as a beneficial, divine purpose for humanity. Don't be fooled. Negative, chaotic forces will always attempt to use intuitive gifts in non-Holy ways. So, the Triabrain definition is used to represent God's will for your success. Plus, it represents guiding everyone toward a beneficial outcome. The following exercises will help you develop ways to bring more intuitive energy through your brain.

Triabrain Telepathy / Claircognizance

What is *Claircognizance*? (Norton, 2014) It is the ability to "know clearly." And *Triabrain telepathy* is a type of *Triabrain* intuition that centers itself on connecting mental messages. Telepathy is the ability to read another brain's thoughts using 'existing pathways.' This method is used to communicate directly between two people by reading or injecting brain activity into the second person. Telepathy has been known for centuries by indigenous peoples. However, research in 2014 validated demonstration of mind-to-mind communication. Neuroscientist Carlos Grau of the University of Barcelona and colleagues set up a clever experiment in which signals picked up by an Electroencephalograph (EEG) from subjects. Their studies proved that telepathy exists.

My Story

Truthfully, I thought this type of intuition was a hoax until it personally happened to me and another rocket scientist in 2001. There was a time in my career where I was assigned to a new department with a manager who did not understand my sincere intentions to do a great job. At first, he and I clashed. Then one day, I was so frustrated that I was on the verge of quitting and went home crying.

Deciding to stick it out, I went to the beach the next day and envisioned myself having a conversation with him. I was at his home expressing my gratitude for his guidance. It was weird; I saw him feeding a boy in a

> *wheelchair. The child was connected to three tubes, including a ventilator used for breathing and a gastrointestinal tube used for eating. I thought it was a dream.*
>
> *When I returned to work, he said, "You came to my mind on Saturday. All I kept hearing was that you were "thankful."*
>
> *I looked at him and said, "Were you feeding your son at the time? Does he have tubes of some sort?"*
>
> *Astonished by my question, my supervisor appeared as if he'd seen a ghost before responding, "Yes, my son has special needs."*
>
> *Suddenly, I felt as if I had seen a ghost. I had no idea this daydream was real-life.*
>
> *After that moment, my supervisor and I became close in our working relationship. We were able to read each other's minds and help fulfill the need to support multi-million-dollar projects, and new rocket engine designs. He is still my mentor today. More than 20 years have passed, yet we remain in contact – but this time via telephone. Incidentally, my mentor is now the CEO of a world-renowned aerospace manufacturing company.*

Oftentimes, while awake, God will give you thoughts. When you can receive and embrace thoughts sent from God, you're safely guided on the path toward innovation. When you have this gift, it can be used both personally and professionally. Telepathy can be used to connect the Godly meaning of experiences in your life and understand the importance of certain events in your current beneficial development. It is extremely important to respect others while using this gift. Never approach someone and tell them what you intuitively know unless they ask and you're guided to provide that information! Your job is to connect the beneficial dots. If you use this gift professionally, you are a person designed to bring innovative ideas into the world. You can be an educator and scholar. You would be an esteemed doctor, lawyer, or private investigator. All are people who successfully connect the dots. You are a person who can connect ideas and present new ways of thought. You are part of a group who specifically create new methods simply from an idea that is presented.

∞ Developing Your Telepathy Exercise ∞

Level One

1. Find a coffee shop or an outside area where you can view people.
2. As each person walks past, look at them. What is the initial thought that pops into your head? Most likely, it is their thought. Watch their movements. What does their movement suggest to you about their thoughts? What thoughts come to you as you look at their heads? Whatever comes to your mind is most likely accurate. Trust it.
3. Say a silent prayer that for the person to become fully aware of their own thoughts.
4. Repeat the process for a week.

Level Two

1. Attend a social event.
2. As you see people who you would like to meet, think, "You seem to be a cool person to meet."
3. As you have certain thoughts about what you would like to experience at the party, release those thoughts to God.
4. See who approaches you. Listen to see if any of your previous thoughts that are repeated back to you in conversation.
5. Say a silent prayer that the person who approaches you is enlightened regarding the source of their thoughts.
6. Repeat the process once a week for 30 days. Meet new people!

Triabrain Precognition / Clairvoyance

So what exactly is precognition? What is Clairvoyance? Both are the ability to have a clear view of a future event that could not otherwise be anticipated through any known process (Wikipedia, Precognition, 2017). Precognition (from the Latin præ-, "before" and cognitio, "acquiring knowledge"), also called future sight, and second sight. Clairvoyance is considered "clear seeing." It is a natural form of intuition that your *Triabrain* possesses. Scientists use this part of their brain to produce innovation. They see an invention before it is physically created. As with other parts of the *Triabrain Theory of Relativity*, your brain can see things independent of time. This category of intuition includes envisioning the past without knowledge of the specifics, which is another part of this *Triabrain* ability as well. It is where we get the commonly used term ***recognition***. "Of course, I recognize you!" Oftentimes, God will reveal to you hidden information about the future (or past) as a way to inform you of the power of your present fractal decisions.

J. W. Dunne

"In the early 20th century, J. W. Dunne, a British aeronautics engineer, experienced several dreams which he regarded as precognitive. He developed techniques to record and analyze them, identifying any correspondences between future experiences and his recorded dreams. Dunne reported his findings in his 1927 book, ***An Experiment with Time****. In it, he alleges that 10% of his dreams appeared to represent some future experience," (Dunne, 1934)*

If you have this clairvoyance, you can use this power personally or professionally. For a personal approach, you consciously see important aspects of your life's journey, and look for signs as they appear. It is important to respect others' free will while using this gift. Some people do not want to hear what you see. Some do. I have noticed that allowing God to present you with an opportunity is the best approach. Never go up to someone and tell them what you see in the future unless they request to hear it! Your job is to see the chain of events that lead you to the best future outcome. If you have this gift, you could be a great strategist and event planner. You can see issues and prevent potential future challenges. You are inventors who create airbags for passengers on the jet. You are the manufacturers that install the right number of lifeboats on cruise ships. You are a person who creates a fire alarm and exits routes during emergencies.

∞ Developing Your Precognition Exercise ∞

1. Buy a journal.
2. As you imagine things that happen in the future, write them down. If you imagine different future technologies, write them down. If you imagine a person inventing new technology, write it down. Write down whatever comes to you. Be like Nostradamus, and write everything down.
3. Give your journal entry a date which you saw in in your "imagination."
4. As you start to see things that happen per your visions, go to that journal entry and record the day in which it came true or was developed.

5. After a month or so of recording your imaginary predictions, start to write down predictions that you can see happening for yourself. Do you receive a promotion? Will you meet the woman of your dreams? Will you go through challenging times? Jot down things that come to you and include the date.
6. You will begin to witness how your clairvoyant gifts predict future events.

Triabrain Remote Viewing

Imagine being a remote computer repair technician. In this vocation, you log on to someone's computer from afar to access their computer files. Such remote repair service can be as far away as another continent. Through technology, this approach would allow you to determine what is and isn't working on the customer's system. You can also see applications that require connection to successfully run the computer. Remote viewing is the same concept.

Basically, remote viewing is a cross between telepathy and precognition, where you see events as they happen in real time. In early spiritualist literature, remote viewing was known as clairvoyance with out-of-body travel or "astral travel." This ability usually occurs when someone is either at complete peace or experiencing severe trauma. Ingo Swann was a prominent American psychic researcher, parapsychologist, artist, and author best-known for his work as co-creator of the remote viewing discipline. More specifically, this discipline became known as the ***Stargate Project***. He coined the term 'remote viewing' as a derivative of protocols originally developed by Rene Warcollier, a French chemical engineer in the early 20th century, as documented in the book, "Mind to Mind," (Swann, 2017)

You will oftentimes experience remote viewing in your daydreams. God will pick you up and take you to places around the world that need your thought energy. Your thoughts help transform energy in the area. If you imagine an event that you've never seen before, chances are you are remote viewing. Or, if you can imagine vivid details of a terrorist attack happening across the globe in a country you've never visited, then God is connecting you to specific places. Here, your positive energy can transform a chaotic situation. The more you are guided to positively focus on others, the more you can receive positive prayers for your own well-being. This chaotic flow is what is meant by *Karma*. Whatever you give returns to you.

For a personal approach, you can travel to any point in time, and dynamically shift that situation. For instance, you can go back in time and determine how to pray for yourself in past or present situations, where you did not know the answer. Or, you can travel into your future, and experience it as if you are already there. In this way, you can remain in the present, while still praying for yourself in the future. You can see yourself performing tasks in the future, as well as, determine what you'll need to do in order to become successful.

It is important to respect others while using this gift. Never tap into someone's life unless you ask permission or are asked to do so. Your job is to simply view things the way God and others may perceive situations. In a professional sense, you can become a counselor who can honestly view issues according to your client's perception. You can be an Intelligence Agent capable of seeing criminal acts in real-time, and protect potential victims. Or, you can become a professor who sees how your students are viewing their own scientific work to better explain their chemistry questions. You can also help search- and-rescue efforts in identifying the location of victims. There are countless ways to apply helpful service to others. More importantly, when you return to your body, you must be willing to be grateful for what you witness in your own life. Gratitude is your personal anchor.

∞ Developing Remote Viewing Exercise ∞

1. Grab a deck of cards. Pick out 10 cards randomly.
2. Spread in a horizontal line and face them down.
3. Sit in a chair, in a quiet, empty place.
4. Close your eyes.
5. Imagine going to the first card in your mind, now turn the card over. Which card do you see?
6. Open your eyes and write down the card that you see.
7. Close your eyes and do the same process for each card.
8. Write down your answers.
9. After writing down the results for the last card, turn over the cards.
10. Record which cards in the deck matched your guess.
11. Do this every three days, for 30 days.

Triabrain Psychometry

Have you ever held the remnants of items recovered from the *Titanic*? Psychometry is a natural ability and one of the easiest to master. This type of *Triabrain* intuition is based on reading the history a person's chaotic path through the energy left on an object. This method has been around for centuries though only recently scientifically documented. "Psychometry" is a term coined by Joseph R. Buchanan in 1842 (from the Greek words psyche, meaning "soul," and metron, meaning "measure."). (Wagner, 2017) He was an American professor of physiology and one of the first scientists to experiment with this skill. Using his students as subjects, Buchanon placed various drugs in glass vials, and then asked the students to identify the drugs merely by holding the vials. The success rate was significantly different than all other results. And the success of the experiment led him to publish the book, ***Journal of Man*** (Buchanon, 1888).

Anyone can receive impressions from objects that have been in another person's *Triabrain* field. By holding the object, anyone can obtain information. This information will render as images, sounds, smells, tastes and even emotions. But it is very important to note, that this energy is not <u>your</u> energy. It is someone else's energy. Therefore, you are supposed to give this energy back to them for their personal use after you read it. Otherwise, the energy will wreak havoc with your own chaotic flow.

If you are someone who can feel things from objects, you can use it to determine what foods, medicines, and nutrients are beneficial for your body. By (feeling) the energy resonating from an object such as an apple, you can determine if your body can absorb this food without difficulty. Everyone's digestive track is different. Some people can eat certain foods, while others are left in digestive pain. You can test which food's energy agrees with your digestion. This verification will support *Triabrain* function. If you are used to buying second-hand items such as clothing purchased at thrift stores, you can test to see if these items are compatible with your *Triabrain* field. If you desire to buy a watch, per se, you can see which watch is best by doing a muscle test (see within this section).

It is important to respect others while using this gift as well. For instance, if you touch an object and acquire someone else's information, never tell her about the energy obtained unless you are asked to provide insight! Your job is to connect the energy with experiences. As for this type of intuition, it is most beneficial in a professional field such as structural safety, where you can use this gift to provide insight regarding hazardous structures. Oftentimes, there is an energy associated with building structures that are about to collapse. Your intuition can make others aware of potential hazards. Another helpful profession is used car sales, where your insight will help match drivers with their personalities. Some cars are better suited for certain drivers due to comfort. Or, you can go into professional organizing. You could help clients clear their clutter by suggesting which items are helpful to remain in their space.

∞ Developing Your Sense of Touch Exercise ∞

1. Find a friend who you socialize with on a regular basis.
2. Ask to hold an object they possess, then ask if it is okay for you to read their *Triabain* imprint. (You can explain the *Triabrain* to your friend).
3. Place this object in the opposite hand that you use for writing.
4. Close your eyes. Feel all the energy that comes to you. Does the object seem to jump up and down in your hand? Is it hot? Is it super cold? What is the energy doing in your hand?
5. Now, feel what it means. Translate the feeling into whatever jumps into your mind. Capture one of two feelings that you are experiencing from the *Triabrain* energy.
6. Open your eyes.
7. Now, honestly share with your trusted friend the message you received.
8. At the same time, silently pray or usher in energy for your friend's well-being.
9. Next, let go of the energy that you felt. Return all the energy that you feel in your body back to your friend by imagining all the energy being sucked out of you like a vacuum. It is given back to your friend's feet, packaged in a wrapped gift to use for their transformation. *By returning this energy specifically to one's feet, you are honoring their existence.
10. Repeat this process with multiple trusted ffriends.

∞ Developing Muscle Testing for Your Correct Diet ∞

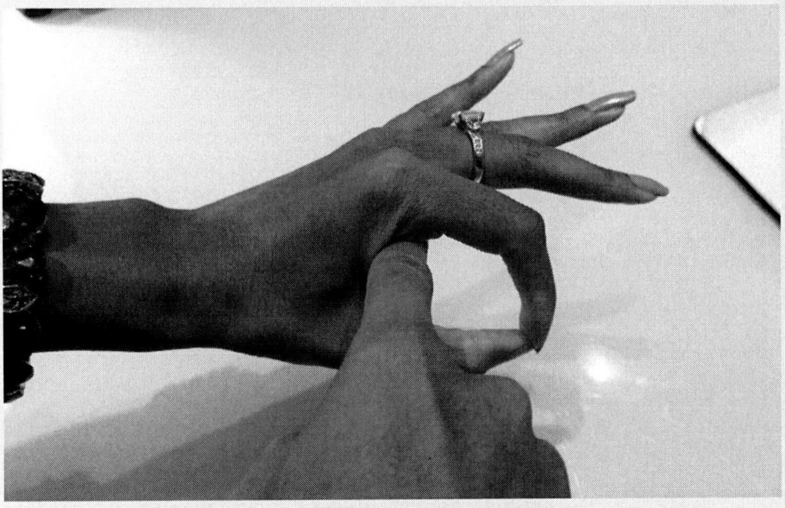

Image 7-3: The starting point will be in the inner circle of your hand connection.

1. Inhale deeply. Allow your pelvis to fill with air. And, plant your feet beneath you. (You may stand or sit)
2. Using the opposite writing hand, connect your index finger and thumb in an "O" position.
3. Close your eyes. Feel all the energy that comes to you.
4. To determine if a particular food is beneficial for your body, place the food next to your stomach area.
5. Repeat Step 1 of the breathing process.
6. Now, feel the inside of your body again. Are you agitated or calm? How do you feel?
7. Ask yourself, "Is this food beneficial to me now?" Meaning, at this moment.
8. Lay the item directly in front of you, take the index finger from the other hand, and place it horizontally on one side of your "O" finger connection. Gently move your finger to the other side and see if you can break open the finger "O." You can use gentle force.
9. If your finger breaks through, the energy from the food is not compatible with your *Triabrain* field. If your finger stays locked within the circle, the food is compatible with your *Triabrain* field.

10. Repeat the process 2 times to confirm your results.
11. Open your eyes.
12. Now, you know how to test what is best for your personal energy.

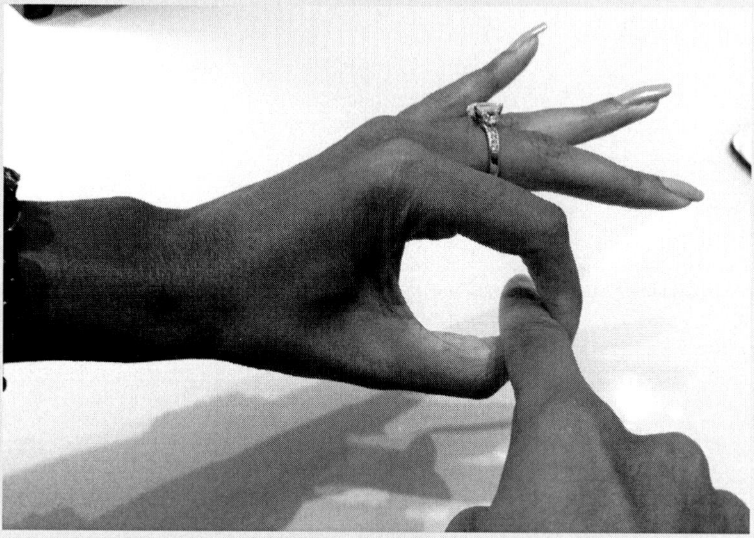

Image 7-4: If your finger fails to break through your hand connection, you are strong in eating that certain type of food.

Triabrain Empathy /Clairsentience

Have you ever sat next to someone and felt uneasy? Or, have you touched someone and immediately felt pain? You are experiencing *clairsentience*. This is a natural *Triabrain* sense like telepathy, but a person can extend (and receive) ones' senses a short distance from one's body. Clairsentience is a type of *Triabrain* intuition that centers itself on body feelings. (Virtue D. , 1998) Clairsentience is read using 'existing pathways.' It is the way *Triabrain* energy travels from person to person.

This form of intuition uses the other five natural senses of touch, hearing, smell, taste, and sight to translate information. Once this skill is cultivated, you can sense someone's feelings from as far as the other side of the room. Oftentimes, God gives you messages on how a person is feeling, so you can pray for them and send uplifting feelings, especially during depression. Frequently, God will help you use this ability to reveal how you are truly feeling when you are attempting to hide from *yourself*.

Again, it is important to respect another's feelings while using this gift. Never go up to someone and tell them how they feel unless asked to do so! Your job is to empathize with others. When you empathize with others, your interaction with the other person allows their receptivity to increase. If you can feel the energy from others, you can become a doctor or healer. Kinesiologists, physical therapists and chiropractors naturally use this skill to determine where emotions are caught in the human body. This is how they can effectively release toxic energy. Or, you can be a judge who introduced a bill that increases empathy. You can work as a pastor, priest, or rabbi who empathizes with your organization. This effort allows introspection that transforms lives.

More importantly, with this skill you must be able to discern feelings that are yours, versus the feelings of someone else. Otherwise, you will go insane. In the next chapter, you will learn how to promote relationships where you are energized, and not drained.

∞ Developing Your Feeling of Touch Exercise ∞

1. At night, touch each part of your body. Touch your legs separately. Your arms. Your nose. Your head. Touch all of your body parts.
2. What is each body part telling you when you touch it?
3. Your thoughts can be found in your body. Do this exercise often and write down the thoughts in conjunction with how you are feeling.

Triabrain Sound / Clairaudience

Have you ever heard a song on the radio and knew the lyrics were speaking directly to you at that very moment? Have you ever heard a calm, peaceful voice in your ear, and followed its beneficial direction? You are experiencing clairaudience, which means clear listening. This type of *Triabrain* intuition is based on hearing sine and cosine waves in vocal frequencies within a chaotic path associated with the energy of noise. Some companies like ***Hemi-Sync***® create brain wave CDs with these binaural beats. This ability allows the brain to receive information when two different, pure-tone sine waves are heard. Both wave frequencies are below 1500 Hz and have a 40 Hz difference between them. Plus, the frequency is heard differently in each ear. People have heard messages since the birth of humanity. Here is one recent experience.

Tom

Tom was in training to be an astronaut and was on the final leg of his qualifying training. He had completed all of his exercises successfully. Yet, there was one particular qualification that he feared. It was swimming. Tom was not the best swimmer. All of his life, he dreamed of becoming an astronaut. That day arrived. Tom's swimming time would make or break his candidacy. When he went into the pool, Tom swam as hard as he could. But, he didn't feel like he was moving fast enough to qualify. Out of nowhere, Tom hears this person swimming next to him. He was unaware of any swimmers simultaneously testing directly next to him in the pool. Tom briefly looked over to see this man he had never seen in his life. Nevertheless, Tom continued swimming.

Then, Tom hears the man say, "You can do this! You can do it!!! You can pick up your speed!!! You have the power and endurance to qualify." The man swims off.

Encouraged, Tom swims speedily with all of his might. He finishes swimming with a time barely within the qualifying mark. However, this time enables Tom to become a NASA astronaut. When he asked the NASA Officials about the mystery man that was swimming and yelling next to him in the pool, no one had an answer. According to NASA Officials, no one else was in the pool with Tom. Tom later went on to fly the Space Shuttle to Space a total of four separate times, and walk in space three separate times as well.

I was honored to sit in Mission Control launching him off one of those occasions.

If you can hear energy, you can use this skill to determine if someone is telling you the truth. You will be able to hear the difference in sine and cosine waves from their vocal chords. You can also hear the confidence in your voice. When you are shaky, you are less confident. When your voice fails to waiver, your inner desires are in tune. Plus, you can tell when you need more information about a certain topic before presentations. Your voice is solid when "you know your stuff." And, you can use this intuition method to hear your guardian angel's voice, who especially watches out for your safety.

You can also use this skill professionally. You could be a person who is a vocal singer, musician or hypnotherapist. These individuals can transform their personal vocal tones to transfer energy. You could become a pilot, able to hear the engine's operations when your visibility is impaired. Or, a railway engineer who can hear the engine in pitch black darkness. As for the story above, Tom was a Navy fighter pilot, who turned into an astronaut.

∞ DEVELOPING YOUR LISTENING EXERCISE ∞

1. Imagine turning on a radio and listening to one of your favorite channels. This channel is one that God wants you to hear. It can be any type of fun music that you enjoy.
2. Can you 'hear' or perceive any words? Any melodies? Have you heard the song before?
3. Do you hear a voice? Is it male? Is it female? Have you heard it before? What is the voice saying? How do you feel when you hear it?
4. Listen to the voice. Do you feel peace in the message or tone?
5. If you don't hear anything at all, think back into your memory. What do you remember hearing in real life that stands out in your mind right now?
6. Now, turn on the radio and see which songs are playing.
7. Repeat this exercise for 30 days.

OR

1. Go to Sleep
2. Upon waking up, what do you hear?
3. Write down what you hear, or record it verbally as soon as you wake up.
4. Repeat this exercise for 30 days.

Triabrain Hysterical Strength / Clairstrength

Have you ever been in a natural disaster and discover the strength that you never knew you possessed? Have you ever heard of a person running to a fire and rescuing a person? Have you seen people overturn a wrecked car? These individuals are taking the energy from a dramatic situation and channeling into their physical body, and they use adrenaline to promote the transfer. This capability is called *Triabrain* Hysterical Strength or "Clairstrength." This supernatural strength usually manifests in the midst of turmoil. Surprisingly, this strength is not "Hysterical" at all. It is grounded in pure loving peace. (Wikipedia, Hysterical Strength, 2017)

Hysterical Strength is a real ability that very few people discuss.

It is a superhuman strength presented at the time of extreme crisis. Record numbers of people have come forward with their personal experiences. A mom jumps in front of a car to save her children. A young climber reaches to catch several climbers before falling off a cliff. A grandmother stops bullets aimed at her grandchildren. You may even hear of men running through flames unharmed. Such stories are amazing. This strength occurs at any age and at any time.

Early science experiments have shown that adrenaline increases the probability of this gift. This strength is the pervading theme for the 1978 TV Series, *The Hulk*. However, science has not fully embraced this ability, because the mechanics are not fully explainable within the brain-to-body connection. Yet, people are fascinated by this type of intuition. It is a gift that saves lives.

Unfortunately, there is no clear way to train for this gift except by being placed "in the fire." There is no way to know how you will react in an extreme situation unless you've previously experienced a crisis. This process is the only way you will know that you possess this ability. I personally know this skill exists. During the 1994 Northridge earthquake, my sisters and I gained Hysterical Strength as we jumped from the second floor to the ground level. I jumped while carrying my younger sister on my back. Nevertheless, every "trial-by-fire" situation is different.

Pastor Jeff Perry

Pastor Jeff is a well-known minister with a congregation of more than 2,000 members in Saint Louis, Missouri, along with nearly 1,000 members in Beverly Hills, California. He also hosts a monthly, "3rd Tuesdays" service for an entertainment-based ministry group at a Beverly Hills location. During services, "Pastor Jeff" often shares his life-changing experiences.

In 2014, Pastor Jeff experienced a boating accident in California with two other pastors. They were sailing at sea and collided with rocks. As a result, Pastor Jeff suffered severe chest injuries, including a broken sternum. Nevertheless, he managed to encourage the other two pastors who suffered life-threatening injuries. Fortunately, everyone survived the accident. However, whenever Pastor Jeff describes the accident, he mentions how God was there, providing strength moment- by-moment. During the times when Pastor Jeff felt he could not maintain physical strength, his uncompromising faith in God supernaturally empowered his body.

Incidentally, this was not the first life-threatening situation Pastor Jeff experienced. Throughout his life, Pastor Jeff has endured a number of traumatic misfortunes. He survived a flood that destroyed his new church in St. Louis, Missouri. And on another occasion, while providing aid in war-torn Kosovo, Pastor Jeff witnessed remnants of appalling war crimes. In each situation, a divine force empowered Pastor Jeff and others to survive. Pastor Jeff credits his incredible strength from God to explain how the Hysterical Strength root in faith helps save people from harm. Each time Pastor Jeff shares his story, Hysterical Strength is transferred to others, equipping them to overcome any situation they may encounter. (Hudson, 2014)

There's no training for Hysterical Strength. It will only reveal itself during a moment of catastrophe. If you have experienced this gift, then you know you are sane. Your purpose on this planet is to help saves lives. There is no way to build this intuitive gift other than being willing to trust that God will honor all your human strength in the midst of a most horrendous crisis. Your strength is exponentially multiplied. The reason why you are given this intuitive gift is to save the promise of a certain beneficial future.

You are placed on this planet to help yourself and others survive accidents and natural disasters. As you help people embrace their life purpose, you are empowered by God. It is not necessary to talk about what you *can* do in dramatic situations. Discussing your gift is not beneficial. Rather, it is most beneficial for you to explain what God demonstrated through you. Numerous individuals will be strengthened by your story. This process is how Hysterical Strength spreads. You can also use this skill professionally. You could be a fire fighter, search-and-rescue officer, lifeguard, or policeman. These individuals faithfully transform their strength to meet the energy of the situation.

Triabrain Telekinesis / Clairmovement

Have you ever looked at something and swore it moved in front of your eyes? Clairmovement is the ability to move physical things clearly without physical touch. The word *telekinesis* (or "psychokinesis") is also used for the same ability (Wikipedia, Pshychokinesis, 2017). It allows you to influence a physical system without ever physically adjusting what you are moving. In this ability, you can move objects and special energy by creating a mental force which is like the energy used in actually moving the object. This brain skill is contingent upon your concentration.

In September 2006, a survey about belief in various religious and paranormal topics was conducted by phone and mail-in questionnaires (Bader, et al., 2006). Among those polled, 1,721 Americans indicated they believed in telekinesis. Of these participants, 28% of males and 31% of females selected "agree" or "strongly agree" with the statement: "It is possible to influence the world through the mind alone." At first, I was skeptical about this type of special gift until my dear friend Wendy shared her experiences.

Wendy

Wendy was in a class that claimed to help people learn to master telekinesis. As a university professor, she is accustomed to taking extra-curricular classes during her recreational time. So, Wendy enrolled in this four-hour seminar on how to master telekinesis by "bending spoons." She thought it would be entertaining. In the class, Wendy learned to move energy from one location to another. In doing so, she was astonished while learning this feat. As she used the techniques shown, Wendy bent a spoon solely using her mental focus, intent, and the movement of energy through the object. Wendy was ecstatic about this enhanced gift when she spoke with me about her latest recreational class. This experience left Wendy yearning to master this skill using other objects.

Although some people would be freaked out regarding the concept of intuition, I cannot emphasize enough the importance of respecting one's free will. For many, the subject of intuition often creates fear. Never approach someone and use your gift of telekinesis unless that action is warranted. Your job is to change environments by maintaining or bringing a sense of peacefulness.

If you truly possess the ability to move things in the air, then it's imperative that you also master the ability to focus when using this gift (Freeman & LLC, 2007-2014). Without concentration, you will never be able to manipulate the energy to cause movement in an object, bend the flame of a candle or change environments without first changing your energy. When activated, every person has the ability to shift environments effortlessly by balancing energy. Your ability extends into careers where your gift can affect countless. As a public speaker, politician and even a sports athlete, you can master movement and shift the energy in an environment due to your focus on energy placement (Freeman & LLC, Learn Telekinesis Training: How to Learn Telekinesis and Develop Your Ability - Concentration Exercise #1, 2007-2014).

∞ Developing Your Ability to Shift Energy ∞

Level One

1. Sit in a chair, with feet on the ground.
2. Feel inside of your body. What energy do you feel? Point to it.
3. Imagine all of that energy pulled out of your organs, tissues and muscles.

4. Imagine its color. Imagine it being completely removed from your body, traveling through the air, then deeply buried in a distant field of dirt.
5. Now imagine a still calming energy entering you in its place. Hold onto that energy and allow it to move into you in the other energy's place.
6. Envision the new energy inside of you.

Level Two

(To be completed after Level ONE is mastered.)

7. Sit at a comfortable distance from the book in a relaxed manner.
8. Then, hold your finger approximately half-way between the book and your eyes. Using your field of vision as your guideline, align the tip of your finger just below and between the two images.

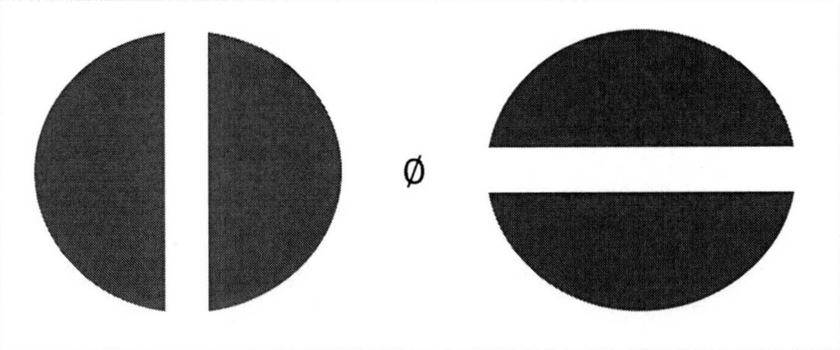

9. Your concentration should be on the tip of your finger.
10. Allow the focus of your eyes to blur slightly.
11. You will begin to see the two images move closer to each other in your field of vision.
12. Your goal is to align the two images on top of each other so that you see an equal armed cross in the center and maintain that alignment for at least 1 minute.
13. Do this exercise on a regular basis. In this exercise, you are moving light waves. This exercise is a tool to help you control your concentration. Sincerely practice this exercise and see if this ability helps you start moving energy.

Triabrain Manifesting / Faith

Faith is the intuitive ability to believe in an event although no physical evidence of it exists. By manifesting intuitive ability, a person can manipulate physical situations and objects from thin air based on sincere intent. These people have the ability to create things from nothing. Consider a computer software developer, inventor, a celebrity. These individuals call material objects or situation into existence. They use what others call "The Law of Attraction." It is simply turning good intentions into positive action. It really is as simple as that.

People who are most effective at this ability fulfill a purpose for healing and advancing mankind. If you have this ability, use it. Manifesting requires you to attract a physical situation in your life that promotes growth for you, as well as others. The purpose of this ability to manifest physical outcomes which are intended for personal and professional growth. Each time something is created from "thin air" (or attracted) God is providing resources. Manifesting is a method to develop awareness so that you can create your desired future. Although other forces cultivate similar abilities, God is the one who allows your manifesting abilities to help many people.

Individuals with faith and manifesting gifts often become powerful educators, business moguls and organizational leaders. They are raised with the purpose of uplifting mankind through their creations. Produced with a loving intent, their manifesting gifts are designed to bless and provide assistance to others. All things manifested are intended to raise awareness and express God's kindness. When a physical outcome appears, consider it a confirmation that God answers intent. When such individuals manifest and attract material things due to their faith, they serve as inspiration for others to do the same.

Matthew

Matthew was a French man who encountered a woman named Jade from the United States. She was in town for a week. Matthew fell deeply in love and yearned to date Jade while she remained in his country. However, he was working as a mechanic and could not afford to take her out on a nice date. Nevertheless, Jade enjoyed spending time with Mathew, and agreed to do simple things based on his finances. On one of the nights, Jade was invited to attend a social dinner with her friends. In turn, she invited Matthew to accompany her. Matthew prayed to God for the income to go with Jade and treat her to a nice evening. He began preparing for the date, while still remaining faithful that God would financially intercede on his behalf. While Matthew was putting on his suit jacket, he found a 100 Euro bill. Prior to this date, Matthew didn't recall seeing or leaving this money in his pocket.

Matthew knew it was a sign from God that God wanted him to enjoy his time with Jade. When Matthew saw Jade, she was extremely happy that he could attend the social. When Matthew told Jade about finding money, she realized how God "works in mysterious ways." They had an unforgettable night.

∞ Developing Manifesting Ability to Bring Forth Physical Outcome ∞

Level One

1. Begin by trying to manifest something small.
2. The object could be anything like an eraser, toothbrush, or pen. These exercises will help build confidence in manifesting physical outcome.
3. Now, spend a couple of minutes thinking about this item. How will you feel when you have it? How will it feel in your hand? Allow your imagination to envision the object in your hand.
4. Now, let it go.
5. Thank God for what is about to happen.
6. Look forward to it unexpectedly appearing in your life.
7. The Law of Attraction will begin happening in other areas of your life.

Level Two

1. Sit in a chair, with feet on the ground.
2. Imagine what you truly desire in your life.
3. In a journal, write down exactly what you seek to experience. Explain it in detail. What does it look like for you? Is there a specific model number? Is it something in which you will create? How does this item/outcome specifically enter your life? Write down every detail you can image about what you desire to attract.
4. If you cannot write it down, imagine that you have it right now in your life. Smell it, feel it, touch it as if it's already here.
5. Now keep a mental thought of you possessing it.

6. Draw what you see. Or, if you cannot draw, find it in a magazine and attach it to your journal entry. In other words, create a vision board.
7. Hold on to this fact that you will attract what you desire.
8. Now, thank God for providing it to you by saying a simple prayer:

"God, you know that I desire ________________ in my life. I trust that you are providing this ______________ or something better for me. I thank you in advance for growing my faith in you as I receive this beneficial gift. God, please give me patience and the ability to see the opportunities for me to live passionately every day in the interim."

INTUITION PRACTICE #3:
Be Open About Your Intuition with Other Intuitive People

Once you name something, you take away the fear and shame from it. This chapter helps you become confident in your newly-discovered intuitive abilities. Now, that you have read the various parts concerning dreams and types of intuition, it is time to start using these talents. Remember, it is best that you remain mindful when sharing your experiences. Not everyone will understand or appreciate the gifts that you bring to the universe. Don't be dismayed by this fact. It is your job to appreciate the gifts for yourself.

Rather than throw your hands up and think that no one understands you, take a different approach. Begin talking about your experiences with people you believe are accepting of this *Triabrain* method. When conversing, don't say, *"I have Metaphysical brain powers. Do you?"* This question instantly turns off your potential listener. Rather, simply say, *"I have experienced a few things that seem amazing. I am curious if you have ever experienced these set of events, too?"*

This conversational entry is amazing because it does two things. It allows you to speak about the results in an "over and beyond" physical way. When people hear about the results, they are more apt to listen. Secondly, the question introduces thought into the other person's *Triabrain* about their own experiences. He begins to see how brain power is being used in extraordinary ways.

If a person is turned off, and not willing to listen, that is fine. Let it go. Find others who are willing to express their experiences. Not everyone is open about their circumstances. And, it will be part of your growth to talk with individuals who are open to learning about your gifts. Plus, it will be important to find people who are willing to show you how to cultivate your gifts. These intuitive gifts are for everyone to use and appreciate. Simply, set your intention to meet like-minded intuitive people who will grow in the same direction. I guarantee you, doors will open.

CONCLUSION

In the use of all of these *Triabrain* intuitive gifts, it is important to recognize the power you bring versus the power someone else brings to a situation. It is through this discernment that you are able to feel secure in following your intuitive guidance. In the next chapter, you will learn which emotions block intuition. Once this concept is mastered, your intuition will explode. In the next chapter, you will also become aware of how certain unresolved emotions can make your intuitive gifts go haywire.

Unleashing Your Right-Brain Power

CHAPTER 8

UNLEASHING YOUR RIGHT-BRAIN POWER

THE BEAUTY IN RELATIONSHIPS

"Everything is energy. And that's all there is to it. Match the frequency of the reality you want and you cannot help but get that reality. It can be no other way. That is not philosophy. This is physics."

-Albert Einstein

When you desire to change the circumstances of your life, it takes much energy to do it. You must change your energy to match what you desire. You must change toxic emotions into healthy feelings to create long-lasting change. Unfortunately, there is no short cut. Many days you will wonder, "*Why on Earth am I spending all this energy???? How long will this last???*"

But, there comes a time when the energy of building your integrity e.g. committing to yourself – empowers you. This integrity empowers you to change your world from the inside out. And you will be forever grateful that you spent the time learning about yourself. The only way to move forward is to be true to you.

Don't be fooled. Chaotic forces, like deep-seated emotions, will lie to you. They will attempt to stall your progress. Painful memories can distort your progressive energy. Your deep emotional pain can hide in your system for decades and wreak havoc in your *Triabrain* connections. Uncomfortable memories reside deep in your system through its own chaotic pathways. Toxic brainbrink is found not only in the brain, but in every part of your living connections. This energy is even in the field around you. Faulty thoughts fail to convert emotions into healthy feelings. In this case, chaotic energy hides in unforeseen places like cockroaches.

Toxic thoughts related to fear may take the form of throat discomfort. Shame may hide in a hip joint. Doubt may mimic your poor indigestion. Sometimes anger can run so deep in your system that it will begin to affect the way your entire face looks. Such intense emotions sometimes trick you into thinking that someone else's pain is yours. You will lose the ability to know where you stand, where you are, and how you truly feel in this vast universe. Your right brain will perceive things inaccurately. Emotions will even make you question what you see and what you do. When you feel pain, emotional issues distort your authentic feelings. These emotional disturbances, based on faulty beliefs, attempt to block how your thoughts and intuition can serve your highest good.

And emotions, like shame, will block your integrity communication with yourself. You will start to see the emotions, like fear, surface in your actions. For example, you select dysfunctional relationships. Fear may make you stay single (or married) for too long. Anger may make you disliked at work. Apathy may make your friendships feel one-sided. So, you will do one of three things: (1.) You will avoid working through emotions; (2.) You will avoid anything that resembles what brought you pain; Or, (3.) You may turn off your feelings altogether in efforts to cope.

I was the third type. I was so great at being a scientist that I turned my feelings off. I shut down most of my feelings when I was 8 years-old. I was a young kid, excited to learn and go to school. I was also highly-creative and very artistic. I watched the 1980's TV show *Fame* and wanted to be a professional dancer. I danced in joy, mimicking the people leaping and twirling on TV. However, my childhood was cut short soon after.

At the age of 8, a deceitful man by the name of Alvin became a "friend of the family." He loved to watch me dance. And when I was 8, I innocently fulfilled his request to dance for him. I was raped by him. The experience was so painful, that I erased it from my memory for 30 years straight. I could not even tell my mother, because I did not remember it myself. I finally remembered the truth a full 30 years later, when I decided to undergo physical therapy. As I healed my back and abdominal area, the truth returned to my conscious memories. This truth came back to the point of overwhelming emotion, because there were many, emotions I hid from myself for 30 years.

For 30 years, I turned off my feelings, but the trapped energy manifested in my body and chaotic actions. I excessively turned to sugar and baked cookies for years thereafter. Unknowingly, I was using sugar as a self-medication! I turned to math and science, because I knew "math" would not lie to me. In my teens, 20's and 30's, I had absolutely no feeling in my abdominal area. My gut feelings turned mute. So, I overate so I could experience feeling stuffed in my stomach area. Pain was better than no feeling at all. For me, it served as a warped sense that I was still alive. In my 20's, I threw myself into launching rockets and graduate school to avoid working through the deep-seated emotions. I completely avoided committed, romantic relationships. Although I had high intellectual an intuitive intelligence, my brain was chemically-stuck in the emotional state of being 8-years-old regarding relationships.

When I learned the *truth*, I was finally ready to process this painful memory. As they say, "When the student is ready, the master will appear." Nevertheless, like countless others, I had to escape the, "Why did this happen to me" mode. It felt like I was 8 all over again, as my thoughts became flooded with a hurricane of emotions. I was looking at myself as an 8-year-old victim instead of viewing myself as a loving adult. Although, I accomplished great things in science, my emotional right brain needed to develop into the same intensity as my left brain. I needed to fully embrace the fact that I did not cause the trauma; rather it was simply a horrifying experience I had to fully overcome. And this incident would serve to repower me decades later.

Remember, this is my story not yours.

All that emotional energy had to go! More importantly, it must be replaced with an energy that was more powerful and flexible. I had to select new feelings to replace the old ways I experienced life. When I did this, I could feel my abdominal area again, and I could walk in heels again. I could dance in peace. I could do all things because I took action based on accepting myself. I chose the feeling of acceptance.

When I learned to accept myself, I had the strength to forgive Alvin. I had no idea where in the world he was located. But, I felt how small and low he truly is: He is a little man, doing low things. I am much bigger than he. As Olympia LePoint, I am a powerful woman. In forgiving him, I took back my power. I regained my mental and magnetic powers. And this magnetic energy removed the toxic emotions from within my mind and body, thereby sending the consequences back to him. For, I sent back the hell that he created for himself. It was not mine. My life is fruitful, exciting, peaceful, meaningful and enlightening. And in turn, I received a new flow of positive energy in the form of bodily feelings. As you may recall, emotions are toxic and feelings are healthy. So, I welcomed these new feelings based on experiencing the truth. The truth in you is called integrity. The truth is simple. I am a grown person able to protect, defend and provide for myself, in a feminine way as a true woman. As for you, you are a grown person able to take ownership over your life. You now have regained your power again as you read these paragraphs.

Feel the shift that is happening within you, too.

Forgiveness is a choice; it is necessary for you to move forward.

RIGHT TRIABRAIN BLUEPRINT FOR RECONNECTION (RTBR)

Have you ever experienced pure joy when deciding to act on a plan? On the flip side, have you remembered a difficult experience, then questioned every next move? Have you ever been so determined to change your situation that you look for any open door? If so, you are using the right *Triabrain*.

The right *Triabrain* represents how your feelings affect your conscious and unconscious decision-making process. This *Triabrain* sector selects and interprets your experiences, and chooses a feeling based on its experience. Your future decision-making is based on your perception of the event. The feeling response is a type of *Triabrain* thought designed to take emotion and convert it to a form of pleasure. This pleasure turns into a sensation that affects the physiological systems (e.g., immune, endocrine, and cardiovascular) of the body that are connected to the *Triabrain*. Neuroimaging studies of emotional self-regulation, psychotherapy, and doctor's placebo effect studies are examples of how feelings influence automatic body reactions and future decision-making.

In Chapter 4 you took the self-test to help determine how your faith brain was disconnected. The following sections give a summary of how each brainbrink can be reversed using the right *Triabrain*. If your primary score was, *"Hiding in You, Only Seeking in Others"*, then you would want to pay close attention to the first *Triabrain* reconnection principle in this section: "*Run to Yourself First, Before Going to Friends & Non-Professionals.*" If your primary score in Chapter 4 was, *"Needing Drama, Lacking Self-Romance"*, you would benefit from reading the second reconnection principle, "*Take Back Your Power in the Form of Choice.*" If your top score was, "*Expecting a Let-Down, Not Re-Directing Power,*" then be prepared to see things in a new way within the third reconnection principle, "*Be honest with yourself and decipher the types of relationships that you ARE attracting versus wanting to build.*" The chart below lays out your plan of action. But first, it is important to understand why your *Triabrain* disconnected in the first place.

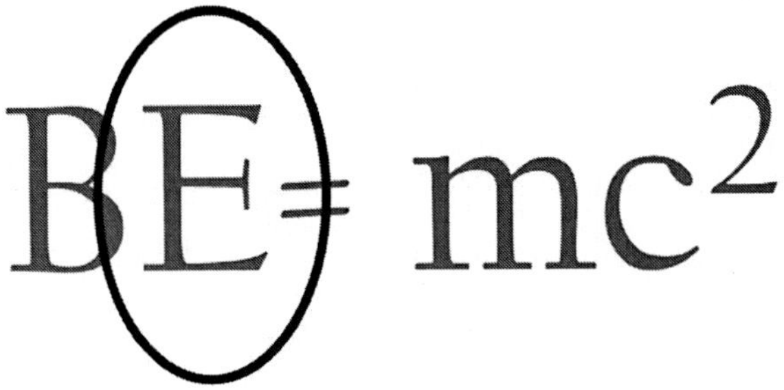

Image 8-1: The Triabrain Theory of Relativity focuses on the energy in your brain that serves to transform an emotion into a feeling that gives you the desire to take action.

Brainbrink Disconnection Toxic Emotions	**Triabrain Reconnection Principle (Right Triabrain Blue Print)**	**Score Index (Results from the Self -Test in Chapter 4)**
4. Hiding in You, Only Seeking in Others	4. Run to Yourself First Before Going to Friends & Non-Professionals.	• Primary focus if your score is 20 and up. • Secondary priority if your score is 15 -19. • Third priority if your score is 0-14
5. Needing Drama, Lacking Self- Romance	5. Take back your power in the form of choice.	• Primary focus if your score is 20 and up. • Secondary priority if your score is 15 -19. • Third priority if your score is 0-14.
4. Expecting A Let-Down, Not Re-Directing Power	6. Be honest with yourself and decipher the types of relationships that you ARE attracting versus wanting to build.	• Primary focus if your score is 20 and up. • Secondary priority if your score is 15 -19. • Third priority if your score is 0-14.

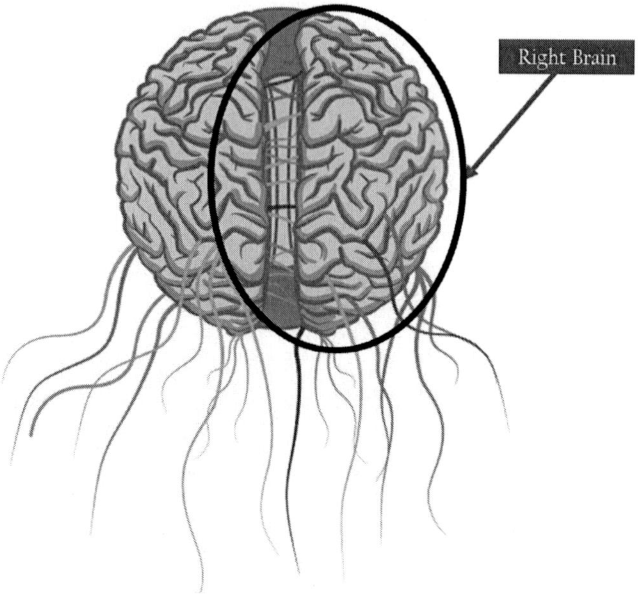

Image 8-2: The Right Expressive Brain

Why on Earth does the right Triabrain disconnect?

Before you can connect the right brain, you must know why it originally disconnected. From the ages of 8-9, a person makes a conscious decision to accept or reject trusting a person who is closest to him or her. In this time frame, the child will encounter a situation that will make them feel as if they were never protected or nurtured. It can be a parent's illness, an emotionally absent parent, an uncle's poor life choice, a mother's work addiction, a mother's cell phone obsession, or a father's affair, where a necessary relationship "feels missing." And in turn, the child internally feels lonely. Forever, this person will feel alone in life, yet it is masked by keeping active. Over-commitment often results, or a person prides himself on "being a lone wolf." And because of this early life experience, he loses touch with his feelings. Nervous system brain responses become shut off or overactive, which causes unhealthy, trapped emotions. Consequently, he will have trouble trusting his own senses and decision-making. The non-expressed energy in feelings alters the brain.

Robert (from Chapter 3)

Robert was 8 years-old when he realized his father had a gambling addiction. His father would spend hours and hours gambling. As a result, his mother was left to pick up the pieces after all family money was blown on "women of the night" and casino games. Robert felt alone and let down by both his parents. He disliked how his father was not there and placed his mother in a stressful situation. At the same time, he was neglected by his mother during traumatic situations. As an adult, Robert vowed never to be with a "woman for hire," and he began distrusting his mother.

Although the experience secretly traumatized him, Robert had trouble making decisions about the women in his life. He never wanted to mistreat a wife, so he stayed away from commitments where he could deeply fall in love with a woman. Then, one day at a restaurant, he met Ann. The moment Robert met Ann he intuitively knew he wanted her as a lifetime partner. Ann was smart, accomplished, kind and caring. She had a feminine strength that refused to accept Robert's shenanigans. She sincerely admired Robert for his strength. Though, the thought of marrying Ann was too overwhelming for Robert to consider, for four years, he wrestled with asking Ann to be his girlfriend. Robert liked his freedom of being single. At the same time, Robert wanted Ann for himself romantically. Robert was overwhelmed with the thought of losing Ann to another man.

RECONNECTION PRINCIPLE: Redirecting Energy = Making Better Decisions and Owning Your True Feelings as a Grown Adult

It is your job to understand that every relationship you experience is an opportunity for you to reconnect with yourself. Like the chaotic mathematical shapes formed in fractal geometry, your relationships with the Creator, yourself and others will generate feelings that must be positively directed. Most importantly, the ability to establish an inner bond with yourself will allow you to no longer practice self-abandonment or self-isolation.

When I speak of integrity, I am referring to the process of committing to self despite the feelings of others. Each time you deepen a relationship with yourself, you gain integrity. You know when energy needs to move out of emotions into healthy feelings. You become more aware of when you can shift the emotions back into feelings that fuel you. In doing so, these feelings serve as powerful brain reshaping forces. They are changing your inner environment.

It is your job to take responsibility for thoughts, feelings and actions. No one makes you think or do anything. It is your power to do what you need to do now. This is the secret to healing yourself from the past. No other person can you unleash your own healing. It is your role to identify how your own thoughts and actions affect your emotional state.

And when you are in relationships with people, the relationship is ever-evolving based on you recognizing your own feelings, and taking appropriate action. Relationships with others are a tool for you to gain a better understanding of yourself. There is the beneficial outcome in every relationship if you realize that relationships are designed to help you make better decisions. Relationships help you to trust yourself and your own decision-making power.

When you convert your emotions into feelings of pursuing your passions, you are also tasked to express yourself in honorable ways. That is, you create opportunities into trust, and trust turns into forgiveness. Forgiveness turns into understanding. And, understanding provides you with bliss to move forward. This transformation creates self-stability. If you accept the opportunity given to you in each relationship, then you have three fractal decisions to make to reconnect your right brain:

1. Forgive the person who betrayed you when you were younger. Mentally take your power back from them, and leave them with their own consequences.
2. Decide to listen to yourself today, and every day from this day forward. Do not run from others, or run to others all the time. Rather, be committed to creating a healthy relationship with yourself first before establishing a relationship with others.
3. Express your passions and find opportunities to connect with others who share the same passions.

This is how to feel better in your brain and in your body.

∞ Forgiving Your Parents Exercise ∞

Allocate at least an hour for this exercise.

1. Find several sheets of paper. Sit in a quiet space, with both feet firmly planted.
2. Think back to a time (or series of times) where you lost complete faith in your parent(s) ability to protect and care for you. Sincerely think back to that moment in time.
3. (ON SHEET#1)
4. Write a letter to either parent sharing how you honestly and currently feel about your experience. Let out of all your thoughts and emotions. No human will ever see this paper except you. Let everything go onto this sheet of paper. (This process may take several sheets of paper.)

5. Now, breathe deeply 10 times, preferably through your nose. Deeply inhale so the air goes as far down into your diaphragm as possible.
6. Now reread the letter. Look at the letter. Feel the letter with all its energy. Any emotion that you feel inside of you, imagine it leaving you and attaching to the letter. Attach to the letter anything that pulls and prevents you from taking care of yourself.
7. Any force that keeps you addicted to things that distract you from your best life, give it to God by *mentally* thinking and feeling, *"I am giving this to you God."* Imagine a pure, white light completely burning through the letter and all its pages.

8. (ON SHEET#2)
9. On new sheets of paper, write a letter to your past self. Tell your past self all the beneficial skills and outcomes that resulted from the horrible experience. Pretend you can go back in time and give this letter to your former self. Share important life lessons that you wish you could tell your former self.
10. Now, when you are ready, forgive your parent (alive or deceased) for placing you in a situation where you learned to distrust. What powerful emotion do you feel needs to be returned to them? Pray that their spirit finds God as they are receiving the energy they gave to you.

11. (ON SHEET#3)
12. Now, when you are ready, forgive yourself from turning away from your parents, "when taking matters into your own hands." This was when you thought that you could do things on your own, but were not ready to take on that adult responsibility.
13. Now make a commitment to you and your past self. Write down how you will commit to working together to look at the beneficial things that come into in your life based on your parents' presence. Remind yourself how you can constantly renew yourself now, and pick yourself back up from any experience.
14. Commit to yourself to be open to ways that you can nurture and protect yourself. Ask your Higher Power for the strength to transform your emotions into feelings to take better care of yourself. And ask your Higher Power to provide you with the strength to walk away from situations that are not in your best interest. Request your Higher Power to connect you with beneficial people whose presence will point you toward your life passions.

15. Your new trust and commitment to yourself is the start of better feelings to come.
16. Keep these sheets of paper for another powerful exercise in the last chapter of this book.

RECONNECTION #1: Run to yourself first before going to Friends and Non-Professionals.

Throughout the ages, women have been taught to find a man who would marry them. Men have been taught to find a wife to build his financial status. Stop. Change that backward thinking. You must first marry yourself. One of the biggest ways that you fail to harness your brain's power is when you give all your power away to others. If you are constantly yearning to be with others, you are basically running away from yourself. One of the major ways that you give your brain's power away is when going to other people (who are not skilled professionals) to determine your plan of action. In doing so, you completely miss the opportunity to learn about yourself and your own desires. You hide from yourself. As a result, the integrity in yourself will never develop. And this integrity is the key ingredient that allows you to overcome any situation. By cultivating your integrity, you break the patterns of the past. To become more powerful, you must "date" yourself. This is the only way to become aware of your own desires. Through spending time with yourself, you will know the "signature" of your energy versus someone else's thoughts, energies or desires. You are the only one who creates beneficial change in your life: No one else.

Though often, highly intellectual people are not taught the importance of emotional intelligence as seen with the story of Trevor.

Trevor

Trevor is a genius. He scored a 153 on an IQ test, and graduated with a degree in Chemical Engineering from an Ivy League School. He went into one of the top consulting firms in the world. Later, Trevor earned his MBA from an Ivy League school as well. He continued to tour the globe solving other people's problems and was respected for his insight.

One day, Trevor decided to buy a new BMW SUV on a lease payment, and needed to make a selection on the best wheels. He completed the financing, and negotiated the best deal. Selecting a wheel style and size were the only remaining items left to address. Trevor first asked his female friend her thoughts on the best wheel design. Then, he proceeded to ask 10 or 15 other people the same question. Trevor spent the longest part of his car purchasing process listening to everyone else's desires, instead of his own. Despite being a highly-intellectual person, Trevor had trouble making decisions in his own life because he did not have a relationship with himself.

Although many with high intellectual aptitude have developed the logical side of their left brain, they may not have developed the personal orientation relating to the right brain. As a result, these individuals will have trouble making decisions. The decision-making process is within the relationship that we have with ourselves, and no one else. If this right *Triabrain* sector is not cultivated and developed, a person will exhibit a brain issue that stalls them him from pursuing the future that is best for him. They will take forever to make a decision, and opportunities will skip over them.

In the Yale University study, *The Emotionally Intelligent Decision Maker: Emotion-Understanding Ability Reduces the Effect of Incidental Anxiety on Risk Taking by Jeremy A. Yip and Stéphane Côté,* it associates past negative experiences with the inability to make decisions (Yip & Côté, 2013). Published with the support of the Department of Psychology, this study explored emotional intelligence, and found it is highly emotional intelligence, not a high intellectual intelligence, that allows a person to have ease in decision-making activities.

In two experiments, the study examined how a core dimension of emotional intelligence, "emotion-understanding ability," facilitates decision-making. Individuals with higher levels of emotion-understanding ability could correctly identify which events caused their emotions and whether their emotions stemmed from events that are unrelated to current decisions.

The study concluded that people with high emotional intelligence (right *Triabrain* development) make better decisions, because they do not let their emotions hinder the process of making wise decisions. Also, those with high emotional intelligence tend to have an observing sego eparate of the brain that allows a person to observe what he is feeling objective, without reacting to it. The process is like "stepping out of emotions" to clearly understand the situation, and feel confident about the decision made.

When a person has unhealthy relationships in their life with themselves or with others, it affects their entire way of being. Simple things become difficult to maintain. Oftentimes, personal care becomes scattered and neglected. Certain friendships become emotionally-draining. And, a person will incorrectly gage the parameters of a friendship/relationship. Many who have trouble with the right *Triabrain* function will turn to the Internet or entertainment for visual stimulation. Often a subconscious act, this effort stimulates right brain activity. Relationships become non-communicative, because right brain focus is hindered.

Removing Fear

You may have a plethora of fears. You fear cats. You fear snakes. You fear heights. You fear relationships. Most often, fears are boiled down to one key component for adults: You fear trusting yourself (and/or God) and you fear to make the wrong choices. Fear is the result of you listening to the wrong person. Fear is a spirit. Fear focuses on your limitations. Fear tricks you into using your faith brain to mistakenly focus on an outcome that is not beneficial. Reject fear! Fear is not yours!

This is FEAR:

<u>F</u>alse
<u>E</u>vidence
<u>A</u>ppearing
<u>R</u>eal

And, its role is to do 3 things:

1. <u>Fear hinders</u> you from using your *Triabrain* power. Fear blocks your intuition and guidance from God.
2. <u>Fear locks</u> your *Triabrain* into a stalled state, where you constantly trigger toxic chemical reactions from the amygdala part of the brain. These reactions will bind your brain together and prevent it from reshaping.
3. <u>Fear tricks you</u> into turning your power against you. Fear makes you create your own hell, where you repeatedly think a dreadful situation will occur.

I wrote about the whole subject of fear in my first book ***Mathaphobia***. In it, I help people name fear. In my book, ***Mathaphobia***, I share how fear can have several names. Fear can take the form of "Quincy the Quitter." This is a person who becomes overwhelmed with the thought of asking for help. "Donna the Over Doer" is another fear personality. She will struggle for excessive hours, over-thinking everything to gain the approval of others. Consequently, Donna never learns the strategy to succeed. "Samuel the Struggler" gets angry when others do not understand the importance of his approaches. He becomes furious when he is misunderstood. "Crystal the Criticizer" blames others when she does something incorrectly. You have power when you can name your fear.

You must find the root cause of your fear. If you simply try to give yourself pep-talks to overcome fear, you will screw yourself over royally. Self-talk is damaging if you do not address the underlying issue of your fear. You cannot remove fear by tricking yourself into believing something that you do not believe 100%. If you try to self-talk yourself out of depression into happiness without investigating the root cause of your issue, you will make yourself mentally-unbalanced. A third of you will believe the worst, another third will cling to what you 'think' is right, and the last third of you will be on the fence about every decision you make. Your confidence will be destroyed in the process.

The only way to reshape your brain is to get down to the root issue of your fear: piece-by-piece. To remove fear, you must learn about the hidden beliefs that eat away at your sanity. Take courage in facing the issue, even if you are not conscious of what you are facing. For most, fear removal is not a one-day, 100% removal process. It takes years to completely remove layers of fear hidden within dark tar-like masses in your *Triabrain*.

I was 8 when I was sexually abused. Fortunately, I overcame that experience. I am not alone. It estimated that 1 out of every 5 women in the world experienced some form of sexual assault (Rape, 2016). For many years, I had no idea that feeling anxious was the direct result of the fear that resulted in sexual abuse (Boulware, 1998). Thus far, I've mentioned the more prevalent common results of how fear presents itself in people who have been sexually mistreated (Gynecology, 2013). Women who've experienced sexual assault often identify with one of the issues below:

- Developing a negative health image (always focusing on "imperfections" and "flaws")
- Difficulty trusting both men and women in close relationships
- Cutting your skin to feel pain in youth
- Excessive partying and risky social behavior
- Depression, anxiety or sadness upon waking
- Fear of intimacy or closeness with men (shying away from relationships)
- Difficulty with feeling sexual sensations
- Compulsive eating of sugar to numb abdominal pain
- Flashbacks of being a specific age for no conscious reason
- Problems concentrating and staying focused on the task at hand
- Sexual promiscuity or a loss of interest in sex

- Unexplained pelvic pain in your lower abdomen as a child, or horrific pelvic pain as an adult
- Excessive overwhelmed feeling when maintaining a normal routine or ordered life

Olivia (Continued from Chapter 4)

One night, Olivia noticed her gums were bleeding. She brushed extra well in that area, and noticed her gum pulsated afterward. Olivia could feel the blood flow from her gums. This sight terrified her. Olivia had already experienced three root canals. Past trauma consumed her thoughts, provoking her to cling to trauma instead of faith. She immediately assumed something was wrong. Olivia vividly recalled childhood reactions when encountering pain. Back then, she feared the outcome if faced with a pressing situation. As an adult, Olivia needed to grow out of believing something was wrong with her. Thus, I had Olivia perform the following exercise. Later she wrote back her results.

∞ LISTEN TO YOUR HIDDEN THOUGHTS EXERCISE ∞

1. Sit back in a chair and breathe deeply for 3 minutes. Breathe as deeply as you can. Eyes are closed.
2. Imagine a bubble around you. It is an invisible bubble that will tell you anything and everything about your body. While inside that bubble, ask to feel the parts of your body where there is tension or fearful thoughts that may be trapped. Search for this area according to where your body releases heat. You will have 1-3 areas that will stand out.
3. Place your right hand on the part of your body where heat is released or your invisible bubble indicates.
4. Now place your hand over each area again. Ask the invisible bubble to indicate areas where hidden thoughts are trapped. Write each thought down on a fresh sheet of paper.
5. Now breathe in deeply, and ask for love, peace, and guidance in your relationship with you. Take your "non-dominant" hand and cross out each thought one at a time on the piece of paper. Use your "non-dominant" hand to replace each thought with whatever comes to you. These are truths. Ask yourself if you're willing to accept these thoughts.

6. Embrace the replacement thoughts and acknowledge them. Program them into your *Triabrain* bubble. Imagine these thoughts now surrounding you.
7. Now, stand up and walk for 2-3 minutes. Thank yourself and the Creator for revealing the truth to you. Your brain and body will naturally adjust based on your new thoughts. These thoughts will bring you back to a place of peace.

Olivia wrote:

"I am getting better at listening to myself. You are right. My tooth was not the issue: it was my emotional state. I still plan to see a dentist for a checkup, but I am no longer in panic. The back of my right skull was not moving, my heart area felt tense and my left groin area was not moving (locked). I sat and listened to the hidden thoughts in these areas, while unaware that I was allowing panic to block my thoughts. Apparently, I needed to know that I am resilient and can adjust to new situations (according to the pain I was experiencing in the back of my head). According to my heart, I could love myself more by getting enough sleep. My groin area indicated the need for me to respect myself more for feeling "girly." Thank you, for helping me discover hidden thoughts in my body."

Reconnecting to Your Subconscious Through Journaling

You must establish a relationship with yourself to know who you are versus the chaos you experience. You benefit from knowing your feelings versus any fearful thoughts you may encounter. You must begin communicating with yourself on a regular basis. If not, you will constantly be drained by taking ownership of energy that is not yours. If this happens, co-dependency will result. You will become involved in an unhealthy enabling situation, providing excessive emotional and/or psychological support.

To express yourself to yourself, you must become knowledgeable about the different types of emotions that you can transform. Each emotion has an opposite feeling. Dr. David R. Hawkins in his book, *Power Versus Force,* created the ***Map of Consciousness***. This map serves as a conscious framework (Hawkins, 1995). Consciousness is not just being physically awake. It is the process of knowing the various parts of you. This awareness includes knowing your thoughts, emotions, sensations, surroundings and the power of your existence. It is a mathematical approach based on kinesiology to represent how you and I view reality.

Map of Consciousness

Developed by David R. Hawkins

The Map of Consciousness is based on a logarithmic scale that spans from 0 to 1000.

Name of Level	Energetic "Frequency"	Associated Emotional State	View of Life
Enlightenment	700-1000	Ineffable	Is
Peace	600	Bliss	Perfect
Joy	540	Serenity	Complete
Love	500	Reverence	Benign
Reason	400	Understanding	Meaningful
Acceptance	350	Forgiveness	Harmonious
Willingness	310	Optimism	Hopeful
Neutrality	250	Trust	Satisfactory
Courage	200	Affirmation	Feasible
Pride	175	Scorn	Demanding
Anger	150	Hate	Antagonistic
Desire	125	Craving	Disappointing
Fear	100	Anxiety	Frightening
Grief	75	Regret	Tragic
Apathy	50	Despair	Hopeless
Guilt	30	Blame	Evil
Shame	20	Humiliation	Miserable

Image 8-3: Dr. David Hawkins Map of Consciousness identifies that pride, anger, desperation, fear, grief, apathy, guilt, and shame reduces personal integrity. In turn, your brain energy is reduced. Note: In Dr. Hawkins' chart, the "emotion" is labeled as "LEVEL" in the left column.

Dr. David R. Hawkins' *Map of Consciousness* suggests that pride, anger, desperation, fear, grief, apathy, guilt, and shame reduces personal integrity. This *Map of Consciousness* identifies that integrity starts with courage and continues to neutrality, willingness, acceptance, and reason. As these feelings increase within you, self-love and joy develop. After extensive time loving yourself, you will gain joy and peace in situations. Subsequently, enlightenment is embodied within your brain and existence, which exudes throughout your *Triabrain* field. Anyone who meets you will be automatically transformed by your presence alone.

Kinesiology was used by Dr. Hawkins to create the *Map of Consciousness* scale from 0 to 1000 points. Per his theory, the map represents the highest consciousness available to humans. The lowest consciousness is shame scoring 20 out of 1000 points. The second lowest is guilt at 30 out of 1000. Fear is in the mid-to-low range as 100 out of 1000, with anger rating slightly higher at 150.

Each of these emotions has opposite feelings on the other side of the spectrum. Once shame is removed it must be replaced by something that has an energy level higher than courage. One such replacement can be peace, which scores 600 out of 1000. Once guilt is removed, you can replace the emotion with joy, which scores 540, for example. Reason combats fear, and reason scores 400. The whole idea is that shame, guilt, apathy, grief, fear, desperation, anger, and pride are all emotions that can be transformed into beneficial feelings for your *Triabrain* connection.

There is no better way to become knowledgeable about your true feelings other than asking your subconscious to help you reach this level of awareness. One way to become self-aware is through journaling. For me, the power of journaling manifested while healing from my own painful memories. Journaling is an excellent practice to simultaneously activate the left and right sides of the brain. This concurrent activity triggers connections. These connections allow the brain to start activating. When your brain actively moves, it breaks up brainbrink and reshapes.

When you typically write information, you are using logic to express time and places of events. You are using your right brain to express emotions. If you are right-handed, you are using parts of your left brain. And if you are left-handed, you are using parts of your right brain. However, when you write with both hands (ambidextrous), you use more than just your left and your right hands. You access your conscious and subconscious mind. To better explain, the conscious mind refers to things that you remember. And the subconscious mind accesses a mental activity that functions just below your threshold of your awareness, where all experiences are stored as sensory data. This is the part of your awareness where memories of fear are stored and repressed.

∞ Right Hand - Left Hand Journaling Exercise ∞.

1. The way tap into your subconscious mind is to perform two actions. First, you write to yourself. Express how you *think* you feel about a certain situation. Express what you consciously are experiencing.
2. Take a break and read the letter back to yourself. Identify emotions that you are experiencing. Shame, guilt, apathy, grief, fear, desperation, anger, and pride are all emotions that can be transformed into beneficial feelings that will serve you.
3. Take a break. Do something that takes your mind off these feelings for 5 minutes.
4. After a 5-minute break, return to your letter. Using your "non-dominant" hand, write a response letter to yourself.
5. Write whatever thoughts come to you. Thoughts will come to your head. Or, you may hear sentences. You will experience heart-filled messages. Write them down. There is no right or wrong way to retrieve messages. Simply capture the feeling or thought that resonates. Write the message. You can trust whatever comes to you in this process because it is you talking to yourself.
6. Read the message that you wrote to yourself.
7. Which feeling did your higher-self tell you that you needed? Enlightenment? Peace? Joy? Love? Reason? Acceptance? Willingness? Neutrality? Courage?
8. Listen to what you are telling yourself and follow that advice. You are using your intuition to bring enlightenment to your path.

Reconnecting to Pleasure

The foundation for the following *Pleasure Principle Exercise* was introduced to me through Sean Wolf of *The Body Restoration Clinic* in San Jose, Calif. He explained that by practicing the *VOILA Method* energy is removed; and it must be replaced with beneficial feelings. Without performing this replacement, there is an open space where toxic brainbrink resided. However, once brainbrink is removed, this open space is "refillable." You have the choice on how to "refill your feelings."

I asked how to avoid refilling this space with toxic emotions again. And Mr. Wolf sent me a video clip from *Harry Potter & The Prisoner of Azkaban*. I was puzzled and asked, "What is this video for?" He said, watch the "*Expecto Petronum*" spell that appears in this movie. *Expecto Petronum* is a defensive charm spell used to protect against Dementors by summoning one's happiest memories.

In Latin, "expecto patronum" means, "I await a patron." What's more, the patron is the Latin translation for the word "protector." In ancient Rome, a "patronum" was a person of authority who helped with all your legal, business and life transactions (Ellen, 2012). This person would argue on your behalf, and you were so confident of their expertise that you didn't fear the outcome. Yes, the patron was your protector. An ancient spirit of peace was given during the most difficult trials.

Although the ***Harry Potter*** movie clip was a fictitious spell, it is adapted to create an effective *Triabrain* reconnection technique, which helps you use the faith sector of your brain in conjunction with your right brain. If you know that you are protected, you regain peace. For, peace helps break up the effects of toxic brainbrink and keeps the *Triabrain's* open space available for more pleasant experiences.

The following exercise is designed to rewire the chemical response in your human brain during fearful situations. This experience helps you NOT create more painful chemical reactions; it fights them off for you. When we experience pleasure in the body, endorphins are released. You can program your brain to do this amid any stressful situation. People who have undergone major life trials will benefit from this exercise the most. For there is a deeper capacity in their brains to hold new pleasant experiences. Within this exercise, you are commanding your brain to release peaceful endorphins in lieu of harmful cortisol.

∞ Expecto Petronum Pleasure Principle ∞

1. You must envision the happiest memory you can recall (the happier the memory, the better your brain neurons will connect).
2. Rub your hands together. Separate them so your hands are 3 inches apart.
3. Look between your hands, feel the energy and think "wonderful moments."
4. Then create circles around your eyes by moving your hands like windshield wipers across your face. Do this for a good 30 seconds. (When you do this exercise for over 30 days, you can skip this step.)

5. Think of pure, loving, holy protection and acceptance while you are thinking of your fondest memory. Is it being with a parent? Is it with a person who passed on to Heaven? What is your fondest memory when you were really young?
6. Hold on to that memory. And let it sink into every fiber in your body.
7. Say "expecto patronum."
8. Overlay that memory with what you see directly in front of you.
9. Tune in the way that your body internally feels as you think of this pleasant memory. Hold on to this feeling through ANY challenging experiences. And overlay that experience over any stressful situation that you undergo in the future.

As mentioned in the previous chapter, overcoming trauma depends on consciously knowing the truth surrounding painful situations. Many times, you may not to know your hidden emotions, unless you delve deep inside of yourself for the answers. And when you take the time to dig deep inside of yourself, you will find out what truly eats away at your being. Removing the energy of fear helps you in knowing the truth. Journaling offers a person the ability to understand his deepest desires and fears. And, the *Expecto Petronum Pleasure* Exercise will help you combat future fearful situations.

RECONNECTION #2: Take back your power in the form of choice.

When your emotions are deeply embedded in your being and your self-help efforts do not work, you would likely benefit from professional counseling. Healing methods are the best investment that you can make into a complete restoration. It is an excellent resource for people who desire to become the best version of them. These people are pulled into the *Success Radius.*

If you have lived in drama with a lack of romance, then your saga can end with professional help! Skilled mental professionals can assist in your efforts to regain your power. Counselors help you make wise decisions when selecting your best future. Therapists also help remove chaotic toxic energy and transform it into peaceful love.

Please note: your friends are not professional counselors. Friends are not the best people to provide advice. Most of your friends struggle with their own problems, and they are not skilled with the medical terminology and brain knowledge that you need. So, do not go to a friend thinking that she or he will solve your problems. Your friends are simply in your life to offer "friendly" support. If you think they will solve your problems, that behavior is a form of codependency. So, there is another approach that will assist on a greater level.

The most effective way to take back your power is through understanding your power of choice. By going to a professional counselor, you can learn about the powerful choices available. I must emphasize the importance of therapeutic resource. When my mother was in her accident, I saw her head bashed open before she went into surgery. Although my spirit is better, I was haunted by visions of seeing my mother's head split open. When I ate, I saw her head. When I studied, I saw her head. When I went to sleep, I saw her head again. I was suffering from a situational type of post-traumatic stress. After receiving counseling, I still remembered the event; however, the experience no longer provoked horrific memories. And when I replayed the event in my mind, I could see the situation as a fact without being attached to it. Counseling will help you remove painful memories, so you can see the situation for what it is, instead of the situation being clouded by fear.

Counselling is the most effective way for you to become aware of your thoughts, hidden beliefs and reasons for your feelings about certain situations. Often referred to as "therapists," these individuals come in many different forms. Licensed Clinical Social Workers (LCSWs): Licensing requirements vary by state, but LCSWs hold graduate degrees and typically have at least two years of clinical social work experience. LCSWs may provide individual, family, or couples therapy. They often work in schools, public health and medical fields, or other community and group settings.

Licensed Addiction Counselors (LACs): LACs are not typically referred to as therapists, but they may practice alongside therapists. Typically, LACs have a bachelor's degree and will have a minimum of one year of training in addiction counseling.

Internationally trained VOILA Practitioners are physical movement counselors. They are not credentialed as mental therapists, but they may practice alongside therapists to bring out emotions at a faster rate using Cranial-Sacral Kinesiology applications. VOILA practitioners identify emotional triggers in the body. Typically, VOILA Practitioners have some medical experience or biological training and will have a minimum of one year of Advanced VOILA Method training.

Licensed Marriage and Family Therapists (LMFTs): LMFTs, who focus primarily on marriage and family therapy, will have a master's degree and typically must complete an internship before practicing. Each one of these medical professionals have the same goal: help you become aware of which emotions are blocking your feelings. These professionals treat a variety of issues.

- Anxiety
- Depression
- Mood issues
- Post-traumatic stress
- Obsessions and compulsions
- Chronic fatigue syndrome (CFS)
- Irritable bowel syndrome (IBS)
- Substance dependency
- Phobias
- Eating disorders
- Persistent pain
- Erratic sleep patterns
- Sexual issues
- Anger management issues

These are the different types of therapy that will help with repowering the brain to effectively function:

- **Cognitive behavioral therapy** - Cognitive behavioral therapy is grounded in the belief that it is a person's perception of events—rather than the events themselves—that determine how he or she will feel and act. Cognitive behavioral therapists believe that by adjusting your thoughts, you can directly influence your emotions and behavior. This adjustment process is referred to as cognitive restructuring. The cognitive behavioral process is based on an educational model where individuals in therapy are made aware of negative reactions and agree to learn new, positive emotional and behavioral reactions to challenging situations. Overwhelming problems are broken down into smaller manageable parts. Clients are shown how to set and reach short-term goals. More importantly, professional therapists help clients readjust thoughts, feelings and reactions to prep future, challenging situations. Changing attitudes and behaviors can help people learn to address specific issues in positive and productive ways (Ellis & Beck, 2007).
- **Eye Movement Desensitization and Reprocessing (EMDR)** - EMDR therapy is an eight-phase approach that identifies and processes memories of negative and traumatic events that contribute to present-day problems. After the person in therapy briefly accesses an unresolved memory, he or she will focus on external stimulus delivered by the therapist. There are two key reasons why EMDR therapy is effective. As you may recall in Chapter 6, eye movements along with how light refracts in the eyes, enhance the efficacy of therapeutic treatment through neurological transformation. These neurological changes assist clients in removing negative memories associated with distress. Scientific research has also indicated that

this type of eye movement is an internal desensitization to the emotional reaction to memory (Shapiro, 2017).

- **Hypnotherapy** – This approach creates a hypnotic state in which the client increases motivation or alters a behavior pattern through hypnosis. The professional consults with the client to determine the nature of the problem. The therapist begins explaining how hypnosis works and what the client will experience. The professional will perform a series of tests to determine degrees of physical and emotional suggestibility. The professional then induces a hypnotic state in the client using individualized methods and techniques of hypnosis based on test results and analysis of client's problem. There are many skilled professionals in self-hypnosis conditioning.
- **VOILA Method Therapy** – This approach merges cranial sacral adjustments with hypnosis and cognitive behavioral therapy to remove physical pain in the body. During the session, the client shares the physical ailment he or she faces. An assessment is made by the professional to determine the root cause of the issue (physical, emotional or mental). The VOILA professional then removes the unconscious thought associated with pain. The professional then helps the client become aware of a new thought selected by the client. A new thought-to-body-cranial movement replaces the toxic emotion and re-creates muscle and joint balance in the body. VOILA Method founder, Joel Crandall, trains kinesiologists, physical therapists, chiropractors and therapists to integrate these techniques in physical assessments.

Ann and Robert

(Continued from Chapter 3)

After their night of passion, Ann chooses to listen to Robert regarding taking preventative measures. Ann heard him loud and clear. She decides to take emergency contraception to avoid pregnancy. This fractal moment served to unlock hidden emotions in Ann which were designed to transform her mental state to success. Ann realized the need to reinvestigate why she thought she needed a husband and a child.

Ann and Robert continued dating for three more months.

Ann took responsibility for her choices and went to a psychological counselor and a VOILA therapist to work through transforming her emotions. In doing so, she began seeing her true desires. She originally believed that motherhood and marriage would offer her maternal life and self-worth. However, through counseling, Ann began seeing innate nurturing traits.

Through therapy, Ann saw that a husband and child were not necessary to validate her womanly worth. Her eyes "opened" to a new self-perception. Ann decided not to focus on marriage or children because her true passion was making a difference through her career. More importantly, she now felt she owed herself the opportunity to see what she could professionally accomplish.

As Ann transformed her emotions into healing feelings, she knew she desired to be the only woman in Robert's life. Ann gave Robert a choice. Ann asked him if he wanted to offer an exclusive dating relationship. If his answer were "Yes," Ann would agree to continue dating Robert. However, if he said, "no," then Ann was intent upon ending the relationship. Robert said, "No," which prompted Ann to take back her power. She said that although she had feelings for Robert, she had to honor herself and leave. Ann thanked Robert for his care and decided that if he were not willing to exclusively date her, another man would welcome this opportunity.

Although Robert masked his true feelings through an angry response, Ann's decision crushes him. He felt upset that Ann did not want to be with him. Her decision caused him to reevaluate himself. Ann's renewed power made Robert realize what he too wanted from life. After Ann left, Robert was with other women but was unsatisfied. He began to see how much he truly desired a supportive, loving person in his life. Robert desired a true woman with joy. He looked at his life and began seeing how unfulfilled he was with his current friends and sexual relationships. Robert's addictions no longer helped him cope.

Through a series of events, Robert decides to enroll in VOILA therapy to overcome past traumatic experiences. Because of this healing process, he learns to become free from addictive behavior. Robert finds honesty self-integrity and satisfaction from daily experiences. As a result, he creates new income revenue based on coaching techniques. More importantly, Robert makes peace with his deceased parents.

Later that year, Robert returns to Ann's life regularly. He asks Ann for the opportunity to date her exclusively. At that moment, Ann has men who are pursuing her. Nevertheless, Ann agrees to date Robert: he was the only man that captured her heart. After receiving VOILA therapy, Robert gains the courage to experience love with one woman. Thus, he forms a devoted relationship with Ann, where they grow together through life's many challenges. Robert supports Ann's celebrity career, while she supports Robert in becoming a business mogul. Together, they are a powerful team that helps humanity. Within two years, Robert asks Ann to be his wife.

A professional can find links to your patterned behavior. Counselors can determine the root sources of your traumatic experience and conclude how cycles operate. Therapists can also determine the psychological interactions between you and the people in your life. Counseling is a great resource to help you regain decision-making abilities. You have options in this life, and therapists can help you make wise decisions.

∞ Finding A Counselor Exercise ∞

1. Decide that you need help from a professional. The professional can be a psychiatrist, a psychologist, or a trauma specialist. It can even be a spiritual counselor such as a pastor, rabbi, priest or another religious leader.
2. Determine your budget and time you will set aside every week to meet with this person. How much time can you create for helping yourself? Go to your calendar and select times when you can regularly meet.
3. Determine your budget for therapy. Set aside money to invest in personal growth. If you have no money, there are still counseling centers willing to work on sliding scales. In other words, many health agencies will offer to help based on your limited budget. To find a list of these individuals, find your nearest hospital, and ask to speak with the social worker on staff. He or she will provide a list of local counselors. If you are a college student, there is free personal counseling available on all campuses. And if you are a full-time employee, there is usually free counseling available for employees. To find locations and available appointment hours, contact your Human Resources benefits department.
4. Write a list of 3 things that you need help doing within the next six months. It can be overcoming break up. Finding a new job. Learning to deal with difficult parents or children. Learning how to study correctly. When you have a plan of action, it becomes easier for someone to help you.
5. Select a person, and ask for help. Help can be in regular talking seasons. It can be through hypnotherapy. It can be within EMDR. It can be through the VOILA Method. In any case, ask about the process for your treatment.
6. Request homework from the person who you choose to visit. And write down what you learned from each session on a separate sheet

of paper. This education can be written in a journal or in a notebook that you can reference for months and years later.

7. Have confidence that your new thoughts will help change the way that you feel inside of yourself.

THE END

RECONNECTION #3: Be honest with yourself and decipher the types of relationships that you are attracting versus wanting to build.

If you no longer want to expect to be let down, you must no longer let yourself down. If you want to connect yourself to the life you desire, you must be 100% honest with who you are now. You are the only person on this planet who can lift yourself up and expect greatness. The relationship you have with yourself is the most powerful, meaningful, influential relationship you can maintain.

Your Relationships Help You Know Yourself

Part of the power to overcome is simple. You must harness the ability to see your relationships as they are, without making them something that they are not. The relationship you have with yourself and the relationship you have with other people cultivate your ability to build inner strength. And your brain's ability to overcome is unleashed by deciphering which relationships promote personal growth.

In life, you must be honest with the types of people you are attracting. As mentioned in Chapter 5, you will always attract three types of people: (1.) Many of them struggle with the same issues as you (in certain areas); (2.) Some overcome issues that you seek to resolve; and (3.) Countless others mirror your persona.

It is your job to determine which types of people you allow in your presence. You must ask yourself some key questions. *Do they have the answer to an issue that you are actively trying to resolve? Are they complaining about a situation they are unwilling to fix? Or, is this person exhibiting characteristics that bother you?* You must be brutally honest with yourself. Through your discernment, you will discover which relationship is draining, and which relationship provides energy on an equal exchange. You will find the path to your success.

People who struggle the same way:

Richard and William both wanted to be a cinematographer. They both graduated from a top film school. Richard was gregarious and an extrovert, where he constantly met people in the industry and frequently offered his resume. On the other hand, William is quiet and considered an introvert. He sent resumes online and sat at home watching movies. Richard got a job and asked William if he attended networking events as well. William felt insecure because of Richard's progression. Within time, William stopped taking Richard's calls and no longer wanted to socialize with him. While attending a party together, William yells at Richard. At this point, William was extremely frustrated by Richard's successful career. William's irritation finally reached the breaking point.

People who help you point the way:

Dawn is a part-time professor who wants to write an autobiography. She meets Sally and discovers Sally owns a book publishing company. Dawn and Sally become friends. Because of their friendship, Dawn learns to start her own business. Sally also learns how to become a community college professor.

People who reflect you:

Christian is frustrated over his job. He is agitated every time he works late hours. When he goes to the grocery store, Christian sees a cashier who also appears discouraged about her current job. Christian realizes his reaction to the cashier is in direct correlation to how he views his job.

In order develop a powerful relationship with yourself, you must be willing to acknowledge how the people you attract mirror yourself. Attraction allows you to draw in the most beautiful chaos principles that exist. When you recognize how people mirror you, you are empowered to make changes to your brain and life.

Brad

Brad is a man who has experienced major issues regarding love and relationships. His mother raised him until the age of 10, at which time his mother gave him away to his grandfather. At the same time, Brad's grandfather desired to raise Brad's other two siblings. His mother was an addict and never raised him. As a result, Brad would seek a mother figure from the women he was dating later in his life.

His first marriage was to a woman who abused prescription drugs during their child's pregnancy. He divorces his first wife then marries another addict. Brad divorces his second wife and marries a third time to another addict.

Through the ups and downs of each marriage, Brad never realizes that he is the addict. He needed love at any cost and failed to see that he could give healthy love to himself.

Returning Another Person's Crap

Let's face it. Sometimes you encounter friends, family members, coworkers or others that inflict their pain on you. You know it is not your emotion. It is solely 100% their funky attitude toward you! They are trying to impose negativity on you. We all know people who behave in this manner. However, they behave, you become upset. Because of their inconsiderate actions, your mood starts to change. Well, there is good news. You don't have to take that crap. You can give it back to them. The following exercise will help you let go of other people's negative energy so that you can move forward in peace.

∞ Give Back Their Crap Exercise ∞

Level One

1. You can be anywhere. Simply focus on your body.
2. Think of your large *Triabrain* bubble surrounding you. Envision your organs and feel where you feel the stress. Is it in your stomach? Hip, neck, shoulder, or back?
3. Place your right hand on the part of your body experiencing stress or pain.
4. Place your left hand on the part of your body where you feel calm.
5. Use your right hand to "suck the energy" from the uneasy area out of your body.
6. Continue to "mentally" remove the agitation until it is eliminated and covering the palm of your right hand.
7. Say, "Cancel, clear, delete from my being."
8. Mentally send the energy from your right hand into the ground and bury it.
9. Thank God (the Creator) for being restored with the new feeling of peace.

Level Two

1. You can be anywhere. Simply focus on your body.
2. Think of your large Triabrain bubble around you. Envision your organs and sense where you feel the stress. Is it in your throat? Ankle, shoulder, or back?
3. Wherever you feel it, imagine pulling it fully out of you.
4. Ask "who it is from."
5. Continue to remove the feeling out of your body until it is 100% out of you.
6. Say, "Cancel, clear, delete," from my being.
7. Now, imagine rolling all that toxic energy into a large area rug.
8. And, now imagine placing the area rug on the ground next to that person's feet.
9. Feel the guarantee. You truly gave it back. And you may receive a surprising response.

Know Your Power in Attracting Energy

You have the power to attract anyone you need into your life. You can use brainpower to help consciously choose your relationships. However, it requires you to change first.

The act of burning has been symbolic for ages to activate new growth and transformation. Burning is a major concept within my Native American heritage. The controlled burning of forests was used profoundly as honoring The Creator. Burning promoted new growth and introduced nutrients needed to sustain a harmonious new life. Burning is also a method of healing. In ceremonies, burning is the pathway leading to harmony with self, the tribe, and the environment. Fire ceremonies are wonderful during a New Moon when you want to introduce newness into your life. The following Native American-inspired exercise is simple and empowering.

∞ Attracting Healthy Relationships Exercise ∞

1. Take out three sheets of paper. Label one paper "Sheet #1". Label the next "Sheet #2". Label the last paper, "Sheet #3."
2. (On Sheet #1) Decide what type of relationship you desire to have in your life. List at least ten qualities of how you desire the other person to act in the relationship. (If it is romantic, define the type of love you desire. If it is for your career, define the type of work relationship you want.)
3. (On Sheet #2) Be honest with yourself. Rewrite the list. Make an honest assessment. Do you show those traits daily within yourself? Go down the list. Place a check mark next to the traits that you exhibit. Place an (an "X") next to the ones that you do not.
4. Answer this question for yourself on Sheet #2: When you do not show the qualities that you seek in other people, what emotions do you experience? Are you angry, fearful, ashamed, distraught, and disappointed? Be real with yourself. How do you feel? Use extra sheets if necessary.
5. (Sheet #3) Now, using your non-dominant hand, write out new emotions. Describe how you desire to feel about yourself. List the actions you will choose to help carry out this new way of life. Let your intuition guide you in your response. Listen to your heart. The words will organically manifest. Simply, write these thoughts. Use extra sheets if necessary.
6. Read over all three sheets of papers.
7. Thank yourself. Pat yourself on the back.
8. Thank God for the opportunity to make adjustments in the upcoming days and years.
9. In an outside open area, take sheets #2 and Sheet #3 and burn them in a shallow pan where you can save all the ashes.
10. Immediately bury the ashes in the dirt after burning the papers. Burying the ashes is a symbol that you are taking the emotion out of you, transforming it through fire, and allowing new growth to happen within you.
11. Keep Sheet #1 with you regularly to remind you of this ongoing transformation.

THE END

Dawn

Dawn's family member was in the hospital, and she felt overwhelmed. She struggled to get up and go to work daily. She wanted to share the truth about what happened, but she kept up a facade. She wanted to appear that she could handle everything. Secretly, Dawn wished that she had more female friends as confidants.

Dawn performed the burning exercise one night. After the exercise, she realized that she was not upfront, and honest with people about her life. Dawn noticed how she continually attracts people who back out on her. She realized that she needs to be honest with herself.

She performed the Attracting Healthy Relationships Exercise. In the morning, she buried the ashes. That day she was running six minutes late to work. Her dean met her in the hall and asked if everything was okay. Dawn lied and said yes. Realizing that she was not open and honest with the person she desired to become, Dawn felt compelled to go to the dean and share the truth. She disclosed that she felt overwhelmed because her family members were facing criminal charges. Dawn apologized for being late to school, she honored her job and the dean's leadership role.

Dawn's sincerity changed her life. The dean listened to her with empathy and offered her psychological counseling through her job. Dawn's decision to be open with herself was the first honest relationship that she formed. The second sincere female relationship was with her dean. Today, Dawn has several sincere female friends who are reliable.

When a person has healthy personal relationships, their life expression is balanced within the right brain. You feel as if you can talk to others and share your emotions freely. You will know how close or far others should be within your personal space. You will have confidence in how you feel about certain situations. You will also know how to add space between you and others when situations are unhealthy. These are ways that the right brain reshapes and connects itself to the faith sector, through your intuition, then to the left side's logic.

You can turn on and reconnect your right brain. In turn, you will begin to have a healthy relationship with yourself and with others in a way that will permanently stimulate you and unleash your brainpower. Plus, you will be able to talk to people one-on-one without the use of cell phones in your hands or pockets.

In the next chapter, you will learn how to connect your left brain with fun and practical exercises. You will learn how to use your resources to create something out of nothing.

Unleashing Your Left-Brain Power

Chapter 9

Unleashing Your Left-Brain Power

The innovation of creating something out of nothing.

Notice these numbers.

I had three weeks of Summer Break from teaching mathematics at the college campus. I was driving 40 miles each way, to and from campus four days-a-week. I was happy to have a least a small bit of a summer vacation. On one of the days off, I decided to visit my sister and niece. While traveling to see them, I started feeling extremely hot. I naturally assumed the air conditioning was not working. So, I called my friend, Nick, and made an appointment to have my car examined on the following day. When driving back home from my sister's home, I started feeling hot again. I don't get sick often: yet I sensed my body was attempting to communicate to me. Something was wrong.

I look at the temperature gauge on the car, and it was on "H" HOT. I had never experienced this gauge reading on the dash of my reliable Honda Accord. Although it had nearly 190,000 freeway miles, my car still operated like it was brand new! My car had 34,000 miles when I purchased it. Since that time, I faithfully performed routine maintenance, including quarterly oil changes. Nevertheless, something major was happening within the interior of the vehicle. As an engineer, I went into a non-logical mode for a "hot second."

Using my Bluetooth, I called my step-dad and said, "Nick, the car is on Hot. What should I do?"

He says, "Where are you?"

I say, "On the freeway."

Nick says, "Get off the freeway! The engine is about to be damaged. Turn the heater on to let the hot air out. Running the heater should help," Nick suggested. He warned, "Don't drive anywhere for a few minutes! How far are you from home? Where are you?"

I respond, "I am an hour and a half away."

Concerned Nick says, "Damn it! Well, you're going to have to wait it out for at least a half hour. Or, as much as 40 minutes."

"Okay, Nick. I have gotten off the freeway. I will wait for the car to cool down. I have the heater on, and it is still on HOT. I am not going to risk driving the car any longer. I will call you back shortly."

Immediately after the phone call, I had to be quick on my feet. I needed to return home safely. Plus, I had an appointment across town in 45 minutes that I was not going to make. I also had a medical appointment the next day. I needed my car. So, I had to find a way out of the situation.

I thought, "*What are my resources?*"

Immediately, I remembered that I had emergency roadside assistance through American Automobile Association (AAA).

I called AAA and met the nicest man, who helped me tow my car back 37 miles. It was after 6 p.m., so the local car rental shops had closed. I had to wait the next day for a rental car, which I paid $25 a day. Afterward, I began to wonder if my car's engine was okay.

I looked online to determine the value of my trusty Honda Accord. According to Blue Book standards, my old car was barely worth a few thousand dollars. I was in the middle of writing a second book, and my finances were going to the book production and marketing. And it was not intended for a car.

I began experiencing anxiety, because I lacked the money to buy a new car. Without knowing the full facts of the situation, I started "freaking out." My Honda had been reliable up to this point. I could not jump to conclusions.

Sometimes, a way out of a situation requires pure logic and deductive reasoning. I sincerely hoped that my car would be okay to transport me from San Pedro back to Sherman Oaks. Nevertheless, wishful thinking would not have physically transported me home unless I took actions. Fantasy thinking would not have provided the strategy to take my car off the road and tow it to the repair shop. Faith needed to be combined with action to transform this situation.

I had a major decision to make: What do I do with my car if repairs cost more than the car's value? Do I invest the money designated for the new book into buying a new car? Or, should I bank on my talents to bring in future income to buy a much better car in months to come?

Weighing out your options logically is sometimes the most direct way to accomplish immediate goals. Measurable results are not a fantasy. Numerical results are methods to pull you closer to the success radius.

After weighing my options, I chose to repair the car. I set a portion of the money aside for the future down payment, if needed. I chose to allow my talents to speak for themselves and secure new speaking gigs within the first 30 days of the book's release. With this money, I could buy a new car outright. This decision to invest resources into a suitable outcome was more beneficial than I could imagine.

The point of this story is simple. Please consider three main take-aways:

1. Your world is not real until it is measurable. Numbers, as you read in this story are key to understanding when to continue or stop.
2. Your passion is not attainable until it transforms into something tangible. Whether it be a car, income, an engine, healthy body, clear mind, or new book, your thoughts are meant to create something innovative.
3. You can have all the great ideas in the world. But if you cannot make your talents work for your benefit, your thoughts are simply worthless. You are worth passion, thought, and love. The result is the birth of innovative greatness.

And you can bank on yourself. For you deserve the finest things life can offer you. The question is, will you connect your talents and logic to reach them?

Plain and simple, you must have corresponding actions to passionately create something that is physical that you can touch, taste and love. This creation is the meaning of innovation.

LEFT TRIABRAIN BLUEPRINT FOR RECONNECTION (FTBR)

The Left *Triabrain* Blueprint represents the brain sector that embraces the physical world while attempting to map and understand relationships between all things in space and time. This brain sector is responsible for all math and science applications, bodily movement and brain activity during task execution. This section of the brain develops logic and advances current technology for advanced survival. This scientific brain's mission is to gain knowledge about the nature of tangible objects in space and time. It regulates logic and creates physical boundaries as a way to efficiently use resources. It builds theories through observations, experimental investigation, and explains theories of physical phenomena. This brain sector interprets and predicts cause and effect behavior, foretelling future events.

In Chapter 4 you took the self-test to help you determine how your faith brain was disconnected. The following parts give a summary of how each brainbrink can be reversed using the left *Triabrain*. If your primary score in that section was, *"Rejecting Logic, Embracing Fantasy,"* then you would want to pay close attention to the first *Triabrain* reconnection principle in this section: *"Decide to investigate the facts of the situation, instead of sugarcoating your reality."* If your primary score in Chapter 4 was, *"Subtracting Science and Only Adding God,"* you would benefit from reading the second reconnection principle, *"Decide to understand the way real life works, including science and math."* If your top score was, *"Overlooking Resources, and Struggling for Scraps,"* then be prepared to see things in a new way within the third reconnection principle, *"Identify and use your resources in new ways, expecting a new replacement."* The chart below lays out your plan of action. But first, it is important to understand why your *Triabrain* disconnected in the first place.

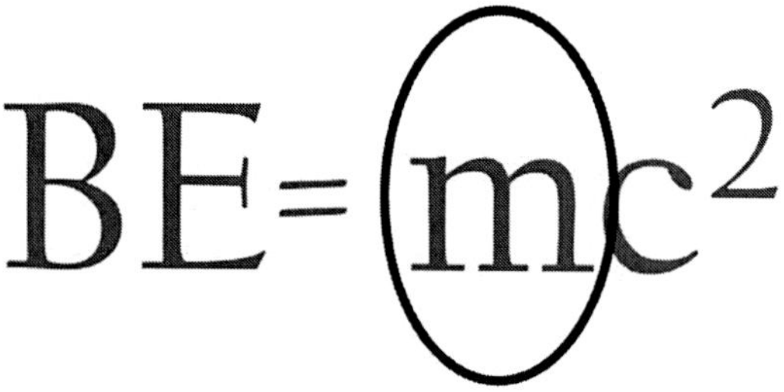

Image 9-1: The Triabrain Theory of Relativity focuses on the mass in your brain that serves to create the pathways and logic needed for action.

Brainbrink Disconnection Toxic Emotions	**Triabrain Reconnection Principle (Left Triabrain Blueprint)**	**Score Index (Results from the Self -Test in Chapter 4)**
1. Rejecting Logic, Embracing Fantasy	1. Decide to investigate the facts of the situation instead of sugarcoating your reality.	• Primary focus if your score is 20 and up. • Secondary priority if your score is 15 -19. • Third priority if your score is 0-14.

2. Subtracting Science, and Only Adding God	2. Decide to understand the way the real life works, including science and math.	• Primary focus if your score is 20 and up. • Secondary priority if your score is 15 -19. • Third priority if your score is 0-14.
3. Overlooking Resources, and Struggling for Scraps	3. Identify and use your resources in new ways, expecting a new replacement.	• Primary focus if your score is 20 and up. • Secondary priority if your score is 15 -19. • Third priority if your score is 0-14.

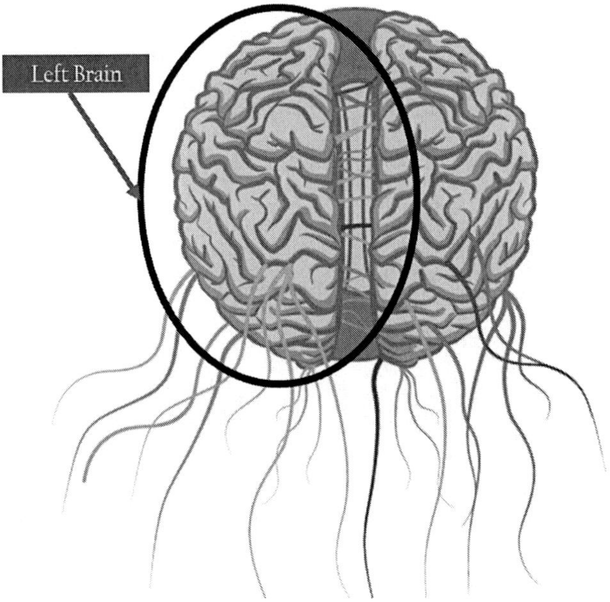

Image 9-2: The Logical Left Brain

Why on Earth does the left Triabrain disconnect?

To reconnect the left brain, you must know what disconnected it in the first place. From the ages of 10 – 17, a person forms their view of how the world will support them or work against their goals. The teen can have no education of science, or be in an environment where science, resources, and logic are highly valued. It does not matter if a teen is from a wealthy home, an impoverished home, or any other situation. The scientific impact is the same.

From the ages of 10 – 17, a person makes a conscious decision to accept or reject her logic and resources. She determines if her resources are enough to succeed in life. Somewhere during this time, the individual will encounter a situation that will make her question her problem-solving skills. It can range from transferring to a new school, experiencing financial hardship at home, dealing with a parent's legal troubles, or failing math and science classes. The person exists in an environment of "lack." In turn, the person loses the ability to allow logical pathways to reveal available resources. Because of this challenging experience, a person's left brain becomes imbalanced.

Reconnection Principle: Realize that Rebuilding Mass = Using of Resources & Science to Solve Problems (Rebuilding the Left Brain)

It is your job to accept that every situation happens for a reason which may or may not be controllable. Each time you endure difficulties, you can use innate gifts for discovering viable resources. It is a chance to prove that you can change your life. There is a beneficial outcome in every situation if you realize the situation is designed to help you secure your brain's adaptiveness. By experiencing obstacles, you are strengthening your executive problem-solving mind. If you accept such tests, you will reconnect your logical left brain. To start the process, you can embrace these three steps:

1. Recognize you have viable resources within yourself and your environment. These conduct energy and point to your success.
2. Physical failures are meant to point in the direction that is most beneficial.
3. People you meet will point to resources and serve as connectors.

∞ Forgiving Your Educational Systems Exercise ∞

Allocate at least an hour for this exercise.

1. Find several sheets of paper. Sit in a quiet space, with feet planted firmly on the floor.
2. Think back to a time (or a series of times) when you lost complete faith in your skills to achieve a goal.

(ON SHEET#1)

3. Write a letter to either a teacher, parent or friend, educational environment or training center who was a part of the discouraging situation. Release all your thoughts and emotions regarding your desire

of being better prepared. No human will ever see this paper except you. Let everything go onto this sheet of paper. (This process may take several sheets of paper.)

4. Now breathe deeply ten times, preferably through your nose. Deeply inhale deep air, expanding far into your groin as possible.
5. Now, reread the letter. Look at the letter. Feel the letter with all its energy. Capture any emotion you feel. Imagine pulling those feelings out of you and attaching them to the letter. Capture any emotion that prevents you from using your resources. Attach those emotions to the letter.
6. For any educational environment or training system that provokes anger, give it to God by *mentally* thinking and feeling, *"I am giving this to you God."* Imagine a pure, white light completely burning through the letter and all its pages.

(ON SHEET#2)

7. Now on new sheets of paper, write a letter to your past self. Tell your past self all the beneficial skills and resources that you wish you would have known when you were undergoing that experience. Pretend you can go back in time and give this letter to your younger self. Share important life lessons you wish you could tell your former self.
8. Now, when you are ready, forgive your teacher(s)/mentor(s) (alive or deceased) for placing you in a situation where you did not know how to find the answer to tough circumstances. What powerful feeling about your resourcefulness did you discover?

(ON SHEET#3)

9. Now, when you are ready, forgive yourself from low, self-esteem thoughts during demanding situations that caused anxiety.
10. Now commit to you and your past self. Write down how you will commit to using every suitable and available resource to find new ways of performing tasks in your life. Remind yourself how you can constantly find new ways to accomplish tasks.
11. And ask God to provide you new insight to use what you already have in building what you will need in the future.
12. Your newfound trust in personal skills will now attract the resources you need to change your life.
13. Keep these sheets of paper for another powerful exercise in the last chapter.

RECONNECTION #1: Decide to investigate the facts of the situation instead of sugar coating your reality.

I always wanted to be a professional speaker. And I continually saw myself speaking in front of large audiences. I was 12 when I envisioned myself helping people through motivational talks. Years passed, and I began my studies in the science field. I attended a university with highly-intelligent people. Fortunately, I gained a corporate engineering job at the location where some of my friends were employed. I distinctly recall one special friend, "Thomas." As with all the other names in this book, I have changed Thomas' name to keep him anonymous.

Thomas was a fellow engineer who I truly admired. A few years older than I, he was a reputable African-American alumnus. He graduated in Engineering from the same campus. Many alumni knew him. Thomas was also well-known at work. Every Christmas, Thomas and his wife would hold get-togethers for Kwanzaa. I was further amazed when he decided to write his first book, while working at the company. I knew that I wanted to be an author and speaker like him.

He mentored numerous people while working at the company. I was amazed. So, I asked him if he could professionally coach me to do the same. Thomas had a great website, an engaging speaking platform and a steady clientele. I was in my mid 20's, and I honestly did not how to communicate my professional needs. He agreed to help me "build" my speaking platform.

Within each subsequent meeting, my fascination began fading. He was ill-prepared to coach anyone, especially me. When I asked him how to purchase a website domain, he gave me his, "Finding Your Purpose," worksheet to complete. When I asked about gaining representation by speaking agencies, Thomas gave me his, "Thinking Positive," worksheet. The third session was even more frustrating. That time, I asked him about developing speaking topics; instead, Thomas helped me with my resume. This was not the "help" I agreed to purchase.

Then the light bulb went off: I was being bamboozled. Thomas was taking my money, and I never gained the things I was purchasing. His coaching was a crock. After building enough courage, I stood up for myself. I told Thomas that I did not want to continue with our coaching services. He was upset. But I did not care. Success needs to be executed.

To become a professional speaker, one must have a message and platform. A person must have a list of topics to discuss. The person must have a website with videos on YouTube. Most importantly, the person must develop a talent to speak. His coaching was smoke-and-mirrors. I decided to investigate the facts on my own. I no longer sugar coated this coaching relationship because Thomas was a friend.

After talking with a fellow employee about my experience, the truth came out about his actions. He operated in dishonesty. Thomas used company time to write his book and coach clients. His wife arranged his additional businesses. He had no clue how to run his own business without help. To make matters worse, Thomas "borrowed" thousands of dollars from at least 20 coworkers to write the book. Incidentally, he's yet to repay anyone.

Sometimes, when the truth comes out, you can't sugarcoat your reality.

With my newfound courage, I decided to take matters into my own hands. Instead of being mad at Thomas, I built my resources. I enrolled in Toastmasters classes and learned the mechanics of public speaking. There, I met two lifelong friends, Justin and Maureen. Maureen helped me become a Rotarian.

I attend National Speakers Association (NSA) meetings to create a speaking platform and market products. I called GoDaddy and purchased a domain for my first website. After networking with other speakers in NSA, I studied their websites for hours. I observed their topic choices and their website designs. I asked my friend Laurie to build a logo for me, and her brother Ed helped build my first website. (By this time, it was 2007 when websites were professionally coded.)

I networked with former employees, and they connected me with a speaker's agency. The agency asked for a speaking video. I had no such thing. Fortunately, by this time, I had left my role as being a rocket scientist, so I could now post items to the web. Not having any video, I asked friends at Toastmasters to sit in the room. There, I could speak on camera to a group.

The speaking agency did not like it. But surprisingly enough, they saw my potential. So, they asked me to create another. This time I contacted Toastmasters friends who worked for Siemens Technology and asked to give a talk for free. A space and audience was needed for filming. My friend agreed. The filming was successful. The agency signed me as a speaker. I also found organizations who wanted to hear my message. From the McDonald House Charities to Rotary Clubs, I found willing audiences to hone my speaking talents. While at Rotary, I met a man who was a member of the Book Publicist in Southern California professional group. He introduced me to people who help authors publish their books. I spent the next two years writing my first book: I published ***Mathaphobia*** in 2013.

After years of building my talents, I was asked to speak for the world-renowned organization, Technology Entertainment and Design LLC (*TEDx Talks*) at the TEDxPCC location in Arcadia, Calif. All the tips I learned from filming videos came into play. I finally experienced the platform I spent years attempting to master. The video was a success, and within the first 30 days, it had over 30,000 views. Now, the video is fast-approaching millions of views. The counter keeps ticking. From the *TEDx Talk*, I become a well-known science expert. If I had not spent the researching how to achieve my goals, none of this success would have happened.

The best part of the story happened while at my local Credit Union a year later. I did not know someone was standing behind me. The teller says, "Olympia, Congratulations on your speaking career! This deposit is a wonderful check for your talents. You will be rich and famous soon! Thomas, do you know this influential speaker in front of you? You once worked together, right?"

I saw it was Thomas. He looks at me with eyes revealing shock. I simply looked at Thomas and smiled. I said, "Yes, I know Thomas. Hello, Thomas. Have a great day."

You must investigate the facts and act. Nothing is going to fall into your lap by wishing and hoping for change. You must get out there and do everything that you can to change your situation. You will meet many who promise you the moon and sky. But, when it comes down to it, you must do anything and everything to use the resources you possess to build the life you desire.

You must get out there and find a way to use everything you've got to change your circumstances!

Creating Contracts for Yourself

No one will take you seriously unless you present a contract and execute it. I have learned this fact in my business as well. To inform others of your "clear-minded" persona, you must spell everything out. Legal systems use contacts. IRS uses receipts, which are merchant contracts. College classes have syllabi to spell out course requirements.

Any place where you work, there will be expectations. If you don't show up on time, there are grounds for dismissal. On a date, there are silent expectations. If a man does not offer to treat you in advance, do not expect him to pay. While traveling, there is the cultural expectation. Say you are in Abu Dhabi in the United Arab Emirates. If you are not aware of the dress code, you face possible jail time. You must know the expectations others have for you. More importantly, you must set personal expectations.

For you to be definitive, you must be clear with yourself and spell out personal expectations. Many times, these expectations are personal goals. When my car overheated, I made a personal commitment. My part-time teaching salary was not going to be enough to afford a new car. I also couldn't afford traveling to beautiful destinations. So, I made a personal contract: I agreed to bring in money to support my long-term goals and business talents.

You have talents as well. Many people know you to be excellent and capable of completing certain tasks. Is it your cooking? Is it your communication skills? Are you a professional at website design? Do you touch people, and they gain healing? You must place a worth to your talent. Otherwise, you will view yourself as worthless. And this thought is not the truth. Your existence is meaningful, and your impact is measurable, in one form or another.

You must establish a value for yourself and talents to recognize your invaluable contributions. There is currency created to show the value in your service trades. Even if no money is exchanging hands, there must be some established contract to indicate your value. Even, God created a contract called the "Ten Commandments" to show Heaven is the ultimate vacation destination!

And you can have multiple contracts with yourself. Will you be in a job for six months only? What year will you write your book? How many vacation destinations will you visit in the next five years? In each case, you need resources to do these things.

∞ DEFINING YOUR CONTRIBUTIONS EXERCISE ∞

1. Get a piece of paper (or write in your notebook or journal).
2. List 3 things in the next three months that you wish to accomplish.
3. List 3 things in the next six months that you want to accomplish.
4. List 3 things in the next year that you desire to accomplish.
5. Now, create a personal contract to accomplish these goals within the next year, and pledge to use all resources you will counter to help fulfill these goals.
6. Keep these results. You will need these results to complete in the exercises below.

Once you create a contract with yourself, it becomes easier to create a contract with others. Your clarity will change your relationships. Plus, your contracts will serve as better communication tools to help you find much-needed resources.

Mark and Joe

Mark has a great idea for a potential TV show. Joe knows TV producers. Mark was a very honest man who truly desired to entertain and teach through inspiring messages. Joe agreed to help Mark expose his talent to producers with a verbal agreement. However, Joe had been burnt before by TV writers. Although Joe knew he could present Mark to suitable producers, Joe felt uneasy because of personal fears.

Mark could sense Joe's hesitance. After much private prayer, Mark was guided to write a contract to indicate his commitment to the writing project. All information discussed would be in one central location, in a contract. When Mark presented the contract, Joe knew that Mark meant business. They later went on to work together for over 30 years.

RECONNECTION #2: Decide to understand the way the real-life works, including science and math.

If you go to court for a lawsuit between business owners, the first question is, "Where is your contract?"

If you have a great idea that others should know, most pose the question, "Where are your blueprints?"

If you desire to advance in your profession, many will ask, "What are your measurable accomplishments."

People take you seriously when you have proof. The proof is a logical way the brain serves to present evidence that a situation is indeed happening. More importantly, you take yourself seriously when you build proof that you are transforming your life. Your brain changes when you comprehend how to quantify things, and you're empowered to understand innovation. (This is why I LOVE being math professor!) When you understand why systems work in general, you gain a greater sense of confidence in predicting your outcome.

Your brain reconnects every time it uses resources and science applications. For this reason, Science, Technology, Engineering and Mathematics (STEM) degrees are extremely influential certifications. These studies trigger the brain to reshape efficiently. STEM education provides higher connections within the *Triabrain* structure. Science evidence follows to support this fact.

Here is one simple example based on math, physics, and gravity. Do you know which tank will fill up first? Do you know the science?

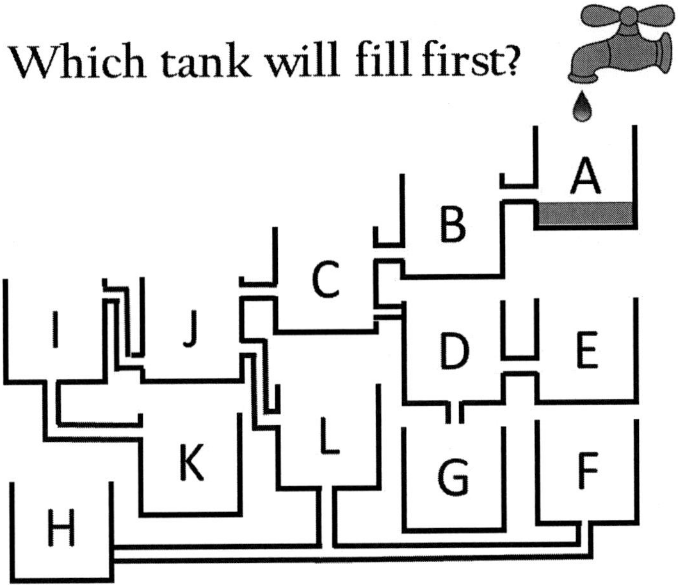

Image 9-3: A basic gravity problem based on the laws of physics.

The answer is ... drum roll, please…

Tank F is the answer. The reason follows the scientific laws of gravity. Water flow will naturally move along a pathway where gravity accelerates its movement. Since tanks D and K have blocks in their pathways, the end options would either be tanks K, or F. Tank J is the only box that both K and F share. When tank J fills, the right exit of J is higher than the left exit. Since J's left exit requires working against the force of gravity to fill box I, tank J would exit contents on the right side faster into tank L. (Tank I would never be filled). So, tank K will never get filled either. On the other hand, since tank J has its right exit higher than its left, the force of gravity accelerates the speed of water to fill tank L faster. In turn tank L points to tank F as the final answer.

Calculate with Math Daily to Reconnect Your Brain

For me, I love math. Its symbols and logic show the truth. This truth is not in any other subject. I love writing, the arts, and psychology. I love rocket science. I love neuroscience. However, math is always different than any other subject I studied. No matter what happened, I could never pretend that I knew the answer. Either I knew it for sure, or I did not. Even though there were multiple ways to find the same result, math always carried integrity. Meaning, math was going to give the correct result. Even if I looked at a problem in 20 million different ways, the result would be the same. Math is real. To me, Math is God's language. The more I could understand the way things worked, the better I understood how the universe operates. Each time that I solved a math equation, I felt confidence in my brain. For each solution, big or small, connected my brain in profound ways. Math showed that my existence alone helped change the world. Math changed the way I saw myself. And Math showed my value, which ultimately could not be measured.

I perceive God and Math to be one. Math is truth and reveals that higher dimensions exist even though we cannot see them. This "Higher Power" relationship is my personal reason why I chose to study math. Each time I learned math, I saw the universal structure to this universe in ways that show everything is connected. Other mathematicians have various personal reasons why they chose mathematics as their expertise. We all have our unique reasons.

For more than 14 billion years, the universe has existed. Some 3,000 of those years, humans applied math to represent and predict natural occurrences within time and space. Before the Greek alphabet, pictures represented math. And, we still use pictures to share the "math story." Throughout time, math translates into various languages. For example, in 2700 B.C., Egyptians used hieroglyphics to demonstrate time, medical procedures, star rotations and continent locations. Later, Greek and Roman empires translated these hieroglyphics into their alphabets. The Mayans devised a counting system that represented very large numbers using only three symbols. Native Americans also created advanced probability calculations for gambling and meteorology. They also created extremely-advanced, mathematical codes for smoke signals. And during World War II, the U.S. military joined forces with the Navajo tribes to create an intricate communication system. The U.S. Marines recruited Navajo men as "Navajo Code Talkers" to transmit the Navajo Codes from 1942-1945. The code was a combination of military language, Navajo words and letters of the alphabet. Finally, the Australian Aborigines also made predictions about seasons and weather. Now, in our 21st Century, we use computers to tell us the "pictures."

Currently, in rocket science, we capitalize on computers and computing software to tell us about the math story in the rocket engine's operation. Sometimes, we use hand calculations. Often, we use computer-based simulations and math-based computer programs. All calculations help us to identify the potential areas for explosion in the Space Shuttle Main Engines. We refer to the desired explosion as engine combustion.

It is a scientifical fact that years of math practice results in a permanent, physical change in the brain's connections. Researcher Dr. Vinod Menon observed that adult brains deal with math equations differently than children's brains. "The stronger the connections, the greater each's ability to retrieve facts from memory," Dr. Vinod Menon, senior author on the study explained to ABC News.

In the study, 28 children between 7 to 9 years old were shown a series of simple addition problems while an MRI machine took scans of their brains (Menon, Qin and Cho). As the children grew, MRI scans showed there were significant physical changes within the hippocampus, the region of the brain commonly associated with memory. The earlier they learned math, the easier it was for memory retrieval (Dovey).

In my first book ***Mathaphobia***, I explain numbers as a language. Mathematics is a language like English, German, Chinese and Spanish. Math is the language of patterns. It represents all universal cause-and-effect relationships in multiple dimensions. These patterns are represented in the language of symbols that comprise mathematics. In the math classes that I teach, I say, "Post a picture of math on social media. You will find that your friends will think you are studying a foreign language. They are right! Because you are!"

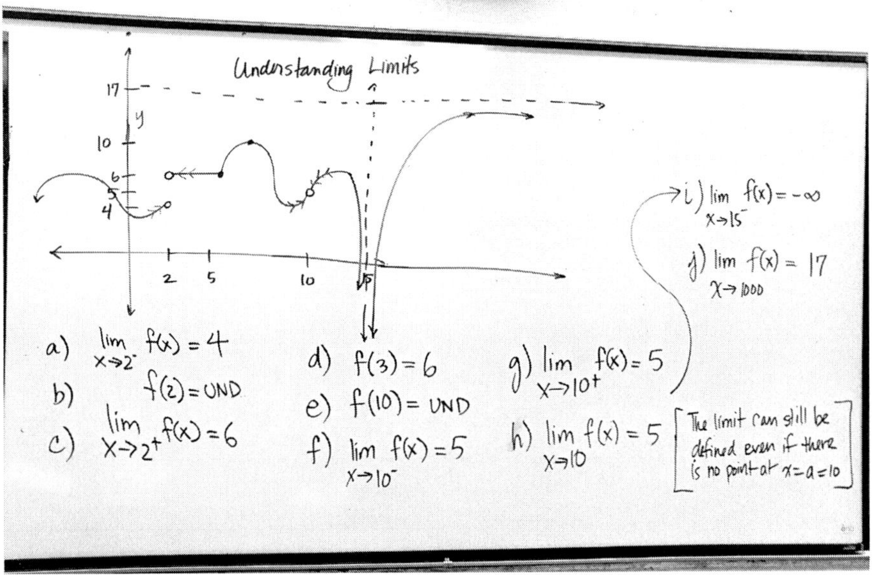

Image 9-4: Photo of Professor Olympia LePoint's lesson on Calculus Limits.

Further, Mathematics is the foundation for every single science, engineering, and technology that exists. As I share in ***Mathaphobia***, Mathematics requires the frontal lobes to fire. When these lobes fire, it causes the brain to reshape. Dr. Josef Parvizi, associate professor of neurology at Stanford

University, proves this mathematical theory on the efficiency of frontal lobes. The researchers in his team pinpointed a group of around 1 million to 2 million cells, located in a region called the inferior temporal gyrus that extends into both sides of the head near the ear canals. These cells firmly responded when numbers and symbols resemble written various numbers (Szalavitz).

> "This is the first ever study to show the existence of a cluster of nerve cells in the human brain that specializes in processing numerals," Dr. Josef Parvizi, associate professor of neurology at Stanford University and the lead author of the study, said in a statement. "It's a dramatic demonstration of our brain circuitry's capacity to change in response to education. No one is born with the innate ability to recognize numerals."

∞ Sudoku Exercise ∞

Fill this 9×9 grid with digits so that each column, each row, and each of the nine 3×3 sub grids that compose the grid contains all of the digits from 1 to 9.

5	3			7				
6			1	9	5			
	9	8					6	
8				6				3
4			8		3			1
7				2				6
	6					2	8	
			4	1	9			5
				8			7	9

Image 9-5: A Sudoku Exercise

∞ DAILY MATH EXERCISE ∞

1. Stand with feet firmly planted on the floor and palms of your hands on the back of your head.
2. Lift your left leg in the air. Touch your right hand to your left knee, and say, "100."
3. Return your feet and hands to the original position.
4. Repeat the process now by lifting and your right leg and connecting your left palm to your right knee. When you touch your hand to your knee, now say, "97."
5. Repeat the process by counting down from 100 to 0 by 3's.
6. Only say the number only when you know it, then your hand can touch.
7. Repeat this process daily, but count down by 2's one day. 5's the next day. And 7's the next. You can down by any number that you like.

Your Digestion = *Triabrain* Connections

What you place inside of your stomach fuels your brain through your digestive system. And one scientist Dr. Daniel Amen has this concept correct. Dr. Daniel Amen is an American psychiatrist and a brain disorder specialist who helps people understand the vital importance of nutrition for brain healing. Dr. Amen's clinics specialize in the use of brain imaging equipment in diagnosing psychiatric disorders (Wikipedia). Amen has studied brain injuries affecting professional athletes, and he is a post-concussion consultant for the National Football League.

The author of the book ***Change Your Brain, Change Your Life***, Dr. Amen shares scientific evidence how anxiety, depression, anger, obsessiveness, or impulsiveness could be related to the how specific structures in your brain work. Further, in his various brain books, Dr. Amen suggests that your diet completely affects how your brain operates. But most people are unaware that the brain affects digestion, and the digestion also affects the brain. As a scientist, I must say that Dr. Amen is correct with the brain's power relative to digestion.

To build the energy in your system, you must have the foundation to do so. You must have water, minerals, protein, and omega fatty acids to energize tissue for healing and rebuilding. Internal combustion happens when each nerve ending transfers energy via neurotransmission. If you think that your brain is just in your head, think again. Your brain extends through roots through your entire system. Neurotransmission also occurs in your digestive tract.

The role of the digestion is to convert the energy you acquire through food and use it for your body. You have four main aspects to rebuild brain mass. It is water, omega fatty acids, minerals, and protein. Every molecule in your body has some percentage of water in it. And studies have shown that water transfers your converted energy.

Water is the most programmable part of your body. Water can be programmed by your thoughts since it retains and transports energy. Specifically, you must know the role of water in your *Triabrain* system. You need water to digest food, dissolve nutrients so that they can pass through the intestinal cell walls into your bloodstream, plus move food along through your intestinal tract. Water carries waste products out of your body. Water provides a medium in which biochemical reactions such as metabolism (digesting food, producing energy, and building tissue) occur. This H_2O sends electrical messages between cells so that your muscles can move, your eyes can see, your brain can process its thoughts. And like the radiator in a car, water regulates body temperature. It cools your body with perspiration on your skin. If you try to drink things other than water – like soda, coffee, tea, power drinks, or smoothies – you will run your brain and organs into the ground. You MUST have water if you want to have a fully functioning *Triabrain*. Water is the only fluid that lubricates your moving parts.

Omega fatty acids are considered essential fatty acids. Omega-3 fatty acid (Alpha-linolenic acid) is an essential fatty acid that plays an important role in brain function and may help you fight against cardiovascular disease. Omega-3 fatty acids are in fish, such as salmon, tuna, halibut, other seafood including algae and krill, some plants, and nut oils. Omega-6 fatty acid (Linoleic Acid) combined with Omega-3 fatty acid produces many health benefits if your Omega-6 to Omega-3 ratio is 2:1. The best sources of Omega-6 are seeds, nuts and grains, green leafy vegetables, like lettuce, broccoli, purslane and kale, and in certain raw vegetable oils. Note, some cooking destroys the benefits of the fatty acids. Some Omega–9 fatty acids are common components of animal fat and vegetable oil. Avocado oil is 70% Omega-9 fatty acid by percentage. Oleic acid in of olive oil, macadamia oil, and other monounsaturated fats are a type of Omega 9. And erucic acid in rapeseed, wallflower seed, and mustard seed are Omega-9 acids. Since oil and water don't mix, this oil is the transportation for your water to reach your brain membranes (Group).

Protein can help you regulate your blood sugar levels. But it's important to eat the right amount and the right kind of protein for brain health benefits.

Proteins provide the amino acids that make up our neurotransmitters. These are the biochemical messengers that carry signals in your entire *Triabrain*, which extends in your entire body. The better the protein, the more efficiently neurotransmitters deliver correct messages. Protein also referred to as amino acids, create serotonin, which is one of the main chemicals which regulate your moods. Eating the right sources of protein helps to boost your levels of serotonin and dopamine energy for sleep regulation.

- Poultry is an excellent source of protein. Organic free-range poultry usually has no antibiotics added to them
- Seafood is an excellent source of protein because it has certain types of brain friendly fats. Fish such as salmon, tuna, sole, halibut are examples
- Milk, cheese, and yogurt are excellent sources of protein, and contain calcium and vitamin D. However, those who suffer from allergic reactions would best gain their protein from other sources
- Eggs are excellent sources of protein for brain health. Eggs yolks help rebuild brain tissue
- Beans are powerful sources of protein. For example, one-half cup of beans contains as much protein as one ounce of broiled steak. Plus, the fiber helps in digestion

Some people can eat red meat easily. I am not one of them. If you are, I recommend lamb as red meat. Although it is high in fat content, the lamb is more easily digestible in the body when compared to beef or pork. And some major athletes rarely eat red meat as they witness that their performance slows. One such athlete is world record holder Scott Jurek, an American ultra marathoner, and New York Times bestselling author of ***Eat & Run.*** Throughout his career, Jurek has been one of the most dominant ultra marathon runners in the world. Jurek has won many of the sport's most prestigious races multiple times, including the Hardrock Hundred (2007), the Badwater Ultramarathon (2005, 2006), the Spartathlon (2006, 2007, 2008), and the Western States 100 Mile Endurance Run (1999–2005). He is a cross country runner who has outrun other athletes in the most extreme weather circumstances. In his book, he believes humans were never supposed to eat animals that they could not outrun and kill with their teeth. Extreme! But Jurek has a valid point!

Minerals

Minerals are a world of their own. My goal is to share the key minerals that we must digest in our bodies to help our *Triabrain-colon* connect faster. The best way I can describe the power of minerals is through lightning. If you have ever studied meteorology, you will know that lightning travels from the ground up to the sky. It is not the sky to the ground. Energy naturally exists in the soil. The reason why trees are usually struck by lighting is that wood from the tree conducts energy under from the ground and extends it to the sky where its branch is closest to a cloud. Flag poles are struck too, because metal conducts energy. Therefore, energy from the ground can readily extend upward. The grounds absorb energy. This fact is why Native American's honor the power of the ground.

Image 9-6: Photo of root and whole grilled vegetables.

Root vegetable and plants carry this energy from the ground and into its molecular structure. This energy is what is converted by your digestive system. It is the natural energy from the ground that you are readily using for your brain's power. It is the most efficient form of digestive energy transfer to you possible. The minerals in the foods conduct energy. Though the presence of water in your body, this natural metal is carried to every water molecule in your system to help you convert the water into the energy that you need. Water is converted through your thoughts. This is the reason why eating whole foods, and vegetables is helpful to your brain.

These minerals travel energy throughout the body by electric impulses:

- **Arsenic** is essential in trace amounts. Arsenic occurs in many minerals, usually in conjunction with sulfur and metals, and as a pure elemental crystal. Arsenic deficiency depresses growth and impairs reproduction.
- **Boron** affects calcium and magnesium metabolism and membrane function. It is essential for efficient absorption of Calcium. Deficiency Symptoms: Osteoporosis, Arthritis.

- **Calcium** is an essential chemical element largely concerned with bones and teeth; needed for blood clotting, transmission of impulses from nerve to muscles, and regulation of the parathyroid gland, which regulates the heartbeat. Lack of calcium leads to osteoporosis.
- **Chlorine** (chloride) is a need for maintaining fluid and electrolyte balance. It enables nutrients to pass into cells and waste to pass out of cells. Deficiency leads to impaired digestion.
- **Chromium** is required for normal glucose absorption and protein synthesis.
- **Cobalt** is an essential part of vitamin B-12. Deficiency leads to nervous disorders.
- **Copper** is an essential nutrient involved in respiration and is an important blood antioxidant. It helps protein metabolize, healing processes. Deficiency leads to elevated cholesterol levels.
- **Fluorine** (fluoride) The major tissues in bones and teeth. Levels in drinking water artificially fluoridated with sodium fluoride which is not natural and can be considered a toxic metal.
- **Gallium** regulates brain chemistry. Helps fight tumors.
- **Iodine** regulates the thyroid gland which the controls the body's metabolic rate. Deficiency of iodine can result in enlarged thyroid or weight gain and breast lumps.
- **Iron** helps carry oxygen to every cell in the body. Iron deficiency also has been associated with the decreased immune function.
- **Lithium** reduces aggression and self-inflicted anxiety.
- **Magnesium** pairs with calcium and potassium. Magnesium is critical to the maintenance of electrical potentials of nerve and muscle membranes and during transmission of impulses across neuromuscular junctions. Magnesium deficiency deficiencies link to heart disease, brain clots, digestive disorders, depression.
- **Manganese** is for blood sugar regulation, healthy nerves, and brain, sex hormone production, normal skeletal development. Deficiency leads to reproductive performance, growth retardation.
- **Molybdenum** aids in processing iron from liver reserves and regulates the metabolism of calcium, magnesium, copper. Deficiencies can result from poor appetite, impaired reproduction, fast heartbeat, visual problems.

- **Nickel** is involved in hormone, lipid and membrane metabolism and cell membrane integrity. Nickel deficiency results in decreased growth, impaired liver function, changes in skin color.
- **Phosphorus** is needed for bone health. It also plays a role in most chemical reactions in the body. Phosphorus deficiency conditions such as muscle weakness, osteoporosis, arthritis, tooth decay.
- **Potassium** is an electrolyte for sodium metabolism. Sodium regulates water balance within the body; are essential for the transport of nutrients into each cell and waste products out of each cell deficiency of potassium is associated with constipation, slow, irregular heart beat, and heart muscle damage
- **Selenium** is an antioxidant that binds toxic metals and promotes growth and fertility. It reduces the risk of cancer, enhances the immune system. Deficiency of selenium is associated with premature aging and increased the risk of cancer.
- **Silicon** is needed for the connective tissues of the body such as tendons, cartilage, blood vessels, nails, skin, and hair. Silicon deficiency first shows as brittle or easily broken nails and dry, splitting hair, and can eventually lead to skull structural abnormalities.
- **Sodium** has the role of electrolyte metabolism. It creates an alkaline balance for the blood and transports nutrients in the elimination of carbon dioxide from the body. Deficiencies result in, muscle cramps and mental confusion.
- **Tin** supports hair growth and reflexes. Deficiency symptoms include symmetrical baldness, reduced response to the five senses.
- **Vanadium** is required for glucose tolerance and the development of bones, cartilage and cellular metabolism. A deficiency may link to reproductive problems and kidney disease, and diabetes.
- **Zinc** enhances the immune system and the spleen; protects against congenital disabilities. Signs of dietary zinc deficiency include sickness and sexual dysfunction, prostate disorders (Clark).

Your digestion is a part of your core body. Meaning, your esophagus, stomach liver, kidneys, small intestines and large colon (which forms your combined digestion) are all geared to help realign themselves based on what is presently entering your body. More importantly, your colon gives your brain the message to readjust the spacing between your organs. That is right. Your digestion even tells your teeth how and where to move. It even tells your hair follicle when to grow. *Triabrain* neurotransmitters and synapsis are also in your small intestines and colon. According to the *Triabrain Theory of*

Relativity, your colon is a mirror image of the crooks and turns in your brain. As your colon changes so do the crooks in your brain. But, your colon and brain stall when it cannot digest food.

If you have gas, for example, the pressure from the gas will create slight formation abnormalities in your colon. Therefore, your colon will tell nearby organs to compensate and readjust to new locations. If gas is not removed, your organs must assume a new position which may cause strain to your body. As a result, the energy that would have been available for you to change your emotion will be stuck in gas pocket! The role of your digestion is to send the command to your organs to move into its proper place. Both the brain and digestion twist and turns a mirror image of one another through *The Triabrain Theory of Relativity*. And when there are conflicting messages, you have digestion discomfort and allergies.

The intelligence in the natural food can adapt to your body, unlike processed foods. The processed food may help you with temporary hunger, but it tricks your brain into thinking your energy need has been satisfied. But in reality, the processed food builds brainbrink and stays in your system undigested. The body experiences mild trauma in trying to digest this "imitation food" which is not naturally biodegradable. As a result, brainbrink trauma can reform in various parts of your colon that transfer to your brain. Or your brain sends the brainbrink to your organ.

This concept was driven home one day when I was working as a rocket scientist. One day, I ate four donuts during a briefing one morning. Then, we went into the Launch Control Room, where I quickly gulped down two cups of coffee. This insane sugar rush helped me for a total of four hours. Then, I started spiraling downward, becoming unbelievably tired for the next few hours. I struggled to keep my eyes wide open and alert. However, this was a HUGE problem, because I was supposed to be alert! I had to prevent launch pad explosions! Gradually, my speech became somewhat slower. Appallingly, it took me a few minutes, instead of a few seconds, to solve problems. Little did I know I was essentially choking off the oxygen supply to my brain!

Sometimes, you unknowingly hinder yourself from brain problem-solving, because you choke your brain of oxygen and water by placing harmful substances in your system. Harmful substances are more than just the typical drugs and alcohol. Substances include sugar, processed foods and soda. Our intake can either starve our *Triabrain* from nutrients or give it energy. The trick is adding as much beneficial energy as possible!

After my sugar-caffeine-high-experience, I suffered severe, allergic reactions for the next few days. I know that two donuts and coffee is nothing for the average person to eat. But, when you are a sensitive person who has experienced trauma, you can be overly-sensitive to ordinary things that others can handle. My sleep pattern was greatly disturbed. I would fall asleep early, and then wake up in the middle of the night with digestion issues. For the next few days, I experienced a "fog-like" mist over my thoughts. Following these abnormal events, I learned my brain was sensitive to sugar and caffeine. I also discovered I was allergic to gluten, peanut oil and yeast found in donuts.

Processed foods make our body work harder to digest food, and they send conflicting messages to the *Triabrain-colon* connection. These messages shift our organs to incorrect locations. More importantly, preservatives in these foods act as poison to the energy conversion. Therefore, the liver tries to isolate preservatives by creating mucus in the body. Simultaneously, the liver sends messages to the hypothalamus in the brain to adjust hormone levels to avoid complete digestion. The brain is tied up in overcompensating for this issue. In turn, your brain slows down its operation and may be susceptible to stall-state thoughts, as discussed in Chapter 3.

While also observing the pattern of my intake, I noticed my brain operated faster when I oxygenated my system with vegetables and whole foods. Vegetable and whole foods have two things that the body needs to conduct energy. They have higher water molecules in its composition. Plus, whole foods have minerals. These minerals are the natural metals that your body needs for energy conduction. I noticed that when I polluted my system with sugar, milk, red meat, my brain appears to take longer to function due to the hormones that the *Triabrain-colon* connection was trying to process. During such circumstances, it felt like I had a learning disability. It is through such experiences that I realized we have power over our thinking capacity based on what we allow in our bodies.

I will offer replacements to help maximize your brain's natural energy capabilities. The following list is based on a simple idea. Some foods cause energy to go haywire, thus promote brainbrink to grow in the entire nervous system. While other foods, add water molecules to our body, which, in turn allows the minerals and water to conduct energy for your thoughts. When your brain is fed, you can be an innovator, capitalizing on your own thinking power. Avoid these pitfalls, if you can:

Remove	Replace
• **Soda/Coffee/Alcohol/Tobacco** Caffeine in coffee and sugar in soda impair the message transfer process (neuron-to-neuron) within the brain. Tobacco use generates free radicals that impair the message transfer process. Abuse of alcohol not only impairs the message transfer process in the same manner as smoking, but also causes the destruction of brain cells.	• **Spring and Alkaline Water.** The ph level in spring and alkaline-based water allows the body to better metabolize oxygen into the bloodstream. The electrolytes found in some sports drinks and waters allow the body to metabolize oxygen as well. Whole food vegetable juices also add chlorophyll to the body, which increases brain function. Green teas without caffeine are also good for the brain. Gum helps people who have a hand-to-mouth complex when under stress. Though gum would eventually have to be removed in time as well.
• **Remove Stress** Stress causes your body to pump out increased levels of the hormone cortisol. Excessive cortisol levels can lead to the destruction of neurons in the hippocampus (the learning and memory center of the brain). Stress hinders the frontal brain lobes from working. As a result, stress activates the same reptilian portion of the brain as mathaphobia®.	• **Meditation and Prayer** Three ways appear to stop the cortisol secretion: exercise, laughter and prayer. The exercise begins to re-establish the hormone regulation in the body, which stops cortisol secretion. In a study done with laughter, patients who laughed daily healed their ailments faster than a group without exposure to laughter. And, studies show that prayer and meditation are effective in reducing cortisol secretion.
• **Sedentary Lifestyle** Sitting too long in one place does not allow blood to flow to our brains efficiently. If you let a car sit in a garage, you will have to start the car to get the fluids moving again. The car fails to operate at its optimum level until it is heated. Your body is the same. When you move your body, blood flows to your brain.	• **Active Lifestyle** Studies of senior citizens who walk regularly showed significant improvement in memory skills compared to sedentary elderly people. Walking also improved their learning ability, concentration, and abstract reasoning. Stroke risk was cut by 57 percent in people who walked as little as 20 minutes per day. Plus, Vitamin D from the sun can increase brain function. Thus, walking in the sun can make you smarter.

• **Processed Foods and Additives**	• **Foods for your Blood Types**
Processed foods make your body work harder to digest food. And, the preservatives in these foods serve as poison to the body. In turn, your brain slows in its operation in learning. This list includes artificial colors, aspartame, BHA (butylated hydroxyanisole), MSG (monosodium glutamate), OLESTRA (Olean), sodium nitrates, sterol esters, sucralose, and sulfites. Using certain preservatives has been known to cause a mild allergic reaction in sensitive people, including Samuel-the-Struggler students. Some animal studies suggest they create a small risk of cancer or tumors; and possible link with hyperactivity and learning disabilities	Good diet and exercise habits reduce the likelihood you'll develop high blood pressure, diabetes and heart disease. Healthy eating according to your blood type can increase proper digestion, which leads to better oxygen flow to your brain.

You can overcome cravings and emotional eating if you realize that your brain is also in your gut. *The Triabrain Theory of Relativity* indicates that the same nerve ending in your head mirror themselves in your digestive system. Through Chaos Theory patterns, your brain is reflected in your digestive system. Your faith brain extends to all organs. And these colon connections have a one-to-one mathematical relationship with your brain.

∞ Digestion Comfort Exercise ∞

Image 9-7: A Stretch to help digestion, with the left hand on the right ankle.

1. Sit in a chair. Place both feet on the ground and sit up as tall as possible.
2. Take your right leg and place your right ankle on your left knee. Bend your right leg so it bends at a right angle.
3. Take your left hand and place it on your ankle.
4. Take your right palm, and meet your right palm with the sole of your feet. Your hand should be over your ankle and not under it.
5. Sit up straight. Breathe through your nose deeply.
6. Keep your tongue on the roof of your mouth.
7. Most importantly, smile. You are enjoying this.
8. When you start to yawn, simply yawn. Then stop. Your digestive tract and your organs have all changed their interior clearance spacing on one side of your body.
9. Repeat the exact same exercise, but now using your left leg.
10. Take your left leg and place your left ankle on your right knee. Bend your left leg so it bends at a right angle.
11. Take your right hand and place it on your ankle.
12. Take your left palm, and meet your left palm with the sole of your foot. Your hand should be over your ankle and not under it.

13. Sit up straight. Breathe through your nose deeply.
14. Keep your tongue on the roof of your mouth.
15. Most importantly, smile. You are enjoying this.
16. When you start to yawn, simply yawn. Then stop. Your digestive tract and your organs have all changed their interior clearance and spacing on the other side of your body.
17. Congratulations, you have helped to realign your digestive system!

Image 9-8: A stretch to help digestion, with the left hand on foot sole.

VOILA as a Way to Heal from Head Injuries

Brainbraink is not just a theory causing the separate of brain mass. As explained in Chapter 4, dark brainbrink glue-like masses serve to impact brain tissue and keep it from reshaping. As seen with NFL players, head injuries serve to separate the brain communication and create brainbrink that can grow and cause major brain issues. Prolonged brainbrink exposure together with traumatic head injuries can lead to degenerative brain disease as explained by Dr. Ann McKee in her study explained in Chapter 4. A major concern exists for anyone in sports like football, soccer, boxing or any other head impact sport. Physical impacts without proper brain-head-therapy treatments are detrimental to your *Triabrain*. There is an innovative scientific method established to help people overcome such head injuries.

VOILA Method of Structural Joint Balancing is the innovative approach. It is unique an innovative way of helping the mind and body connect in healing itself. It restores the brain to muscle communication. VOILA Assessment is systematic, yet dynamic with assessments that are done throughout all structural keystones in the body. It is a tool used to treat people who have experienced physical pain from accidents, and pains associated with emotional distress.

The method teaches physical rehabilitation professionals ways to assess and balance the cranial bones together with the body's structural keystones. While moving energy flow throughout the *Triabrain* full body system, VOILA gives new core strength, equilibrium, and removes brainbrink dark masses (as seen in NFL players). In turn, the brain-to-body reconnection will jumpstart the brain's physical reshaping ability. I truly have witnessed firsthand that VOILA reverses head injury issues.

The VOILA Method focuses itself on the engineering of the human body relative to thoughts, feelings and actions. One such example of the VOILA method explains the role of cerebrospinal fluid. The VOILA method helps rebalance this fluid. As Joel Crandall states with the VOILA Method:

> "The cerebrospinal fluid (CSF) is a major part of the extracellular fluid of the CNS. The CSF fills the ventricles to 'float' the brain, the spinal canal and the subarachnoid space and is controlled by the SphenoBasilar Valve. The sphenobasilar valve controls the CSF and pressure throughout the Cranials and the CORE.
>
> We rely on exercise to keep your heart and lungs healthy. But if you have experienced a head injury in the past, exercise can sometimes be harmful. This is because exercise can increase the amount of cerebrospinal fluid or CSF pressure in your brain. There is a sequence of pumps to help this function.

- **Heart - Blood pressure pump** - Heart pumps blood in a closed system through the Arteries and veins feeding the Brain and the body (Organs and muscles.) If you lose pressure in this pump system, you might also lose lose strength and possible catastrophic failure.
- **Lungs- O2/CO2 Pump** - The diaphragmatic pump increases and decreases volume to produce a lower and higher pressure so air can come into and out of the system.
- **Cell Membrane Pumps** - The most commonly known is the Sodium-Potassium pump. Roughly a third of the ATP made by our cells is spent to power the sodium-potassium pump.
- **Muscles- The Calcium Pump** - Every time you move a muscle, it requires the combined action of trillions of myosin motors.

There are far more pumps in the body. If these electrical circuits and pumps are not functioning efficiently to create the correct pressure, muscles do not function efficiently. If you lose electricity or pressure in these systems, you will lose equilibrium, strength, mobility and stability. In extreme situations, you may lose life! It's not about muscles! The VOILA Method balances all cerebrospinal fluid and helps the pumps operate, the brain can heal from injuries."

Ref: http://www.voilamethod.com/single-post/2016/05/14/Pressure-Systems-of-the-Body

The VOILA system uses pressure points and the synchronization of diaphragm VOILA adjustments to produce nominal, inner body temperatures and pressures. These environments allow the body to naturally trigger its immune system to remove toxins and recalibrate brain fire. More information is available on VOILAMethod.com

RECONNECTION #3: Identify and use your resources in new ways, expecting new replacement.

In life, the only way that you will see your progress is when you are mentally tested. Now this mental testing takes form in 3 ways. Your thoughts and beliefs will be challenged as chaos arises. Your feelings will be challenged as you witness world events that are not pleasant. Further, your actions will be challenged. You will muster up all your strength to act in doing something opposite from your normal routine. In these entire tests, you will strengthen the mass in your brain. You will strengthen the connections within your *Triabrain* and you will strengthen the connections from your brain-to-body. Lastly your internal connections will change your environment.

To pass the tests and build healthy connections in your *Triabrain*, you must learn to use your resources wisely. When you use your resources, you are reshaping your brain's pathways. These physical resources give you the energy boost to throw you into your success radius. The following techniques will help you use your resources. Plus, they will help you remove the clutter that simply bogs you down.

The Millionaire Mindset to Using Resources

I applied to the University of Southern California (USC) for an Aerospace Engineering degree in 1993. I was told, "No." I was not accepted into the university. I also applied to California State University at Northridge for a Mathematics degree in 1993. I was accepted into the university. Later, I worked as an aerospace engineer at the same company with many USC

Aerospace Engineering graduates. We were being paid relatively the same. Since I went to a state school, I avoided high-priced loan repayments. And I could save money.

First off, there is no such thing as the word "No." You will go to people, and they will turn you down. You may think one approach will work, and it doesn't. That is fine. Replace the word "No" with the question "How?" When I was a rocket scientist, I experienced challenges, because I was a woman, and a young person of color. I realized that when I heard the word "no," it was simply a prompt to find a better method in reaching the same goal. "No" points you to a better opportunity for the same outcome.

Second, failure is a gift. When I authorized Space Shuttle Main Engine tests, our job was to *FIND* the failures. We tested the engine so it *would* fail. There was no other way to secure a safe mission unless you prevented future roadblocks. Your life is no different. You must allow failing for your success. In failing, you find the steps to avoid. The sooner you fail, the earlier you can make corrections. The best mathematicians are the ones who correct their mistakes. Take it from me. I failed Algebra, Geometry, Calculus and Chemistry in high school. But I took the classes over and learned from my mistakes. You can do the same for your life. Take each failure as a gift that points you to find the proper way of doing things. Every scientist knows that when you find a failure early, it allows you to find the answer faster. You must simply do the opposite of the failing steps!

Thirdly, you already have everything that you need to succeed. You are not lacking anything. Use whatever resource you have at your disposal even if it doesn't look like it will help you at first. As an example, I fashioned modeled in my teens and saved every penny for rent and to buy school books. This mission was to earn my bachelor's degree in Mathematics. You have everything you need to make major shifts in your life.

You have the means to transform yourself. Whether it be at a night school or a university, you can find ways to educate yourself. The people in your life are brought to you so they can connect you to the right people. You are never at a shortage of connections. Someone always knows "someone" who has what you need. Most importantly, success is not limited. There is enough success to go around. Resources are enough to go around. When you think that someone is taking your fame, money or connections, think again. You already have what you need to thrive.

Remember the "Defining Your Contributions Exercise" at the beginning of this chapter? Go to your writing. Look at the three things that you desire to accomplish in the next 3 months. List 4 things that you will need to do it. Now, let's use the following T-Table exercise to build your resource plan.

∞ The "T-Table" Resources Plan ∞

1. Define what you wish to accomplish.
2. Create a large "T on the paper" where the left column lists the traditional resources that you will need. The right column represents the current resources that are already available to you.
3. List the resources that you will need to accomplish your goal in the left column.
4. Now think of the resources that you currently have. Match those to the resource that you need to the right.
5. An example is below.
6. Do this T -Table for each goal that you created within the "Defining Your Contributions Exercise."

Goal: ______________________________

Needed	Current Resources

Image 9-9: A T- Table to list your resources.

A completed sample T-Table looks like this:

Goal: To Build a Website and have online followers

Needed	Current Resources
1. A Website	1. Can create a new social media account at no cost
2. A graphic designer	2. Can use PowerPoint to create logos
3. Online followers	3. Ask my friends to like the site, and tell their friends about the new site

Image 9-10: A completed T- Table to list your resources.

Clearing Your Space

Suppose you wanted to clear your desk. To organize first, you place papers in all corners of your desk. Your goal is to throw out papers and make the desk neater. If your clearing is interrupted, the papers will lay in many locations. All these papers take up more space. Every time you look at the papers, your head turns! Only when you remove the papers, you feel peace.

With the *Triabrain Theory of Relativity*, your reality is based on the light that hits your eyes. If you are around things that take up space, your brain is being bombarded by light restrictions. Your brain is working twice as hard to identify your location in space. As a result, your *Triabrain* misfires. As your brain clears, your space clears. As your space clears, your brain can hold more peace.

Physical objects interfere with your *Triabrain* field. The magnetism from the papers themselves literally pull on your *Triabrain* magnetic field. This concept comes from Einstein's gravitational lensing theory. In his theory of general relativity, Albert Einstein described how massive objects could tug on light, and even pull at the fabric of space-time. Put simply: When you have unorganized papers or items, you will perceive these objects as huge things that pull on your space and time. The clutter pulls on your own energy. They warp your senses. When you clear your space regularly, your brain has a chance to rest and reshape.

Image 9-11: A clear space reflects light and activates Triabrain connections.

∞ The Open Space Plan ∞

1. Set 1-hour maximum.
2. Find an area in your home or office that needs to be organized.
3. Create 3 piles. One pile is for you to keep items. The middle pile is for you to throw out. The last pile is for you to donate.
4. When you pick up an item, ask yourself, "Do I need this? Have I used this item within the last 3 years?"
   - If the answer is no, place it in the throw away or donate pile. Only donate things that are in good shape. If it is torn or old, throw it out.
5. When think that you need it, ask yourself, "What do I need this for?"
6. If it takes you more than 3 minutes to find the answer, throw it out.
7. When you pick up a piece of paper that makes you feel uneasy, ask yourself, "*Do I need this for legal purposes, or taxes?*"
   - If the answer is no, throw it out.
8. Only keep the things that you need and feel good in keeping.
9. Do this process 3 times a week.

I hope this chapter answered your questions about how to apply science for yourself. You can harness the power that you need if you use your resources wisely. Most importantly, you have a goal-oriented mindset. Your actions pull you into your success radius. I am confident that you will literally create innovation in your life with these tools.

∞ Answer to The Sudoku Exercise ∞

5	3	4	6	7	8	9	1	2
6	7	2	1	9	5	3	4	8
1	9	8	3	4	2	5	6	7
8	5	9	7	6	1	4	2	3
4	2	6	8	5	3	7	9	1
7	1	3	9	2	4	8	5	6
9	6	1	5	3	7	2	8	4
2	8	7	4	1	9	6	3	5
3	4	5	2	8	6	1	7	9

Image 9-12: The Sudoku Exercise Answer from Image 9-5.

The Power in a Woman's Touch

CHAPTER 10

THE POWER IN A WOMAN'S TOUCH

If you are a woman reading ***Answers Unleashed*** from cover-to-cover, this is one major bravo moment! There are two things that you should know. First, I applaud you as a powerful woman in this universe. Meaning, you are a wonderful mother who cares about your children. You are a kind sibling who cares about your family members. You are a beautiful aunt. You are an educated grandmother. You are an inspiring teacher. You are a wise wife. You are a woman in the truest form. Women birth extraordinary things, out of nothing. This is your gift. You have the natural ability to manifest anything you desire – simply because you are a woman.

Yes, you are a woman! I hear you roar!

However, your roar can become a whimper when you question your power as a woman.

The second thing you should know is vital to your transformation. Oftentimes, when you participate in brain healing and transformation exercises, you will be tricked into questioning your worth as a woman in every sense of your being. You will be posed with subtle and not-so-subtle questions about your womanly importance on this Earth.

If you are young and single, you will wonder why you are not "lovable enough to have a boyfriend."

If you are married with no children, you may feel like something is wrong with you if you have no children.

If you are married with children, you may wonder, *"What if I wasn't a mom? Would I be able to be hot, sexy and single?"* Or you may think, *"What if I am doing things to screw up my kids for a lifetime?"*

And if you are a single mother, you may wonder, *"Why doesn't anyone love me enough to help me, like I take care of my child?"*

And if you are a female teen, you will wonder, *"Why am I not popular?"*

If you are a career woman at work, you will wonder, *"Why don't any of the men listen to me?"*

If you are in a relationship that is not leading to marriage, you will wonder, *"Why hasn't he asked me to be his wife?"*

If you are at work, you may think, *"Why haven't I advanced further in my position at work? Am I good enough?"*

Each thought is a trick to make you relinquish your power as a woman. Being a woman is 100% complete power on its own. Unfortunately, society and traumatic experiences have hindered your ability to understand the true brainpower you unleash to rebirth situations. For years, your identity has always been associated with a man in your life, or your ability to give birth to children. Even your identity has been your ability to be a good wife.

Here is the truth: It is okay for you to be just who you are in this universe. It is okay not yearning for more love. You are worthy of love and passion.

As a woman, this part of the book is specifically designed to help you validate your worth, while transforming your *Triabrain's* power.

When you experience healing transformation, your feminine identity will be targeted. Negative chaotic forces will attempt to fool you into using your power against yourself as you take active steps to change your life. Such negativity may manifest when you perform exercises in this book. Negative thoughts can creep up as though they are your own ideas. These negative thoughts can appear as you read this book, seek psychological counseling or practice the VOILA healing method. These forces will even creep up as you attempt to adjust for healthier eating habits. Beware – these forces are sneaky!

Deception also includes what you may see in the media. You may see disgraceful news about presidential candidates groping other women, and your mind can unleash panic instead of peace. In various print and commercial advertisements, you may view how you should "look" or "act" as a woman, and immediately unleash unworthiness instead of feminine power. Such thoughts may even trigger negative programming that you first learned as a young girl from a skewed parental upbringing. You may even perceive relationships as toxic, where you constantly feel as if you are not being heard, or even told the truth. Some unleash disbelief instead of faith. These are all forms of chaotic forces attempting to sabotage your own feminine intuition. If you are not aware of how you can remove these negative thoughts, you will forever harm yourself with paralyzing perceptions.

Here is the fact: when you learn how to direct your thoughts towards self-love, you are equally as powerful compared to any man. As a woman, you have a unique feminine biology, which makes you naturally capable of manifesting life. Birth happens when your uterus (or uterus area) and brain are connected. Even if you no longer have a uterus, the same area still interconnects the beauty in your life. More importantly, you're created to rebirth new circumstances into your own being.

Think of the female biological make up for a moment. Your uterus ingests outside male protein and synthesizes it. After nine months of thinking about your creation, you birth powerful situations through your life. This internal ability is so awe-inspiring that a human being can be formed. Think about this concept for a few moments. Even if you no longer have your uterus, you still have the scientific make up to transform any and everything that comes into your world. Meditate on this theory a little more. You can do far more than birth children.

As a woman, your brain performs EXACTLY the same birthing function as a uterus. You ingest thoughts, feelings and physical touch, and then powerfully transform them. You are uniquely designed to be incubators for change. You also birth global advancements – known as *innovation*.

Women have taught men how to be innovators by demonstrating the meaning of birth.

I decided to add a chapter about women acknowledging self-worth, because I went through hell-and-back when I personally endured healing and brain transformation. Thankfully, my mentor, Bonnie, helped me cope with challenging experiences. Unfortunately, no one in my family became an innovator. So, I was tasked with learning how to use womanly powers to unleash greatness.

For years, I thought that my success was predicated on the thoughts of men. I wondered, *"Did men like my performance at work? Did men think I was sexy, or 'marriage material?' Why couldn't I find a husband and have a child? Why can't a man see me as his equal?"* Ultimately, I realized this self-doubt consistently arose in the middle of deep, mental cleansing. I was removing negative memories that no longer had a role in my life.

I even tightly grasped my awards to exemplify my "so-called" importance. I kept Space Flight Awards and other accolades on my walls to boost my self-confidence. I falsely believed I could rely on these plaques instead of internally connecting to my feminine brain. I share this personal story because I experienced an epiphany. I realized I was never going to be equal to a man. For I am a woman purposefully created. As a woman by design, I am the improved version of man. I no longer worry about what men think. I discovered how to harness my brain's power in mastering my own thoughts.

Women, by nature, reflect innovation. Don't let anyone ever tell you otherwise.

As you undergo this brain transformation process (or any other healing process), it will uproot the feminine identity that you previously owned. You must be willing and ready to deal with what will surface about how you perceive yourself. You may have been sexually mistreated or abused. You may have been neglected by parents. You may have been discriminated against or even devalued in many situations because you were not "one of the boys." Such painful memories will reveal themselves for your complete healing. There will be times where you'll awake in the middle of the night after vivid, emotional dreams, where you cannot sleep due to extreme discomfort.

At this point in time, you will wonder, "*Why on Earth am I putting myself through this transformation?*"

If there is one piece of advice I will give, never give up. Healing is powerful. Your healing is designed to transform emotions into beneficial feelings for your growth. Your pain will be transformed into freedom. You are never trapped as a woman. You can set yourself free. You do not need anyone to grant your freedom except you!

To reclaim your freedom, you must identify which category you are experiencing in your healing process. I devised four types of actions/chaotic thoughts that attempt to distract your focus. Your subconscious will provide insight as to which category you are experiencing.

1. **You turn to men for validation.** In this case you instinctively want to call your husband, a boyfriend or even male friend to validate if something is true, instead of asking yourself. You may also turn to male leaders for guidance in lieu of female role models. The act of turning to a man makes you feel more feminine. And you may feel the urge to talk to men extensively during this brain transformation person. In reality, by constantly talking to men, you are clinging to the masculine part of your thoughts.
2. **You feel inadequate (or overly-focused) in regards to your sex, or sexual desires**. You may feel the need to do one of two things: You may crave physical intimacy with men (or others). Or, you may overly cling to female friends for support. You will feel the need to get "glammed up" with respect to your appearance. Others may feel the need to avoid admiration from the opposite sex. Either way, you are not balanced in your natural seductive power.
3. **You try to nurture, "or save" others.** You may find a man who you "know" will change into a "better" person. And you seek to focus on his well-being more than your own. You may excessively protect

a boss, a pastor, or a romantic interest. You will find your purpose in making someone else's life easier. And in turn, you are cleverly neglecting your own life.

4. **You reject your feminine thoughts, expressions and actions.** You will not see the point in women's support groups. Or, you refuse to validate your own emotions and actions. You don't see the need in keeping a journal or creating a vision board. Many feel uncomfortable defending their passions. You may overly contribute to organizations to ensure you're "ranking" as the best mom, girlfriend, spouse or employee that can possibly exist. All these actions lead to burn out.

Congratulations Ladies! Welcome to the club! We have ALL been there! Being a woman is powerful. And the brain energy we exude is potent! Own it! There are ways to direct this power into better avenues that will fill you with self-love. It is time to take your own power back. In doing so, you reverse obsession and stress, without sending your power into "the abyss." I offer these three exercises. One is mental, one is emotional, and one is physical to help recharge and redirect your true brain's power.

TAKE OWNERSHIP — FAITH EXERCISE

You may not be accustomed to taking ownership in changing a situation, while searching for an answer. Many spiritual women may turn to God, Jesus, the Creator, Buddha, Allah, Mother Earth or the Universe to change a situation. This is wonderful! If you are strictly considering God to accomplish things based on your limited abilities, you are giving your power away. Take ownership of your power. You with a Higher Force can change any situation. Through your daily intuition, God (the Creator) provides guidance. You have a choice. You can choose situations that are most beneficial, while changing your circumstances.

If you are a woman who believes you can manipulate a situation to obtain your desire, then this is misdirected use of your natural seduction abilities. We women are notorious for this behavior. You may think that if you control the situation, everything will supernaturally change for you. Did you know that you have the authority to change circumstances without manipulation? Your integrity changes situations for the better. Don't stick with an unfaithful man! Don't be intimidated in a job situation, where you have valuable skills. Speak to the Source about a troublesome issue instead of gossiping with friends. Don't misdirect your power; use your power to benefit your life. You have the ability to develop self-love through your fractal decisions. You have choices.

You have the power to listen to your hidden thoughts. But you often are not aware of these messages. The following exercise is designed to help you reconnect with your feminine, Godly power to help you focus on making the right choices in your life.

∞ WOMANLY GUIDANCE ∞

1. Pray to God, (or your holy power) to give you guidance in all situations. Pray for the ability to feel the knowledge inside of your being. Ask God to remove any fear or doubt of the information received, and replace it with acceptance.
2. Ask God to provide you with opportunities and the capability to see them.
3. Own your ability to make wise choices based on whatever you are shown with your new knowledge. Reassure The Creator that you can make both tough and simple decisions with newfound wisdom.
4. Feel your *Triabrain* field around you. Circle your hands to feel energy encasing your being. Everywhere you go, feel it. This is your power. Anytime someone steps within a 2-foot radius of you, know that power exudes from your physical being. Own this power.
5. Act wisely when God presents you with an opportunity to change a situation.

Owning your power is a life-long process. It does not come overnight. However, with this exercise, you will begin to develop a sense of self-awareness. So, you can realize your decision-making power. This is called authority.

LISTEN TO YOURSELF FIRST — FEELING EXERCISE

Oftentimes, women in various types of relationships will encounter those unwilling to meet their expectations. When expectations are unmet, most women equate the answer, "no" with being unloved. Some ladies become angry. Others are notorious for trying to change another person's mind. This is an attempt to control and manipulate the situation. Loving yourself is never controlling a situation: it is committing to personal desires and settling for nothing less.

Loving yourself is simple. But to love yourself, you must first learn to listen to yourself despite what others may think. Love is integrity – the ability to commit to your desired goals, despite challenges. Completely loving yourself means never committing to things which are not in your best interest. Loving yourself means honoring your values and standing up for them. This act shows the world that you define your own life.

∞ WOMANLY NOTES ∞

PART 1: - Journal

1. Take out your journal. Express your feeling about the current situation. Explain what may have triggered these emotions that you are encountering. Be 100% honest regarding your feelings. No one will read this journal except you. So, you must be 100% real with yourself.
2. Wait 10 minutes. Then, read your journal entry. Summarize how you feel in one main sentence at the end. (It may take time to construct this part).
3. Now, take out a separate sheet of paper. Using your non-dominant hand, write a letter to yourself. This response is to the entry you just wrote. Write every thought that enters your mind. You can feel and/or "hear" the words from your heart.
4. Read this letter. Embrace what you have just learned about yourself. Commit to caring for yourself. Make note of your needs. The author of this letter is your "inner child," yearning for attention. Decide what regular steps you'll take to meet the needs of your "inner child."
5. Perform "A Right-Hand Touch Exercise" (Directly below).
6. Now, be clear with yourself and others by expressing your true expectations.
7. After you've completed "A Right-Hand Touch" Exercise, set time aside to discuss unmet needs with the person unwilling to work with you. Give that person the opportunity to change. Listen to them as well. Never assume you know their thoughts. Ask for clarification, and repeat their words for confirmation. Ask directly if he or she is willing to work with you so your needs are met in the relationship. If it is a man, do not accept anything less. If it is a woman, do not accept anything less. If it is a child, do not accept anything less. Hopefully you get the point. You now have the option to change the situation to meet your standards. Take that option. By doing so, you take back your power.

8. Buy a flower or flowers for yourself every week for the next 30 days. Continue if you desire. Or, plant a flower and water it regularly. Give yourself the gift of "smelling the roses" and cherishing your existence.

Remember, if someone walks away, accept his decision. He is honest to you and himself. If you walk away, you are exhibiting self-love. Love means possessing the integrity to walk in honesty.

A WOMAN'S RIGHT-HAND TOUCH — PHYSICAL EXERCISE

A woman is endowed with the ability to achieve something that a man cannot. She can give birth to a human being. It is the absolute power that women own. This power is in her intricate DNA brain patterns. Each birth impacts the world. From a biological standpoint, a woman's body gives the world a nurturing force that makes the world a better place. This force is woven into a woman's natural genetic design.

Women not only give birth to humans, women give birth to great ideas! As women, we help others birth their remarkable inventions. We change the world by our existence: just like we connect human tissue to form babies in our bodies, and interweave ideas in our brains for innovation. How you choose to use this birthing power is your prerogative. You can give birth to a child. You can write books. You can create organizations. You can be a world adventurer. You can be a public speaker. You can invent major scientific technology used by humanity. You can inspire change through major philanthropy. You can heal parts of your body. All birthing power is contingent upon cherishing your feminine DNA and connecting organs. Take ownership of this power that is exclusive to women. In order to cherish yourself, you must recognize the parts of you that are unique.

Part of my *Triabrain Theory of Relativity* is that a woman's right hand has the ability to change the DNA in everyone. Think of a mother's loving touch. Consider a husband's desire to be touched by his wife. Think of a woman's hand in her cooking. Even if you are left-handed, I am a firm believer that the right hand of a woman harnesses the power that scientists have yet to discover. The following exercise will repower your femininity.

∞ WOMAN TO MIND EXERCISE ∞

1. Rub your hands together. Pull your hands apart around 3-4 inches and feel the tingling in your hands. Look at the energy inside of your hands and program the energy by saying: "*True Love. True Integrity. True Feelings. True Nurture.*"
2. Choose a position. Lie down. Stand up. Or sit down. Take both hands and rub them over your entire body as if you are caring for a newborn baby, which is yourself. Spend 10 minutes simply touching your body from head-to-toe. Touch your entire body – every inch.
3. Take your right hand and place it on your forehead. Take your left hand and place it on your womb. Imagine energy from your womb traveling to your head, connecting to your right hand. Sit there for 1 minute, simply touching your right hand on your head. Feel your brain receive *True love. True integrity. True Feelings. True Nurture.*
4. Now, consider a relationship you have with another person (male or female). Realize what you want and need from that situation.
5. Feel Peace within you.

A WOMAN'S EMOTIONAL EXPERIENCE WHEN UNDERGOING HEALING

In the previous chapter, I speak about the *VOILA Method* developed by Joel Crandall. And, in my opinion, this is one of the best methods to shift your brainpower in a rapid manner. *VOILA* uses physics, energy and spiritual work together to help your brain-to-body restructure itself from the inside out. There are several processes to achieve healing: This reshaping requires physiological counseling, trauma therapy, energy work like acupuncture and *VOILA*. But with any healing process, there are usually events happening simultaneously which usually freaks a woman out. In some healing sessions, mild and gentle adjustments will seem easy-to-handle for days after the treatment. On the other hand, there are some cases where drastic responses leave a woman questioning if the healing process is indeed working.

With respect to healing affects that may manifest from this book, there will be some people who experience minor shifts in their brainpower. Others may experience enormous shifts in their brainpower. It all depends on your subconscious intent. Your awareness enlivens after practicing recommended exercises to expose memories deeply hidden in your consciousness. Your results depend on how you were impacted by the original experience. Only you and The Creator will know how your experience has impacted you on a mind, spirit and bodily level.

This fact is also true for the VOILA method. From my personal experience, as well as speaking with other women who have undergone the VOILA process, this method provides beneficial results. Pain is also exposed and removed in order to invoke healing. Please note: It is not solely the VOILA method that leads to healing per se, but it is your consciousness allowing any preferred healing (or other) method to help you. Just like when you cut yourself and experience discomfort while your finger mends, your healing will uproot unpleasant feelings during this process. Although these experiences may bring temporary discomfort, please know that such distressing experiences are <u>only</u> temporary. Any negative emotions that surface does not mean you are losing your sanity. Any "disturbing" dream does not mean your house will burn down! Please do not run out and do anything drastic based on how you feel for the next 30 days.

I was taught to wait 30 days before making any major decisions like buying a car, leaving my job, or getting married. This time is meant to be temporarily discomforting, because your core awareness is changing for the better. Uncomfortable feelings will pass. If you regularly attend therapy treatments, the continued release of hidden feelings will increase your level of discomfort. These feelings will pass as well. Some will attempt to throw you their pain, while you are releasing your trauma. If you experience deep anxiety when around others, I offer the following exercise:

∞ "TAKE IT BACK" EXERCISE ∞

1. Identify which part of your body hurts or resonates in pain. Where are you feeling stress?
2. Claim the truth. Say, "This pain is not mine, nor is it supposed to be inside of me. That pain was the past. I am now removing it, and replacing it."
3. Take your right hand. Place it on your womb.
4. Now place your right hand on your head. Then take your same right hand and move it to the area on your body where you feel pain.
5. Imagine your hand "sucking" the pain out of your body like a magnet. All negative energy is removed by your powerful hand. The pain energy now covers your hand.

6. Now take your hand, and look at a dirt or grass area (or simply "envision this place").
7. Next, take your hand and completely throw all this energy from your hand, and bury it into the Earth.
8. Give thanks to God for allowing you to bury the pain and give birth to new life.
9. Imagine The Holy Power giving you back peace with a gentle lightning bolt of energy (as read in Chapter 6).

Below is a list of experiences. The left column is the "Uncomfortable Experiences." The middle column lists "Disconnected Thoughts" that we have during healing experience. These "Disconnected Thoughts" do not convert energy for your full healing. However, as you replace each thought with this intuitive message, your brain can reconnect any "broken pathways." This chart offers deep, inner peace as you choose to heal yourself.

Uncomfortable Experience	Disconnecting Thought	The Science Truth and Divine Message
Vivid or disturbing dreams	What does this dream mean? What if this event happens?	Your brain is experiencing more blood flow than usual. Your brain is converting energy from experiences and processing it for beneficial future thoughts and actions. Write down each dream and allow yourself to know that there is a beneficial message in each dream designed to help you. By writing down the dream, you remove the energy from the brain, so your subconscious can continue to work on healing your body and focus on other pressing requirements for the day. (Chapter 6) Your dreams are gifts to you from God through your *Triabrain*. God wants you to pray and ask what you need to acknowledge in this dream. You will always receive an answer.

Sinus pressure or sinus drainage	I am sick. I must find cold or allergy medicine to stop the incessant sinus drainage.	Toxins associated with past thought are draining through your brain's lymphatic system. Just wait a few days as your body and core muscles realign with your head. God is always protecting you through your intuition, and your head needs to be clear to receive these messages.
Feel severe fatigue	I must get out and do what's required to make money. I cannot spend time resting. I havc work to do.	Depending on the severity of the toxins removed, your body requires rest and energy associated with sleep to activate your immune system. This rids your body of toxins and categorizes your memory process. Your body feels the need for rest. Time allocated for rest will be beneficial. When you spend the time to rest and heal, God honors this process with higher abundance.
Severe dehydration and chills 2-3 days after treatment	I am sick, and have the flu. What did I do to myself by deciding to receive treatment?	Water is needed in your body. Protein is needed in your body for repair. Possibly, take drainage supplements that are best suited for your body. Deep toxins from your muscle tissue are being released from its attachment to previous thoughts. As you change your thoughts, your body drains toxins through your lymphatic system, which includes your sweat glands and bowels. Your feeling of dehydration indicates your need to replace your water intake. God loves you so much He is removing crap from you.
Feel uncomfortable around others	I must get away from people who make me feel this way.	Your brain is receptive to new, physical waves near and surrounding you. You are feeling the difference in energy within situations. You sense when you feel secure in environments versus when you are giving too much of your energy. God desires you to be in places where you are balanced, or make efforts to balance out situations.

Allergies associated with eating foods 3-5 days after treatment	Something is wrong with me, and I cannot eat all the foods that I used to. I do not feel safe when eating any more.	Mucus and inflammation are being removed from your digestion. This removal is making you more aware of foods that give you energy versus foods that cause digestive discomfort. God shows that everyone is made uniquely. You can see how your body was created. You will begin to feel safe again as you start to trust yourself and your intuition.
Breast Pain Occurs When You Have Certain Thoughts	How I am going to handle this situation with ___________? (Fill in the blank with anyone other than yourself.)	Your breasts are signally the need for nursing yourself, telling you that your feminine health is associated with your thoughts and actions. Health is taking care of yourself and your own life FIRST. Maintaining good health includes going for regular breast exams. God wants you, as a woman, to first take care of your own life. You serve as a role model for others through how you nurture, femininely protect, and care for yourself.
Feel pressure in the uterus and lower abdomen when sitting, standing or laying in certain positions	I desire sensual/sexual affection from ___________........ (Fill in the blank with anyone other than yourself.)	Your body is realigning your physical stance and a solid grounding in spinal movement, and hip-to-joint movements. Deep breathing radiates through your body again. Or, it triggers when you are not breathing deeply. You would benefit from building more pleasure in your life, where you are the one who creates it. God is communicating that He is always with you. So, breathe deeply and do not overly desire things in your life before its natural arrival (birthing) time.

Overwhelming disgust for certain people	I can't believe __________ could do that. I can't handle when __________ does that. (Fill in the blank with anyone else other than yourself.)	You physically see the world through your beliefs, and how your eyes reflect light back to you. Your brain is identifying qualities within yourself that make you upset. Ask yourself how these qualities are exhibited through your actions and hidden thoughts. Ask to see what beneficial things are about that person. God uses other people in our lives to teach us about who we are, or can become.
A severely agitated feeling (and/or upsetting internal feeling) when someone comes near you.	I will stay here. I should not have to move, I was here first.	It is okay to leave the situation (or help them). Some people's energy is toxic. They will drain you of your energy if you allow it. Some have an energetic field that is not balanced with yours. Journaling your feelings about the situation will reveal what you were intuitively sensing. God's natural intuition shows you have a choice in protecting and maintaining your growth and balanced energy.
Many people are attracted to you and seek your presence.	I am excited to have all these people close to me. Or I am not happy that all these people approaching me.	As discussed in Chapter 6, your physical *Triabrain* waves have become stronger in its combined energy signal. Treatments have allowed blockages to be released from your system. And you have attracted two types of people: those who have been healed and people searching for healing (they will do anything to gain your energy). God desires you to value all people, yet be discerning in the types of people you allow close to you (mentally, spiritually and physically). Your God-given intuition will guide you through this process.

In short, you are a woman naturally endowed with unique, feminine intuition. Let the answers come to you. I hope you have enjoyed this chapter. And, I pray this chapter helps you to understand your self-worth as a woman. You bring love to the world. You carry rebirth to the planet. Most importantly, you bring innovation. Love yourself. For I love you, too. Sincerely, Olympia!

SUCCESSFUL ENDINGS

CHAPTER 11

SUCCESSFUL ENDINGS

Sometimes your life turns out in a way that you would never expect. You may exit a prestigious job, and enter your life calling. You may meet a man at a restaurant who turns out to be your life-long supportive partner. You may have a child and get a divorce, to later marry the "real" father of your child. You may start a simple script based on an intuitive nudge, and your idea becomes the next block buster film. You may survive a boating accident, and inspire others to seek a Higher Power due to your divinely-given superhuman abilities during survival. You may be led to simply place your hand on another's for comfort, and their body heals from cancer due to your faith. You may experience a personal violation, yet the incident ignites a superhuman power to help humanity. This is the beauty in chaos. Sometimes, you will never know how everything works together for your ultimate good. But, the Higher Power knows.

The shift depends on your decision to change the situation into one which will be most beneficial.

Through this book my goal is to help you reflect on your past and realize that everything that happened to you (good and bad) was designed to help reclaim your power. Through the chaotic situations that happen in your life, your brain can, indeed, connect faster. A miracle is just around your corner: you are alive when aware of your choices. Your life can positively change in the blink of an eye through your powerful decisions. No decision is right or wrong, because of your sincerity in wanting to benefit this earth. When you seek the major Creator, everything in your life is designed to help you grow. Even the most chaotic situations can turn out to inspire at its end.

Through this writing, ***Answers Unleashed*** will serve to help you reshape your own brain. Trauma memories will no longer haunt you. The *Triabrain* and the *Triabrain Theory of Relativity* are brand new concepts. With its applications, anyone can use science and faith to reshape their brain and ultimately transform his or her life.

As you read with the ***Answers Unleashed Triabrain Theory of Relativity***, you are introduced to a new aspect of brain function called the "faith sector." In addition to the brain's left and right hemispheres, the faith sector presents the understanding of intuition and its assistance in decision-making. We've explored how thoughts can transform energy. As you may recall, thoughts are not only in your head. Thoughts reside throughout your *Triabrain* connections. Thoughts can manifest in any part of your body, and your ***Triabrain*** field. And each thought is responsible for shifting an event to a purpose, an emotion to a feeling, and a desire into an action. During this entire process, your faith brain's connections ignite your intuition. Your natural intuition connects you to higher knowledge, and it helps guide you in making wise decisions at the most fundamental level. With intuitional, emotional, and scientific intelligence, you can make the most powerful, life-changing decisions. You will achieve success. You will create world-renowned inventions. This concept combines faith, science and intuition, which is a new combination in how to understand the brain's functionality. You have witnessed how the ideal function of the *Triabrain* works, versus how chaos can separate it into dark, disconnecting masses called *brainbrink.*

The book also clearly defines the branch of Mathematics called Chaos Theory. The meaning of it is explained by real people who share their stories in efforts to help master using chaos to your benefit. I am deeply grateful for the use of real life NASA science in describing how chaos has two endings: "Beneficial" or "Stalling." And it is your free will that determines how you will interact with chaos in a significant way. There are success radii and death radii at every turn. These paths will either pull you into innovation, or stall you from it.

Further brainbrink happens when Chaos separates your brain and keeps you from healthy thoughts. There are bad habits and unhealthy thinking that take control of your thoughts and actions. Unbeknownst to you, the brain's habit center, called the striatum, can take your hidden, painful memories and run your behaviors without any conscious awareness. One common example is someone who goes on autopilot when driving to work. She may be totally unaware that he has entered the freeway, and has driven 30 miles with cars rushing 70 miles per hour past her. She isn't aware of her actions until after she exits the freeway and nearly hits a pedestrian. Unless a person is willing to use mental awareness to change their automatic drive habits, and replace it with a new healthier operation in thinking, there is no way to reshape your brain and regain awareness.

This book helps anyone become aware of how painful memories and habits turn off the brain's powerful executive mind. Mindfulness, which is the ability to have a clear-minded awareness of your own thoughts and actions, is delivered in this book. When you become aware that you have choices, called fractal moments, you can make decisions that reshape your brain. This is the whole meaning of self-directed neuroplasticity.

With practical applications using the *Triabrain Theory of Relativity*, a person can turn on their sensory motor cortex and their executive thoughts for innovation. Whether the advancement is scientific innovation or personal success, ***Answers Unleashed*** provides the recipe to jumpstart the brain with a unique combination of faith, intuition, psychology and science. This ground-breaking theory serves to reconnect the prefrontal cortex and striatum together for mental awareness.

I hope you've enjoyed these personal stories. It is my hope that you transform chaos in your brain to unleash success! As I share my own personal stories in becoming an award-winning rocket scientist, my goal is for healing energy to transfer into your brain!

My passion for brain health is inspired by my mother and sister's healing after their separate brain surgeries. ***Answers Unleashed*** delivers infectious brain-shifting energy, which explodes through numerous, real-life triumphant, lifesaving examples. I know many of you are wondering about the ending of certain characters in the book. Here is a quick summary:

- Auriel and Isis survived the accident and both become a mother-daughter force that inspires many across the world.
- Pamela and Crystal find new ways of healing and working with their brain after traumatic head injuries. Crystal returns to work as an accountant.
- After Timothy's face is burned, he becomes a well-known actor and soap star in Europe.
- Olivia becomes a world-renowned healer, helping others "stay in their bodies" and heal from cancers.
- Vanna is now married to the man who wants be a husband and father to her child.
- Joel Crandall goes on to establish VOILA centers around the world.
- Robert eventually asks Ann to marry him. They support each other in becoming multi-millionaires and global philanthropists.
- Stephen, the aerospace manager, continues in the field, and eventually becomes CEO of one of the largest aerospace companies in the world.

- Dennis continues with a higher NASA position and ensures the safe flight for new launches.
- Lars sets up coaching facilities across the United States to help athletes gain peak performance for the Olympics.
- Executive Ronald was removed from politics. And he eventually found God.
- Pastor Jeff later leads thousands to accept Jesus Christ, while helping countless overcome life's adversities through faith.
- Antoinette returned to college, started her own business, and made millions from her inventions.
- Alan eventually found practical ways to handle his life. He is now working in a job that requires his logic and continuous problem solving.
- Shonia took care of medical issues and began feeling self-reliant, never having to ask someone else for help with personal care.
- Years later, Glen would accept God's existence, and attend church regularly, while building his companies.
- Charlene went on to write her first book with the help of her workshop attendee. And she is in the process of writing more.
- Blake met his fiancée in my Calculus math class.
- NASA engineers develop a replacement to the Space Shuttle and are planning to fly people to Mars.
- Krystal later became a well-known scientist.
- Susan is divorced, living on her own and working in the field of codependence counseling.
- Brian continues to run, is a proud father, and appreciates his daughter's DNA.
- Joy, author of INVENTING JOY, has made multi-billions from her decision to study science on her own.
- Zena has overcome sexual trauma and now coaches other women in regaining internal peace through meditative practices.
- Miss P. is now working with Zena and has created an international supplement chain of whole food products with her son and grandson.
- Tim is happily married to his wife and are expecting their first child.
- Pamela's daughter (me) later went on to write a series of best-selling ***Answers Unleashed*** books that prompts media acclaim with a TV show, Radio program, and international self-healing conference.

If are a person who cares and wants to leave a legacy in this world, this book is for you. If you are a person who wants to see beneficial things come from tough situations, this book is for you. And if you are a person who wants to attract healthier people into your world, this book is for you. I highly recommend ***Answers Unleashed*** as a fun, easy to read, self-help neuroscience book for every young person looking to better their life. My intention is to follow the dream I was given and provide timely direction at your most critical hour. This book is designed for university students, professionals, counseling centers, and people seeking to overcome painful memories.

∞ FINAL BRAIN EXERCISE ∞

For Chapters 6, 8, 9, and 10 "Forging Exercises."

1. Take a heavy-duty steel tall kitchen pot with its lid.
2. Grab several matches.
3. Tear a few sheets of aluminum foil, and place a sheet inside the bottom of the pan.
4. Take your sheet of paper from each of the exercises.
5. Go outside in a well-lit area clear of dry brush.
6. Think or say, "I am giving these Sheets to the highest form or Life to help me transform all my experiences into strength for the past, present, and future. I give anything that was unsaid or unwritten to the Holy Spirit as well."
7. I give these writing to The Holy Creator for rebirth.
8. Rip up the papers.
9. Burn each paper. Watch each one burn. Make sure that every sheet of paper burns.
10. Imagine a white light circling and cleansing your entire being as you watch the papers burn.
11. Within no more than 72 hours: Find a plant or an open dirt to dig a hole into the dirt.
12. Dig a hole and place all the ashes from the burnt pieces of paper and bury them.
13. Think of this saying as you are burning the paper, "May the earth and heaven provide rebirth to me and others."
14. Thank God for the new life that you will begin from this day forward.

When you read this book, do not turn to me for answers: rather turn to The Highest Source. When picking up the pages, do not reach out to me to solve your problem, reach out to your *Triabrain* connection and intuition as your guide. When you ponder each story, do not view the story as your own, but relate the stories to your life experiences. See how you can change your immediate future. And when you are tempted to think I, Olympia LePoint, know all the answers, stop yourself and realize that I am human like you. We are all in this learning process together. I do not know everything, and neither do you. We all have our own gifts to share. Together we can support each other in making a difference.

I am a guide. I am not the one who will make changes in your life: it will be you who will make the changes for yourself. Do not think, "What would I do?" But, consider, "What would YOU do to establish a better outcome?" Your teacher will not make changes in your life: rather it will be the role of your beautiful mind. Your therapist or mentor will not change your life, though it's your will to succeed that gives you strength to make changes. God will not solely make changes in your life. But your sincere heart invested in Him will empower the Red Sea to part. Your heavenly-assistance and scientific logic will transform your life. I am merely pointing you to the Source and helping you find the answers for yourself. As you read this book, my powerful intention is that healing will come upon you and ignite in such a life-changing powerful way, that every force which attempts to work against you will be halted and sent to the Holy Light. May you be set free to live a purposeful life.

My intention is that every time you hold this book, may God provide answers that you bring to fruition. May his book serve as your connecting source to innovative methods that unleash healing power to reshape your world. May this book's contents explode into every DNA molecule to heal your brain from the inside out. Let your newly-found energy move into beneficial action. May your actions help reshape your mind. I call upon heaven and the earth to help you in your own journey. And for everyone who reads this book, I powerfully call forth your Spirit to be realigned and reignited. May the light that shines through you illuminate during the darkest hour and give you ultimate pleasure in arriving to your success. May your brain reshaping begin.

With deepest love,

Olympia LePoint

Olympia LePoint

BIBLIOGRAPHY

"FractlMan", J. W. (2009, January 19). *fractalfoundation.org/?s=what+is+chaos+theory*. Retrieved November 17, 2016, from fractalfoundation.org.

A Neuroscience Bombshell - Human Brain is Capable of Storing the Entire World Wide Web. (2016). *Science New Journal.*

ABC News Go. (2005, June 30). Retrieved from http://abcnews.go.com/Health/story?id=871969: http://abcnews.go.com/Health/story?id=871969

Administration, N. A. (2000, July 27). NASA Image of Russia's Lena River: How Chaos Fractal Mathematics is Viewed in Nature. *Earth Observatory*. Sakha, Russia: National Aeronautic and Space Administration. Retrieved from https://earthobservatory.nasa.gov/IOTD/view.php?id=2704

Allen, D. A. (Director). (1982-1987). *Fame (TV Series)* [Motion Picture]. USA: MGM Television. Retrieved August 5, 2017, from https://en.wikipedia.org/wiki/Fame_ (1982_TV_series)

Bader, C., Dougherty, K., Froese, P., Johnson, B., Mencken, F. C., Park, J. Z., & Stark, R. (2006). *American Piety in the 21st Century: New Insights to the Depth and Complexity of Religion in the US.* Baylor University, The Baylor Institute for Studies of Religion and Department of Sociology, Baylor University. Waco: John M. Templeton Foundation. Retrieved July 27, 2017, from http://www.baylor.edu/content/services/document.php/33304.pdf

Boulware, C. M. (1998, January 1). *Adult Survivors of Childhood Sexual Abuse.* Retrieved from http://www.psychotherapist.net/adultsurvivors.html: http://www.psychotherapist.net/adultsurvivors.html

Bryer, T., & Gibbs, A. (2016, June 6). *Why I Turned Down Elvis Presley*. Retrieved June 27, 2017, from CNBC Meets: http://www.cnbc.com/2016/06/01/dolly-parton-the-time-i-turned-down-elvis-presley.html

Buchanon, J. R. (1888). *Journal of Man* (Vol. 1). Cincinatti, OH, USA: J.R. Buchanon. Retrieved July 27, 2017, from https://www.thoughtco.com/need-to-know-info-about-psychometry-2593072

Calvin, B. C. (2017, April 8). *The Washington Times*. Retrieved July 25, 2017, from The Washington Times: http://www.washingtontimes.com/news/2017/apr/8/anti-suicide-bills-moves-forward-in-montana-legisl/

Capra Jr, F., Schumacher, M. (Producers), Mann, S. (Writer), & Lester, M. L. (Director). (1984). *Firestarter* [Motion Picture]. USA: Universal Pictures. Retrieved from https://en.wikipedia.org/wiki/Firestarter_(film)

Clark, T. (2011, January 1). *Mineral Functions in the Body*. Retrieved November 17, 2016, from TJ Clark: http://www.tjclark.com.au/Library+old/Colloidal+Minerals/Mineral+Functions+in+the+Body.html

Dovey, D. (2014, August 18). *Math Skills in Childhood Can Permanently Affect Brain Formation Later in Life*. (Newsweek Group) Retrieved November 17, 2016, from Medical Daily.com: http://www.medicaldaily.com/math-skills-childhood-can-permanently-affect-brain-formation-later-life-298516

Dunne, J. (1934). *An Experiment with Time* (3rd ed.). Hampton, VA, USA: Hampton Roads Publishing Co. Retrieved July 27, 2017, from https://en.wikipedia.org/wiki/Precognition

Ellen. (2012, August 12). *The Meaning of "Expecto Patronum": From Hogwarts to Ancient Rome!* Retrieved August 7, 2017, from owlcation.com: https://owlcation.com/misc/expecto-patronum-meaning

Ellis, A., & Beck, A. T. (2007, January). *Cognitive Behavioral Therapy*. Retrieved August 8, 2017, from GoodTherapy.org: http://www.goodtherapy.org/learn-about-therapy/types/cognitive-behavioral-therapy

Falk, D. (2013, October 27). Neuroscientists discover new 'mini-neural computer' in the brain. (U. o. Medicine, Ed.) *University of North Carolina School of Medicine*. Retrieved May 20, 2017, from Science Daily: www.sciencedaily.com/releases/2013/10/131027185027.htm

Freeman, D., & LLC, A. i. (2007-2014, January 1). *Learn Telekinesis Training: How to Learn Telekinesis and Develop Your Abilities*. Retrieved July 27, 2017, from Learn Telekinesis Training: http://www.learn-telekinesis-training.com/telekinesis-concentration-exercise-1.php

Freeman, D., & LLC, A. i. (2007-2014, January 1). *Learn Telekinesis Training: How to Learn Telekinsis and Develop Your Ability - Concentration Exercise #1*. Retrieved July 27, 2017, from Learn Telekinesis Training: http://www.learn-telekinesis-training.com/telekinesis-concentration-exercise-1.php#1

Garrity, J. M., & MacMillan, W. a. (2017, January 1). Structure and Function of the Eyes. *Merck Manual Consumer Version*, p. 1. Retrieved July 29, 2017, from Merck Manual Consumer Version: https://www.merckmanuals.com/home/eye-disorders/biology-of-the-eyes/structure-and-function-of-the-eyes

Grazer, B., Howard, R. (Producers), Goldsmith, A. (Writer), & Howard, R. (Director). (2001). *A Beautiful Mind* [Motion Picture]. USA: Universal Pictures. Retrieved from https://en.wikipedia.org/wiki/A_Beautiful_Mind_(film)

Group, E. M. (2009, March 18). *The Health Benefits of Omega 3, 6, 9 Fatty Acids and EPA & DHA*. Retrieved November 17, 2016, from The Global Healing Center: https://www.globalhealingcenter.com/natural-health/benefits-of-omega-3-6-9-fatty-acids/

Gynecology, T. A. (2013, October). *Committee on Health Care for Undeserved Women*. Washington D.C.: The American College of Obstetricians and Gynecologists. doi:https://www.acog.org/-/media/Committee-Opinions/Committee-on-Health-Care-for-Underserved-Women/co576.pdf?dmc=1&ts=20151210T1146271646

Hari, J. (2015, June). *"Everything You Think You Know About Addictions is Wrong"*. (J. Hari, Performer) TEDGlobal London, London, England, United Kingdom. Retrieved November 2017, 2016, from https://www.ted.com/talks/johann_hari_everything_you_think_you_know_about_addiction_is_wrong

Hari, J. E. (2015). *Scream: The First and Last Days of the War on Drugs*. London: Bloomsbury. Retrieved January 17, 2017, from https://en.wikipedia.org/wiki/Johann_Hari

Harra, C. P. (2013, July 6). *35 Affirmations That Will Change Your Life.* Retrieved November 17, 2016, from HuffPost: http://www.huffingtonpost.com/dr-carmen-harra/affirmations_b_3527028.html

Hawkins, D. R. (1995). *Power Versus Force: The Hidden Determinants of Human Behavior.* Australia: Hay House. Retrieved from https://www.hayhouse.com

Henshaw, S. D. (2015, August 6). *Why Positive Affirmations Don't Work.* Retrieved November 17, 2016, from PsychCentral: https://psychcentral.com/blog/archives/2014/03/20/why-positive-affirmations-dont-work/

Hudson, K. (2014, January 29). *Pastor Jeff Perry Injured in Boating Accident.* Retrieved August 1, 2017, from Fox 2 News St. Louis: http://fox2now.com/.../pastor-jeff-perry-injured-in-boating-.../

Laboratory, J. P. (2017, June 2). Travel Trajectories Near Mars Using Chaos Theory. *Jet Propulsion Laboratory News.* Outerspace: Jet Propulsion Laboratory. Retrieved from https://www.jpl.nasa.gov/news/news.php?feature=5747

Leaf, C. P. (2015). *Switch on Your Brain: The Key to Peak Happiness, Thinking and Health.* Great Plains, Michigan: Baker Publishing Group. Retrieved from http://www.eagleswings.co.zw/Free%20Books/Sanctification%20of%20the%20Heart%204th%20Edition.pdf

LePoint, O. (2014, August 4). Lucy, a Thrilling Science Misinterpretation. *HuffPost*, p. 3.

LePoint, O. (2014, August 4). Movie Review: Lucy, a Thrilling Science Misinterpretation. *The Huffington Post*, p. 3.

LePoint, O. (2015, October 23). Martian Movie Review by a Rocket Scientist. *The Huffington Post.* New York, New York, USA: The Huffington Post. Retrieved from HuffPost: http://www.huffingtonpost.com/olympia-lepoint/the-martian-movie-review-_2_b_8344242.html

LePoint, O. (2016, February 1). *http://answersunleashed.com/.* Retrieved May 20, 2017

LePoint, O. (2016, July 8). The Triabrain and Answers Unleashed. *The Huffington Post*, p. 5.

LePoint, O. (2017, June 20). Fire on 118 . *Answers Unleashed.* (O. LePoint, Ed.) Northridge, CA: OL Consultanting Corporation.

Mangano, J. (2017, January 1). *http://joymangano.com/.* Retrieved from http://joymangano.com/: http://joymangano.com/

McKee, Ann, M.D.; Jesse Mez, MD, MS; Daniel H. Daneshvar, MD, Ph.D; Patrick T. Kiernan, BA; Bobak Abdolmohammadi, BA; Victor E. Alvarez, MD; Bertrand R. Huber, MD, Ph.D; Michael L. Alosco, Ph.D; Todd M. Solomon, Ph.D; Christopher J. Nowins. (2017, July 25). Clinicopathological Evaluation of Chronic Trauma Encephalopathy in Players of American Football. *The Journal of the American Medical Association*, 318(4):360-370. doi:10.1001/jama.2017.8334

Men W, F. D. (2014, April 24). The Corpus Callosum of Albert Einstein's Brain: Another Clue to His High Intelligence. *Brain*, p. 137 (pt 4). doi:10.1093/brain/awt252

Menon, V., Qin, S., Cho, S., T, C., & Geary, R.-L. M. (2014). Hippocampal-neocotical functional reorganization underlies children's development. *Nature Neuroscience.*

Miller, I., & Swinney, G. (2001). http://www.oocities.org/iona_m/ChaosTheory/CTintro.html. (I. Miller, Ed.) *CHAOSOPY Journal*, 1-3. Retrieved November 17, 2016, from http://www.oocities.org/iona_m/ChaosTheory/CTintro.html

Monash, P. (Producer), Cohen, L. D. (Writer), & De Palma, B. (Director). (1976). *Carrie* [Motion Picture]. USA: United Artists. Retrieved from https://en.wikipedia.org/wiki/Carrie_(1976_film)

Newberg, A. B. (2013). *The Metaphysical Mind: Probing the Biology of Philosphical Thought.* Philadephia, Pennsylvania: CreateSpace Independent Publishing Platform. Retrieved January 17, 2016, from https://www.amazon.com/The-Metaphysical-Mind-Probing-Philosophical/dp/1494396742

Newberg, A. B. (2014, June 5). *What Happens to the Brain During Spiritual Experiences.* Retrieved January 17, 2016, from The Atlantic: http://www.theatlantic.com/health/archive/2014/06/what-happens-to-brains-during-spiritual-experiences/361882/

Norton, J. (2014, September 5). Scientists Claim "Telepathy" Success After Sending Mental Messages From One Person to Another 4,000 Miles Away. *Daily Mail*, p. 1. Retrieved July 27,2017,from http://www.dailymail.co.uk/news/article-2745797/Scientists-claim-telepathy-success-sending-mental-message-one-person-4-000-miles-away.html#ixzz4nJWQ47ct

Parriot, J. D., Johnson, K., Corea, N. (Producers), Lee, S., Kirby, J., Johnson, K. (Writers), & Johnson, K. (Director). (1977-1982). *The Incredible Hulk* [Motion Picture]. USA: NBC Universal Television Distribution. Retrieved from https://en.wikipedia.org/wiki/The_Incredible_Hulk_(1978_TV_series)

Rape, A. &. (2016, January 1). *Adult Survivors of Child Sexual Abuse.* Retrieved August 14, 2017, from Rape, Abuse, & Incest National Network: https://www.rainn.org/articles/adult-survivors-child-sexual-abuse

Schwartz, J. M. (2015, October 27). *"The Neuroscience of Habit".* (J. M. Schwartz, Performer) The Concourse, Chatswood, Ashford, Australia. Retrieved January 17, 2017, from https://www.youtube.com/watch?v=S0-NmxR3Lcg

Senay, I., Albarracin, D., & Noguchi, K. (2010). *Motivating Goal-Directed Behavior Through Introspective Self-Talk: The Role of the Interrogative Form of Simple Future Tense.* Psychological Science. Retrieved November 17, 2016

Shapiro, F. M. (2017, July 21). *Eye Movement and Desensitization and Reprocessing Therapy (EMDR).* Retrieved from GoodTherapy.org: http://www.goodtherapy.org/learn-about-therapy/types/eye-movement-desensitization-and-reprocessing

Sperry, R. W. (1945, Dec 20). The problem of central nervous reorganization after nerve regeneration and muscle transposition. *The Quarterly Review of Biology Vol 20*, pp. 311-369. Retrieved April 23, April

Staff, H. S. (2017, June 28). *Types and Stages of Sleep - REM.* Retrieved July 4, 2017, from How Sleep Works: https://www.howsleepworks.com/types_rem.html

Swann, I. (2017, January 1). *Remote Viewing.* Retrieved July 27, 2017, from Crystalinks.com: http://www.crystalinks.com/remote_viewing.html

Szalavitz, M. (2013, April 23). Your Brain on Math. Retrieved from http://healthland.time.com/2013/04/23/your-brain-on-math

Virtue, D. (1998). Ways to Increase Your Clairsentience. *InnerSelf*, 1. Retrieved July 27, 2017, from http://innerself.com/content/personal/intuition-awareness/intuitive-awareness/6364-ways-to-increase-your-clairsentience.html

Virtue, D. P., & Bunick, N. (1998). *Divine Guidance: How to Have a Dialogue with God and Your Guardian Angels* (1st ed.). Carlsbad, CA, USA: Renaissance Books. Retrieved from https://www.barnesandnoble.com/p/divine-guidance-doreen-virtue/1111651466/2675005069970?st=PLA&sid=BNB_DRS_Marketplace+Shopping+Books_00000000&2sid=-Google_&sourceId=PLGoP4094&k_clickid=3x4094

Wagner, S. (2017, January 28). *What Is Psychometry? A Phenomenon Where A Person Can Sense the Past With Touch.* Retrieved July 27, 2017, from ThoughtCo: https://www.thoughtco.com/need-to-know-info-about-psychometry-2593072

Ward, J., Williams, J., & Manchester, S. (2017, July 25). 110 N.F.L. Brains. *The New York Times.* Retrieved August 6, 2017, from https://www.nytimes.com/interactive/2017/07/25/sports/football/nfl-cte.html?rref=collection%2Ftimestopic%2FHead%20Injuries%20in%20Football&action=click&contentCollection=sports&region=stream&module=stream_unit&version=latest&contentPlacement=8&pgtype=coll

Wikipedia. (2017, August 8). *Chronic Traumatic Encephalopathy.* Retrieved August 9, 2017, from Wikipedia.com: https://en.wikipedia.org/wiki/Chronic_traumatic_encephalopathy

Wikipedia. (2017, August 15). *Daniel Amen.* Retrieved August 8, 2016, from Wikipedia: https://en.wikipedia.org/wiki/Daniel_Amen

Wikipedia. (2017, July 1). *Hysterical Strength.* Retrieved July 27, 2017, from Wikipedia: https://en.wikipedia.org/wiki/Hysterical_strength

Wikipedia. (2017, July 26). *Metaphysics.* Retrieved July 25, 2017, from Wikipedia.com: https://en.wikipedia.org/wiki/Metaphysics

Wikipedia. (2017, July 28). *Precognition.* Retrieved July 27, 2017, from Wikipedia: https://en.wikipedia.org/wiki/Precognition

Wikipedia. (2017, July 26). *Pshychokinesis.* Retrieved July 27, 2017, from Wikipedia.org: https://en.wikipedia.org/wiki/Psychokinesis

Yip, J. A., & Côté, S. (2013). The Emotionally Intelligent Decision Maker: Emotion-Understanding Ability Reduces the Effect of Incidental Anxiety on Risk Taking. *Association for Psychological Science, 24*(1), 48-55. Retrieved November 17, 2016, from http://pss.sagepub.com/content/24/1/48

About Olympia LePoint

Hailed the "Modern Day Hidden Figure" by ***People Magazine*** in 2017, Olympia LePoint is an award-winning rocket scientist and author who is unleashing the brain's power through her rocket science and neuroscience expertise. LePoint is an internationally-recognized leader within Math and Science fields through her *TEDx Talk* "Reprogramming Your Brain to Overcome Fear." LePoint is the author of books ***Answers Unleashed: The Science of Unleashing Your Brain's Power*** and ***Mathaphobia: How You Can Overcome Your Math Fears and Become a Rocket Scientist.*** LePoint helped launch NASA's *Endeavour*, *Discovery*, *Columbia,* and *Atlantis* Space Shuttles, in a total of 28 missions to Space. LePoint's Mission Control Room (ROSC) seat is an exhibit at the California Science Center in Los Angeles, California. As a "Modern Day Hidden Figure", LePoint won numerous professional excellence awards including the "Boeing Professional Excellence Award" and "Engineer of the Year, Modern Day Technology Leader Award." From the ages of 21-30, Olympia LePoint was one of the youngest leaders to help launch NASA's Space Shuttle to success. LePoint earned Bachelor's and Master's degrees in Mathematics as a Notable Alumna from California State University Northridge. LePoint is an alumnus from Alexander Hamilton Performing Arts Academy led by world renown producer James (Jim) Berk.

People Magazine featured Olympia LePoint for the 89th Academy Awards. The national publication shares Olympia LePoint's triumphant, real life story in becoming a "Modern Day Hidden Figure." LePoint has been featured on the TV shows "Between the Lines" on PBS, "Living San Diego" on the CW network, NBC News, CBS Evening News, KTLA Morning News, Dr. Drew's "Life Changers," TED Talks, "Kaplan at Night," "Jump Shipp" on The Halogen Network, and "Christians OnDemand" episodes. As a former fashion model, LePoint has graced the cover of several magazines including ***Porter Ranch Magazine*** for her beauty and genius intelligence.

As a seasoned journalist and interviewer, LePoint writes blogs on ***The Huffington Post*** and is the celebrity interviewer in the movie Arrested Development Documentary Project. As the executive producer and writer of the talk show "Answers Unleashed," LePoint uses her rocket science experience to remap the human brain to create a new structure she calls the *Triabrain* and the *Triabrain Theory of Relativity*, which profoundly describes how anyone can use science and faith to reshape their brain and ultimately transform his life. LePoint is powerfully transforming lives through her professional speaking and entertainment talents.